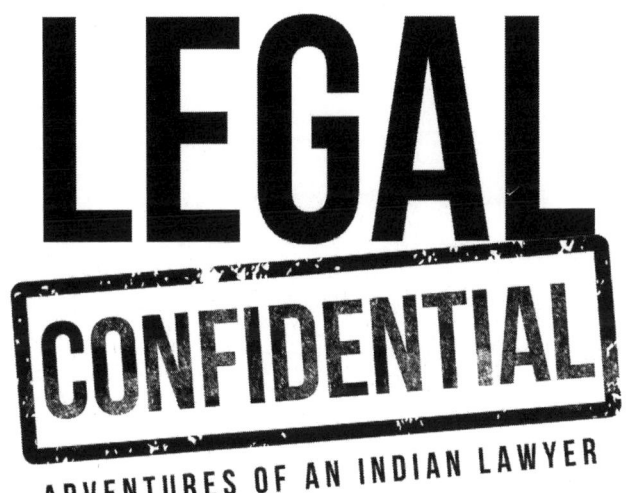

LEGAL CONFIDENTIAL

ADVENTURES OF AN INDIAN LAWYER

RANJEEV C. DUBEY

PENGUIN
BUSINESS

An imprint of Penguin Random House

PENGUIN BUSINESS

USA | Canada | UK | Ireland | Australia
New Zealand | India | South Africa | China | Singapore

Portfolio is part of the Penguin Random House group of companies
whose addresses can be found at global.penguinrandomhouse.com

Published by Penguin Random House India Pvt. Ltd
4th Floor, Capital Tower 1, MG Road,
Gurugram 122 002, Haryana, India

First published in Portfolio by Penguin Books India 2015
This edition published in Penguin Business by Penguin Random House India 2024

Copyright © Ranjeev C. Dubey 2015

ISBN 9780670088393

Typeset in Adobe Garamond Pro by Manipal Digital Systems, Manipal
Printed at Replika Press Pvt. Ltd, India

www.penguin.co.in

This is a legitimate digitally printed version of the book and therefore might not
have certain extra finishing on the cover.

Contents

Part III: Rocking Steady

For Rhea and Rohin,
without whom there would be considerably less to live for,
and nothing to explain

Author's Note

I passed my LLB exam in the summer of 1980. The next year, I was admitted to the Bar. I have been a practising lawyer ever since. I had very clear reasons for wanting to become a lawyer. I now know they were not good reasons. Even though later I knew better, I continued to practise as a lawyer and found new reasons along the way. These reasons changed radically over the years.

Why did I want to become a lawyer in the first place? I used to read a bit of detective fiction in those days. It was all about bringing offenders to justice, and justice seemed important. Then again, growing up in the years when Mrs Indira Gandhi declared the Emergency and muzzled the judicial system, I deeply felt that personal liberty couldn't be taken for granted any more. There were a bunch of other reasons too, and I will return to this topic later on. It helped that my philosophy began to lean towards liberalism. When you truly cherish a bunch of ideals, it just makes sense to simply find a workplace that doesn't clash with them. I decided to undertake the pursuit of liberty and justice for a living.

I learnt soon enough that justice didn't necessarily have a great deal to do with the legal system. I also learnt that justice was not of paramount interest to many service providers of the legal system. Last, and definitely most importantly, I learnt that the last thing the service providers in the justice machine wanted to do was be just to *each other*. It was a dog-eat-dog world of self-serving street fighting, no quarter was asked for or given, and the winner took all. When the velvet gloves came off, there was blood on every hand. It took twenty years for the reality of the legal world to sink in. When it did finally permeate to the depths of my soul, I enthusiastically embraced the ethical void. This book will tell you how I did this, and why. It is about that journey.

Now, you might ask why *you* would want to hear about my journey. I can think of many reasons. For one, most people still don't understand what the justice machine is really about. To live in this aggressive hostile world, and not understand the law, is a lot worse than hobbling about on two wooden legs. If you find yourself confronting the legal world—which is possible by merely jumping a red light at the traffic signal—you need to understand the plot that will invariably unfold. Then there is the business of managing your expectations. What should you do if someone does you in? What do you think the justice machine will do for you? To answer these questions, you need to understand how the justice machine works. Finally, there is a lot of esoteric gobbledegook and sanctimonious claptrap broadcasted by elements of the justice machine. It helps if you know enough about it to cut to the real chase. Knowledge is power!

So in a nutshell, I set out to write this book because I thought you, my dear readers, would benefit vicariously from my tryst with legal destiny, or perhaps from the story of my experiments with legal truths! Naturally, there are limits to what I can explain or even recall about the world of courtrooms and lawyers. I have tried to tell my story, but this does not mean that I have accurately portrayed either my life or the courts of the time. Capturing the whole sole truth would be impossible—for three reasons.

First, in my view, all events, when recalled, are retrospectively reconstructed. Subsequent knowledge is used to reinterpret the past. This is a continuous process. As we evolve as human beings, our understanding—our assessment—of events changes to better align our history with our updated values.

Second, everyone nurses ideological biases. We all experience life through the prism of our biases the same way a computer is limited by the architecture of the programs it runs. I am okay with that.

Third, I am now fifty-eight years old. Middle-aged minds are not as agile as their younger versions, and a declining memory does not help. We inadvertently compress events, distort them, see what we want to see and disregard the rest. What emerged in my case is this book.

This brings me to all the people I have described. I rarely see heroic qualities in people, but this does not mean that you cannot admire someone I do not admire. It also does not mean that those I admire(d) are not flawed in other ways. We all have our own yardsticks to evaluate people. Besides, my sense of who people are may have very little to do with who they are, and a great deal more to do with who I am. This is why I have changed some names in this book. Hopefully, this protects those who were present in the events described in the book, but see them differently.

If you find yourself in this book, I say this: you may think that I am wrong about you, but I reacted as I read you and that really is all there is to our mutual history. I reserve the right to be wrong. Besides, if you have an appetite for philosophical musings, you will agree that at the end of the day, there are no truths; there are only narratives. If you are a lawyer, you already know this. There are no truths, only pleadings, and evidence, and no matter what the judge decides, there is always an appeal. It is true that this process ends eventually but since I am an Indian lawyer, it does not end in my lifetime. This book is my personal narrative. If you disagree, do feel free to write your own book.

If writing your own book doesn't work for you, allow me to make you another offer. I have reserved unlimited space on my website ranjeevdubey.com for those who wish to place an alternative version of events described in this book for my readers. I will, if you so desire, publish your contribution under your name or the name used in this book, whatever you prefer.

At the end, may I timorously suggest that the universe is a vast and inexplicable place. In the total scheme of things, we are nothing, just dust and bones. In a hundred years, we will all be forgotten. Being offended is childish. None of it matters very much. So have fun with the book, and treat it as Krishna's *Leela*.

Part I:
The Doghouse Years

1

The Learning Years

I had two years of experience as a lawyer when I suddenly found myself handling a number of divorce cases. The story began when I represented Mrs Hardeep Kaur against a charge of marital cruelty. She was seventy-eight, had a forbidding moustache and very bad knees. Her middle-aged daughter-in-law wrestled her into court every time the case came up for hearings. Clearly, the old girl had always been built for comfort, not speed, but her cantankerous eighty-two-year-old husband found no joy in her embrace. Despite his immaculately tied turban and his flowing white beard, he was something of a Dirty Harry on steroids, always looking to 'make his day' on some imaginary provocation. He out-yelled his lawyer at every hearing, generally about not very much at all. He picked on the opposing lawyer (which was me) and the judge too, leaving everyone holding their sides and falling about laughing.

Mrs Hardeep Kaur's children didn't see the humour in it though. All of them—the old man, my client, the kids and the grandkids—lived in the same 500-square-yard bungalow in Green Park. They ate out of a common kitchen. It was a happy joint family, but the old man wanted a divorce. That put the kids in the impossible position of defending their mother against their father. The grandchildren—one of whom was my age—said that the old sardarji was seriously south of sanity. I was fascinated by the idea that the legal system had no institutional mechanism to stop geriatric loonies from suing for divorce long after their prostates had given up the ghost. The whole system was designed to promote litigation. And litigation, once started, could go on forever. At that point of my life, I pretty much stopped reading fiction. With this stuff going on around me, who needed a made-up story?

Hardeep Kaur's case didn't progress very much of course. Neither judge nor defendant wanted it decided. In time, I realized that the old *surd* didn't want it ended either: he was in search of emotional catharsis, not resolution. I made some professional progress riding on the back of that case. A joke can be a great foundation for a career. As the years went by, I got more and more of the same. A lot of my clients were women. I particularly recall a woman whose husband was a DTC bus driver. He liked to gamble, and since he didn't win much, there was never enough money at home. She picked up some jobs as a housemaid to cover the bills—sweeping floors and washing dishes in the Karol Bagh area—but he didn't like her going out to work. Their marriage went downhill and one day, he sued her for adultery. He claimed to have come home early and stumbled on her getting it on with the neighbour. There were no witnesses.

It was a bullshit story on the face of it, the kind of story a third-rate lawyer would cook up and hope to brazen it out. Adultery is notoriously hard to prove in India, unless the woman gets pregnant and her husband is in another country the whole time: like the much-loved Nepali cook with his pregnant wife at home! I was pretty cocky about the case. The problem with cocky is that you know you can win, so you start to get reckless. Inevitably, I royally messed up the bus driver's cross-examination. Let me explain. You can't get a divorce under Hindu law only because your wife is found naked in bed with a guy watching *Kaun Banega Crorepati*. For adultery to be proved, you have to prove penile penetration. In my youthful exuberance, that is where I took the guy's cross-examination.

'So when you pushed the door,' I asked the guy, 'wasn't it locked?'

'Jhuggi doors don't have locks, sahib,' his eyes twinkled. No alarm bell went off in my naive head.

'So, when you entered, what was your wife wearing?'

'She was as naked as the skull of her bald lover, sahib,' he giggled.

The judge cringed. He stopped the stenographer and commanded him to write: 'They were in a compromising position.'

'So where were they at the time?'

'Both were in bed, sahib!'

The judge was now red. He commanded the stenographer to write: 'They were in a compromising position.'

'Who was lying on the left side of the bed?'

'He was on top of her, sahib!' The guy was laughing.

The judge held his head in embarrassment. He commanded the stenographer to write: 'They were in a compromising position.'

I was too far gone to care.

'What was he doing when you saw him?'

'He had put it in and was "taking hers", sahib.'

The judge couldn't believe this was happening to him. 'Write, they were in a compromising position,' he barked. Then he turned to me. 'Vakil Sahib, client *bacha rahe ho, ya maze le rahe ho?* (Are you protecting the client, or entertaining yourself?)

Here's the deal. If a man claims he stumbled on to his wife getting it on with someone, all you need do is go on and on cross-examining him about the lack of witnesses. You can ask him how is it possible that when tiny mud huts stand shoulder to shoulder in a jhuggi colony full of unemployed adults and unsupervised kids, his wife found this beautiful patch of scrumptiously screw-worthy solitude to commit adultery. You can ask him why you should possibly believe such a nakedly self-serving story. You can assail his character. You can suggest he is a morally challenged loser who gambled away his family fortune and cannot be trusted. Heck, you can call him a lying bastard and a rake. What you cannot and should never do is help him flesh out and detail his story. You must never ask a question the answer to which you do not already know. You should definitely never explore your profound insights into legal principles and let that dictate your cross-examination. At the end of the day, what a judge thinks of a witness is all about human sensibility, not legal principles: it's to the man inside the judge to whom you must appeal. I had messed up big time.

It wasn't the end of the world: many lawyers lose nearly won cases, but this one remains by far the worst cross-examination I have ever conducted. Mercifully, no harm was done. One year later, when the matter was finally argued before another judge, the whole testimony was nothing but a series of statements saying 'They were in a compromising position', which meant nothing. I buried my blunder under the previous judge's embarrassment and saved the client from damnation. That's the thing about being a lawyer. Everyone gets paid to do a job right, but how many have so much fun doing it?

Occasionally I got to represent a male client in an adultery case. Once a shopkeeper from Chandni Chowk—portly, swarthy but rather lacking in self-confidence—wanted a divorce because his wife was carrying on with his unmarried younger brother. They lived in one happy joint family somewhere in Dariba Kalan. The moment he walked out the door for work, she scampered across to the teenager's room and they locked themselves in for hours. He had known about the affair for a long time: he came to see me because he could find no way to end it. 'Doesn't your family know?' I asked. 'Of course, they do,' he told me. 'So what do they say?' He was crestfallen. 'They say that if you can't satisfy your wife, you cannot complain if your brother does.' 'What does your wife say?' 'She says, "I visit your brother because he makes me happy but I am your wife and it's your duty to 'maintain' me."' 'Doesn't she recognize that it is wrong for her to sleep with your brother?' 'No, she says all this goes on in other families all the time so what is the problem?' 'Have you told your family that you want a divorce?' 'Yes, and they do not approve.' 'What do they say?' 'They say that marriage is a *janam janam ka bandhan* [a bond that spans lifetimes], which small things should not be able to change.' It was all culturally insightful stuff, and better than reality TV; better even than pornography!

It didn't end well though. I filed the case and we had a couple of hearings. The wife showed up with half of my client's family supporting her. They didn't say anything: just stood behind her and glared at my client through the hearing. As far as they were concerned, what went on between husband, wife and brother-in-law was private, whereas washing dirty linen in public humiliated the whole family. They were quite ready to produce six witnesses to say that the wife never visited the guy when the husband was at work. Six months later, he stopped coming. Eventually somebody told the court he had committed suicide.

~

The divorce practice monkey circus had to end sometime. For me, Sharmila was the last one. I guess either the disgust or the self-loathing finally got to me. Sharmila was one of those irresistible self-possessed girls the hotel industry loves to employ. She was beautiful in a characteristically Bong way. She had the curves to launch a thousand Khajuraho temples and her light chocolate skin was clear and smooth as soft clay. She didn't mince words either. Her husband was a nice guy, no question, but he was a crashing bore. She had been married seven years and she knew exactly what her life would add up to if she didn't get out right now. Her parents couldn't comprehend her problem. Her mother-in-law hung on to her skirt and begged her not to do this. Sharmila characterized herself as a very good daughter-in-law, a reasonably exciting wife and an absolute bitch in bed.

'I want to experience life completely, Ranjeev', she told me candidly. 'I sleep with who I like, when I like, where I like. And I want this life without strings or guilt.' In time, she asked about my fees, adding that the hotel industry doesn't pay well but she liked me, etc. I got her the divorce.

Talking of divorce cases, here's one I couldn't do because the lady in question wouldn't let me. I knew Sandy Dutta socially. He was one of those charismatically impish young men with mischief in his eyes, piercings in his earlobes and a big, banging chopper bike in the driveway. His charm was irresistible. I thought his wife Ruma was a complete woman. She was a competent interior designer, a talented landscape photographer, an avid trekker and a nurturing soccer mom. She radiated great inner beauty. We intermittently heard of trouble in their paradise. He drank too much and he was rumoured to be abusive. They fell out eventually and filed fourteen cases against each other. He accused her of infidelity, which no one seemed to believe. The guy he accused wasn't just a close friend: he was a thorough gentleman trying to help her. Other people who tried to help her also had to bite a legal bullet: Ruma's brother-in-law got arrested for stealing

Sandy's jeep, even though Sandy had lent it to him. When it came to anger management, Sandy was a full contact litigation client!

Ruma consulted me once but settled for a woman lawyer to represent her. The case dragged on for a decade and then, when enough legal fees had been paid, they settled it out of court. That happens often enough. This ancient land with its 5000-year-old living culture regularly calls for blood: when enough has been spilt, the parties reach a compromise, or one of them dies.

I heard Sandy's side of the story a decade later when he came by to see me about something else. He said he hadn't been angry about being cuckolded by his best friend. He was angry because he had been manipulated into a vasectomy before he was cuckolded! He blamed his father-in-law. 'I admired the Colonel, yaar,' he thumped the table. 'We had two kids and the bastard said, "Why are you assaulting my daughter's hormones with these birth control pills?" So off I went to Dehra Doon and twenty-four hours later, I was dry as a funeral drum. All I got to show was Rs 500 and a 2-kg tin of *shuddh* desi ghee while my buddy got to hump my fertile wife.'

By this time, he had remarried several times. His current wife was a lot younger, and the daughter of a powerful politician. She didn't think her parents would ever say yes to this much-married rake so she ran off to Delhi with him. The girl's father reported a kidnapping, and an arrest warrant turned up at his door. In turn, he stalled the warrant with a well-aimed bribe and produced his new bride in a local court to prove she had accompanied him willingly. You could say the girl's parents were pissed off. They bided their time. A year later, they found out he was attending a wedding in their town. This time, his estranged mother-in-law filed a complaint stating that he had molested her! The warrant of arrest landed up at the mandap of the wedding. Fortunately, Sandy's host could retaliate with some heavy pull so Sandy could slip away. By the time the same warrants reached Delhi, he had his anticipatory bail in hand.

Sandy is what every lawyer will call a dream client. Successful law practice is always about getting yourself a bunch of Sandies! They can be individuals, they can be companies, but for one reason or another, they always need lawyers. Many top-gun lawyers have made their careers riding on the back of just one client. The best character profile of a client is the guy who likes to live on the edge of legality and financial solvency. You get them aplenty. It's not that they can't make a profit doing things legally, working the percentages. They just have to run close to the edge. They over-leverage their business till it totters in bad times. They illegally shore up the stock prices of their publicly listed company. They trade in their own company's shares on the side. They creatively interpret regulations and run a dodgy business model with a respectable external face. When the crap hits the fan—and it always does—they run to the lawyer. Never say no to clients who can't say no to some crappy get-rich-quick scheme they know will blow up in their faces.

~

When I look back at my career and recall all the crazy characters I have represented, I ask myself if this is why I became a lawyer. For sure I didn't become a lawyer just because I thought it was good fun. Not that I mind that it turned out that way. What's there not to love about having fun being a lawyer? Unfortunately, a lot of it was also not fun; it was incredibly hard work with not enough sleep and no money at all. Of course, most people didn't have money at the time so who cared? It was a great time to be young, not least because of the tectonic cultural shifts going on. Asha Bhonsle and Robert Plant delivered screaming solos from the same radio station. Dope and dupattas were purchased from the same pavement in Chandni Chowk. Jamawars and jeans were worn together in winter. Meanwhile, urbanization and mass migration were shattering the old joint family social structure. Everyone, even my dad, wore a bell-bottom safari suit. The soft-focus Punjabi wannabe Bong superstar hero—and I mean Rajesh Khanna—was done and dusted: reduced to special appearances and a procession of remakes of Tamil hits. The Angry Young Man was well established, to a point where he was making movies about his own real-life marital infidelities! The politics was deafening, and exciting. Indira Gandhi had kicked India's tryst with destiny squarely in the belly with the Emergency. After her ouster in 1977 (the year I joined the LLB programme at Delhi University), a Jurassic idealist (Morarji Desai) ran the country assisted by a motley crew of ideological oddballs, caste jugglers and court jesters. That didn't last either. The country went to the polls in January 1980 and the old girl was back. That is when cynicism became the new normal in Indian politics. This is the year I became a lawyer.

I don't recall puffing out my chest because I had completed my law degree. Everyone remembered that India had recently been screwed over by lawyers. That gallery of eminence included Bengal's Chief Minister Siddhartha Shankar Ray who advised Indira Gandhi to declare the Emergency, President Fakhruddin Ali Ahmed who signed the order, 'kitchen cabinet henchman' D.P. Dhar who ran a parallel government during the Emergency, newly promoted Chief Justice A.N. Ray who leapfrogged over three of his seniors so that he could write odes to Mrs Gandhi in his judgments, and indeed much of the Supreme Court of India with the notable exception of Justice H.R. Khanna.

Law at the time was a family profession of fathers, children and cousins, all with uncles who were judges. You always needed a godfather to go to. If you didn't have a godfather, your faith in the Godfather (who art in heaven) greatly exceeded your common sense. I had a potential godfather, even if it was a long shot. A distant aunt had married Uncle Syal who struggled for thirty years to run an inherited business in terminal decline. When it finally went belly up, he joined the maverick law firm of Duli Chand Singhania.

Uncle Syal was amused that I wanted to be a lawyer. He didn't think a pretty kid from a snooty school in Rajasthan would survive a brutal contact sport like law practice in India. I wasn't going to be daunted. He had no job for me but he had good advice. 'You are not a lawyer till you have learnt to survive in the Tees Hazari courts,' he told me. 'This is the only place for you to test your mettle as a man, and as a lawyer. Besides,' he added for good measure, 'unless you want to depend on your father for a very long time, this is the only place a young lawyer can make a small living.'

He was right, of course. Throwing me in at the deep end was one way of testing my survival spirit. If I didn't make the cut, I could always tuck my tail in and go home to Dad's business. As a career launch, it was a huge improvement over becoming a *basta* vakil (a bag-carrier), carrying files for a hotshot Supreme Court senior for the rest of my life, standing behind him cheering and applauding his brilliant arguments just to get at the sorry crumbs he would throw me when the mood took him. I needed to find someone to work for.

This was a tough one. Every successful trial-court lawyer those days had dozens of juniors. Like the largest and most dominant carnivorous dinosaur with its long powerful tail, the worth of a lawyer was measured mainly in terms of the number of juniors who followed him from court to court. What chance had I to learn anything when so many attention-seeking juniors played groupie with the hotshots? When so many love you, is it the same? What about the competent but less successful lawyers? They had a certain amount of work, it's true, and besides, youngsters could interact with this class of senior: perhaps learn something. I joined one for a bit—without pay I'll have you know—and found this wasn't true. The client hired them because of the personalized service they provided. Their juniors never had the chance to represent the client in court. All the juniors ever did was run ahead of the senior as he went from court to court to tell the judge that the big boss was arriving, or was on his legs in another court, or had a runny tummy and wasn't going to show. It was a dog-shit job for dummies: like playing a plastic trumpet for a fake Mughal emperor in a budget Bollywood costume drama of the 1940s. In six months, I was ready to slash my wrists.

It was about this time that I noticed that over on the other side of Tees Hazari's Central Hall, there sat a beatific old man who always had this Buddha smile. On a particularly bad day, I stepped up to him and asked him what he thought of the profession. He was encouraging. 'It's the profession of kings, my son,' he declared. 'To be a lawyer is to be a master of your destiny. You need not bow to any man. If you don't like a client, there is always another. If a judge doesn't like you, there is always an appeal to be filed. No one can say anything to you.' I must have looked encouraged because he continued, 'Remember also that lawyers command a lot of respect.' 'Respect?' I countered, waving my arms at the riff-raff in the Central Hall. 'Make no mistake, my boy,' he warned me, 'in society, it is fear that begets respect. Everyone fears a lawyer.' He paused reflectively. 'There is one problem though,' he shrugged. 'When you have teeth, you have no chickpeas to eat. By the time you get your hands on the chickpeas, you have no teeth left to eat them with!'

Thirty years later, I recall his prophetic words and chuckle. I didn't know it then, but my luck was about to change very quickly.

2

The Yearning Years

I pretend to be an atheist but I do believe in miracles. Veena at that time, in that place, was that miracle. She was a batchmate from the Law Faculty of Delhi University. She was one of those self-confident, eternally optimistic girls from a middle-class Janakpuri-type family. She had boundless energy, great faith in God, and a warm helpful nature. She looked a bit like the actress Reena Roy—who you will remember was an economy-class Zeenat Aman—but she had way more oomph. She could gas even better than she could bewitch, but like Sonakshi Sinha, she captivated everyone. She rescued me from depression when she took me to see her senior: S.R. Yadav.

Yadav Sahib was a kindly man, with a soft demeanour. Much like the Dalai Lama, he never got round to learning how to be cynical. He hired me on the spot for Rs 500 a month. It was somewhat less than the rent I paid for my Safdarjang Enclave *barsati* but to be paid at all in those days was a kind of privilege. I loved that second-floor barsati for its commanding views and open vistas. I'm not kidding about the open vistas: even the roofless loo had a view. When it rained, I used an old green army raincoat to conduct my business. The boss lived close by in Hauz Khas and it took me less than ten minutes from my place to his. South Delhi was a sleepy suburban paradise those days: the Maruti revolution still four years away.

Finding Yadav Sahib was outstanding good luck. Law is a bitch of a profession when you start. There is far too much to know and you can't begin to function till you know a great many things. Youngsters get mauled in and out of court all the time. Like a bar fight in those spaghetti westerns, a young lawyer's main qualification is knowing how to take it on the chin and go crashing to the floor, then get up, knock the dust off and step back into the ring for another. Yadav Sahib's kindness dulled the pain. He was what in those days was called a Bank Panel Lawyer. India's largest banks at the time ran all their litigation through their pre-approved panel of lawyers. Any banker looking to file a case ran down the panel list and picked the lawyer he liked. To the lawyer, appointment to a panel meant a steady supply of low-value cases. If you managed to get on to one of these panels, you need never look for work elsewhere.

Low value and high quantities are magic for youngsters. Seniors didn't bother with the low-end stuff and large numbers meant high-speed experience. It helped that Yadav Sahib ran a substantial High Court practice too. He didn't show up in Tees Hazari till after lunch and by then, I could headbutt my way through twenty cases or more. Veena supported my ambitions. She was a people person and let me lead the grunt work. With masses of drafting to be done, appearances to be made, arguments to be addressed and cross-examinations to be conducted, I spent two years in Yadav Sahib's chamber thrashing about in a feeding frenzy like a killer whale in a sea full of dolphins.

To be a panel lawyer back then was to provide free home-delivered legal service to the client. Although Indira Gandhi had nationalized banks in 1969, it wasn't till she declared the Emergency in 1975 that her redistributive policies went ballistic. In her finance minister, she found a pliant groupie with an admirable devotion to his master's voice. He took public money from banks and distributed it to millions of poor people in highly politicized 'loan melas'. There were a lot of people to distribute money to. Sanjay Gandhi's slum-clearing initiatives had created a succession of new resettlement colonies—Dakshinpuri, Kalyanpuri, Jahangirpuri and Trilokpuri, amongst others—and banks were intimidated into indiscriminately distributing housing loans to displaced jhuggi-dwellers. This was great for the country liquor industry. Many, flush with cash, drowned in drink, and when finally sober, sold the possession of the plot for cash to drown in some more.

By 1980, it was clear that the loans were never going to be repaid. Most leading Indian banks were awash in red. The Reserve Bank of India was livid. Bank cases started to hit the courts and money started to flow into the coffers of panel lawyers. We filed recovery cases by the bushel on standard printed formats, the few blanks filled with a typewriter.

This was a great time to be the general manager of a bank branch in a resettlement colony. Given the brain-dead nature of the work, bank managers didn't pick lawyers for their devastating intellect. Kickbacks were built into the billing structure. Much of this money transformed into the finest Punjabi baroque houses in bank-sponsored cooperative colonies in West Delhi. It was all very transparent and upfront, or so I soon learnt. The first time I went to collect papers from a bank branch over an old case, the manager treated me like his prodigal nephew coming home. He sweet-talked me over sickly sweet milky tea and kept up a happy banter in Punjabi-English till I was encouraged to pitch for more work. His pleasure at the pitch was palpable. '*Oji* most welcome,' said he, 'but setting *te karoge na?*' (Translating roughly, will you 'set' me?). Bewildered, I nodded. That pleased him. '*Te karo,*' he said, and sat back expectantly.

There was this mysterious silence in the room for the next minute or so while I floundered about thinking of what to say. What on earth was he talking about? Eventually, he put me out of my misery by changing the topic. As the visit turned rapidly frostier, I realized I had worn out my welcome. That evening, I asked the boss what 'setting' meant. He was very amused: profit sharing, he revealed. Not every bank manager was in it for the 'setting' of course. Some spent their evenings with a successful panel lawyer in his chamber behind Tees Hazari. This guy kept a liberal stock of whisky in his chamber. Right about 5.30 p.m., as the courts started to empty, bank managers would toddle in and the party would begin. Reportedly another panel lawyer let bank managers use his chamber for rendezvous with local hookers.

I find it easy to believe the hooker story. A fair smattering of lawyers used to hook up with tarts in chambers in those days. I recall staying back late in my chamber once to find a garishly made-up young lady pop her head in the door and ask if I had '*koi* [any] requirement' in broken English. She was short, thin, dressed in a bright floral synthetic sari, the pallu dropped over her forearm, her blouse cut very low over very firm breasts. I noticed all this in a flash but I didn't get it. 'Requirement?' I echoed, stupidly. She cocked an eyebrow, tilting her head to one side, smiling. 'I'm not hungry,' I told her, thinking she was hustling samosas for the canteen next door. 'Let me know when you are,' she said, and glided by. In an hour, she was back. 'Are you hungry now?' she asked point-blank. I still didn't get it. 'No,' I said, vaguely irritated. 'What makes you think I would be?' She didn't bat an eyelid. 'In my work, babu,' she said, 'everyone gets hungry sooner or later!'

The penny did finally drop but by then, she had laughed hard and waved me goodbye. For someone in a brutal profession, her repartee and her optimism were not lost on me, nor the endearing flick of her delicate wrists. For years, before Dominos Pizzas stole her line, she would come by whenever she found me working late and ask, 'Babu, hungry *kya*?' I regret only that I never engaged with her. You don't have to want to sleep with every girl you want to get to know.

~

With old-school seniors like Yadav Sahib, delivery of quality service was the main path to progress. Yadav Sahib wanted honest hard work and integrity at the job, and I gave him that. Days for juniors were long then, as they are now. Bad logistics made a hard life harder. Youngsters in barsatis didn't own refrigerators. I woke up at seven every morning and joined the Mother Dairy Milk Booth line within minutes. Filling a vacuum flask with a half-litre of milk, I purchased one egg, two slices of bread and a small *tikki* (cube) of butter for breakfast every day, seven days a week. The egg was boiled over the cheap open-coil electric heater in six minutes. By 7.45 a.m., I was out of my barsati zooming out to Hauz Khas. Visiting the boss in the morning was important. There were files to be picked up, and he always had advice on how to handle the day's work.

The bike ride from Hauz Khas to Tees Hazari took about forty-five minutes back then. It took a lot longer in the monsoons when I used that same army-issue raincoat to hunker behind the handlebars of my steely Yezdi motorcycle and skate my way through the slush, the flowing drain water and the couldn't-care-less spray of arrogant car owners to arrive wet and dripping in the Tees Hazari courts. The rain ran down the collar in the gap between crash helmet and raincoat, and up the seat as I sat astride the metal beast. The success of the parka was measured largely in terms of how dry my belly button was when I arrived! There were many July mornings when I sloshed puddles behind me, waddling across the length of Tees Hazari like a drowning Cheshire cat in black shoes oozing some unspeakable gooey slush that looked as if it came out of the backside of a pig with a bad tummy because I hadn't had the time to drain them out. The show had to go on, rain or no rain.

The hours of work were frantic and one got the chance to observe a fascinating cast of characters. Tees Hazari then had a fair number of very honourable men whose calm legal expertise still leaves me breathless. Cyril Joseph specialized in marriage and divorce, and clearly the money was always in the latter! He was a compassionate man with a great sense of fair play. Then there was A.K. Srivastava, a thorough gentleman who never lost his temper, bullied anyone or otherwise disrespected either client or brother lawyer. The much-admired Ishwar Sahai Endlaw was perhaps the epitome of restrained respectability. He never raised his voice, never thumped a table, never ripped off a client and still won most of his cases. In watching these gentlemen, we youngsters somehow picked up a clear sense of what kind of lawyer we should try to be. That type has passed, that time has passed, and indeed the market for that kind of sensibility has passed.

At the other end of the spectrum were colourful people like the Kavel brothers. They ran a one-stop shop for skulduggery. Do you want a fake rent receipt so you can occupy someone's house illegally in Vasant Vihar? No problem. Do you want a guaranteed stay order no matter what your case? Sure, you got it. Then there was Tiger Randhawa, an aggressive Jat with piercing eyes, living up to his name. He could get any house vacated in six months. He made sure the court notice of any case he filed never reached the tenant. He then rushed through procedure till he had his judgment. He then hired goons to help throw the sorry sod out before the guy knew what had hit him.

In an even higher category was a waspy young man with a *makkhi moonch* ('toothbrush moustache', made famous by Hitler)—the spitting image of R.K. Laxman's Common Man—who later achieved great success in the Delhi High Court. He could get any order you wanted, you heard people say. He had a lot of clients and a lot of cash. His black Premier Padmini—the car, not the starlet of the time—carried a large sticker of a bird unfurling its wings across the entire width of its bonnet. Tees Hazari, even then, was full of delicious ironies.

This flotilla of success was peppered with a much larger gaggle of losers and also-rans. For two months before Yadav Sahib, I worked for the kindly Mr Jagga who was too decent to be corrupt and too dumb to be cunning. Tees Hazari trapped mediocre lawyers and slowly ground them into the dust till they believed passionately in their own nothingness. You saw them carrying the burden of their failure on their bent shoulders. They walked without authority, they spoke softly and they bobbed their heads forward in subtle submission as they greeted their successful colleagues in the corridors.

In any thinking man's profession, you are either disturbingly egomaniacal or you have terrifyingly low self-esteem. The low self-esteem created all kinds of destructive outlets. Some worked on the margins of legality: liaising for dirty cops, fixing courts, forging documents and hobnobbing with mobsters. Others embraced confrontation and disruption, spearheading strikes and confrontations with public authorities, heralding a new era in the history of the Delhi Bar.

Tees Hazari transformed considerably in the 1980s. The easy going Mughlai *tehzeeb* (Mughal elegance) gave way to a brasher popular culture. On the one hand, many of Delhi's rural residents had by now sold their lands for serious money and exchanged their dhotis for denims purchased in Mohan Singh Market by the side of Regal cinema. The uneducated amongst that lot drove taxis; those with college degrees became property dealers, or lawyers! At the other end were Partition-era refugees from West Pakistan. Theirs was a no-holds-barred get-ahead culture of aggression and insensitivity. It wasn't to do with their character: it stemmed from what they had endured to survive the slaughter, and what they felt they needed to do to get back to the social status they once had. Many old-timers stood aghast, alienated, unable to function in the hostile tenor of the times. Brinkmanship in Bar elections became the norm, and when the extremists won, they were compelled to deliver on the innate belligerence of their position.

What we got then was a perverse kind of politics, serial agitations over all manner of trivial issues. Tees Hazari was racked those days with acrimonious *morchas* and *andolan*s of an intensity that bore no relationship to the seriousness of the grievance. Small flashpoints led to large agitations. Lawyers struck work all the time, disrupting the judiciary, delaying cases and sending the clients into despair. I particularly remember the case of Rajesh Agnihotri, a lawyer who was arrested for theft in 1988. The cops produced him in court the next day without removing his handcuffs. It could have been deliberate; lawyers mauled cops in court all the time. The Tees Hazari lawyers went bananas. Rabble-rousers came out of the woodwork and let fly their flatulent rhetorical hot air. Kiran Bedi reacted a week later by lathi-charging the lawyers. A municipal councillor sympathetic to her views then brought truckloads of hooligans to Tees Hazari. Lawyers and goondas clashed in a pitched battle. We then had weeks and weeks of strikes till the authorities backed down.

The government reacted crudely to this new reality. They announced the relocation of the lower courts into five different buildings, one in each of Delhi's districts, half-heartedly projecting it as taking justice closer to the people. The Bar scoffed at the double-talking jive, denouncing it as a conspiracy to divide and rule. The courts shut down for weeks. Court bifurcation would have distributed the work more widely amongst lawyers: those with little work would have benefited, but they had no voice. I joined the profession to practise law, but I spent a lot of time twiddling my thumbs as lawyers locked court gates to enforce their strikes.

When the courts did function—about half the time they should have—I had myself a crash course in amoral pragmatism. I was bewildered by the idea that the legal community rarely looked at the rights and wrongs of any legal issue. As far as lawyers were concerned, there was the law, and then there were the loopholes. If they could fit the facts of their case into a loophole, well, that was great. If they could not, they could change the facts to fit the loophole. When it comes to helping your client win a point, the truth had no space between two cynical lawyers and a bewildered court. No one tarried a moment before lying through their teeth, posturing about things they knew were untrue, or putting on an emotional drama based on complete fabrications. Within two years, I had become an existential nihilist: there was no objective truth in the world, only random data reinterpreted and packaged into a court case. I had discovered the ethical void.

More than the ethical void, the lack of compassion was frightening. Senior Bar members treated youngsters like dirt. There was no sense of community, only predators holding knives behind their backs. A large gaggle of youngsters spent most of their time feeling incompetent and intimidated. There was just so much to know and, till they did, they were nobodies getting mauled by every senior lawyer because he could. Compassionate judges were the exception, more than the rule. Rent Controller Mrs Kanwal Inder was one of them. She protected youngsters from intimidation all the time, and rendered judgment without worrying about the stature of the hotshot appearing before her or the antics he got up to. Fortunately, she was not the only judge who did that.

For the most part, the judges were either too tired or overworked to care. A few were just plain corrupt. The lawyers knew everything about it: who had fixed whom and in what case, at what price, through which fixer. Corrupt judges got up to all kinds of antics. We had one caught red-handed accepting money in his chamber in Tees Hazari. We had another caught drinking with a farmhouse owner whose case he was hearing. We had yet another who took the money, then returned it after taking a higher sum from the other guy! Many judges had allegations thrown at them, though, clearly, there were some who were spotless. District Judge P.S. Sharma comes readily to mind. Everyone admired the man for his integrity. The price he paid for his honour was not obvious to me till I drove past him one day on my way to court in my newly acquired Maruti while he rode a scooter. Salaries being what they were, honour and humiliation were interchangeable. Years later, a young judge told me he was regularly heckled by undertrials on bail when he took his daily ride to court on a DTC bus. The bus was all he could afford, and there were days he feared for his life. Judges didn't demand or get Kalashnikov-toting guards back then.

~

Court work generally finished by 4 p.m. The action then moved over to Yadav Sahib's office next to Golcha cinema in Daryaganj.

Daryaganj was a great place to be at the time for at least three good reasons. First, it had some outstanding street food in the by-lanes. If you had the money, typical Delhi street stuff like papri, golgappas and tikkis were delightful, to say nothing of Moti Mahal's tandoori chicken farther up the road towards the Red Fort. If you wanted to go seriously retro-chic, you could walk up this road as far as the overbridge, turn left for Urdu Bazaar Road, hold your nose as you hurried past the masses of slithery scales and entrails of the fish market by the side of Jama Masjid and then turn left again into Matia Mahal till you hit Karim's. On a pleasant winter afternoon, when the pedestrian traffic was thin, you could walk the distance in fifteen minutes. Then, as now, it had to be mutton korma and roti—nahari (slow-cooked lentil mutton) if it was that time of the year. I remember interviewing one of the owners many years later when I moonlighted as a travel writer. The guy said his forefathers had learnt their cooking in the kitchens of Bahadur Shah Zafar, the last Mughal emperor. All masalas were ground at home from raw ingredients by the women in the family to secret recipes passed down from generation to generation. But he didn't see himself as offering Bahadur Shahi cuisine. What makes your food less than royal, I asked. He was thoughtful. 'We don't massage our goats with saffron oil for a year before we slaughter them,' he regretfully admitted!

The second reason to love Daryaganj was the shopping, of which the best were the books. You had no credentials as a literary type unless you were a regular visitor to its Sunday book bazaar. I used to skip meals to have the money to buy books I knew I would never read: Joyce's *Ulysses*, Tolstoy's *War and Peace* and above all, Sartre's *Being and Nothingness*. Without books like these on the shelf, how could you possibly attract any girls? Daryaganj also had about half of Delhi's aquarium shops: I visited at least three of them weekly, driving the owners nuts asking prices of stuff

I could not possibly afford. You won't believe the prices either: 50 paise for a pair of guppies, one rupee for a pair of goldfish, swordtails or mollies, and two rupees a pair for most cichlids including angelfish. Multiply that by a hundred for today's prices and you know what the cost of living was in those days. Daryaganj also had Delhi's first exclusive tea boutique in Sanjay Kapur's Aap Ki Pasand. You could taste the stuff before you bought it, and if you were just desperate for a cup of tea, you didn't have to buy a packet afterwards either! On a bad day, you could walk down to one of the many pharmacies across the road and buy yourself something to end the misery that was life for many Indians in those hopeless years.

The reason I loved Daryaganj most was that it condensed in a microcosm what Delhi had been and what Delhi was becoming. Chandni Chowk didn't change easily, but Daryaganj, at the very edge of Old Delhi, was quick to reveal its transformation. The 1980s saw the rise of the Middle Eastern body shoppers, agents who sent masses of unskilled workers to help transform small hamlets in the Arabian Peninsula to the glass-tower metropolises they have become now. Khan was a small-timer in a poky office one floor above Yadav Sahib's chamber when I joined him. By the time I left two years later, he had become Khanjee Enterprises. With this wealth came a vastly improved office, which in the murky buildings of Daryaganj meant all-round illegal encroachment. Not that it changed either his paan-spitting or the smell of cheap attar he sprinkled liberally about himself and his office.

Every evening after work, I picked up dal worth 50 paise from the dhaba below the office on my way home. Dal with four slices of bread was about as good a meal as a struggling lawyer could expect for dinner. Help was cheap and plentiful but you had to be at home long enough to use that help. I had a particularly trying time with the quarrelsome maids my kindly landlady fixed for me. Somehow, local Jat ladies always turned out to be pre-mixed tantrums on two legs waiting for provocation. Eventually she got me a ghaghra-clad gypsy from Rajasthan who took to bumming cheap cigarettes off me and sitting by my bedside on the floor early every morning regaling me with incoherent stories of her varied misfortunes. She was an abandoned wife, an unwanted daughter-in-law and a destitute woman. She wanted me to use my irresistible legal acumen to help her extract money from her ex-husband. I told her she needed to spend money to get money. She said she had no money to spend but if I could help her, I could *khushi manao* (celebrate happiness) with her! I guess everyone thinks single men in barsatis are fair game. Khushwant Singh would have been pleased.

I was rather impressed by her fair-mindedness in offering me just compensation for legal service, and had her clean my barsati for all the time I was there. She was one of the few who actually offered to pay me, one way or another; most relatives in Delhi only wanted legal service and anger-management sessions for free. Some were displeased when I could not win the crappy senseless cases they forced me to file and handle for free. It was a lonely life, but there was something in being the Marlboro Man. Amitabh Bachchan's rendition of his father's poem 'Kabhie Kabhie' was rather a hit those days. The hero's dialogue about conversations between him and his loneliness (*'main aur meri tanhai aksar baaten karte rehta hain'*) encouraged me to get myself a small Pomeranian pup whom I called Tanhai. Sadly, she whined incessantly all day while I was away, driving my landlady nuts. I had to give her away to Veena's cousin who broke my heart by changing her name to Sherry.

My two years of apprenticeship came to an end for the same reason that most jobs do. Some of it was fatigue. I was just so tired so much of the time. I had to travel long distances, work long hours and couldn't even afford enough nutritious food to eat. Some of it was boredom. I was doing the same job day after day and I didn't see growth any time soon. A lot of it was the quest for independence. It's a lawyer thing, as true then as it is now. Lawyers want to be masters of their destiny. I know law firm managers will tell you a different story. To succeed, you will hear us say, you need to be a great team player and a brilliant cog in the machine. This is self-serving rubbish of course. We want you to work like a dog and make us money. We will tell you what we need to tell you so that you will pull up your gumboots and shovel our garbage. If you want to go to places these same managing partners have been and more besides, you have to be your own person, even if you work for a law firm. Independence of spirit and originality of thinking are the hallmarks of all good lawyers, no exceptions.

So almost exactly two years after I came to work for Yadav Sahib, I bid him goodbye. He regretted my departure deeply, but he was an angel about it. With not a cent to my name or a client in my pocket, I went off singing 'Hum Honge Kamyaab'. It was the ultimate triumph of optimism over common sense. Thereupon began the grunt overs of my life's test match. I practised in the trial courts for ten more years. It laid the foundation of the career I later cobbled together. What running that law practice in the Tees Hazari courts meant in practical terms is the story that comes up next.

3

The Burning Years

Jobs, like marriage, are package deals. If you want to be an independent lawyer, you need an office. Departure from Yadav Sahib's chamber put me out on the street. Where was my office? Enter Uncle Syal again. He had no use for a chamber space he had on the Criminal Side of Tees Hazari. I shouldn't call it the Criminal Side. As advocacy experienced upward mobility in the pecking order of professions, Tees Hazari's Criminal Side chambers were elegantly renamed the Western Wing! The reality didn't change though. If you think of lawyers' chambers as air-conditioned high-rise buildings, it's time for a total review. Lawyers' chambers in my kind of India meant long rows of platforms a foot off the ground, built of highly adulterated cement by the municipal corporation in the dusty backyard of a trial court. These were then demarcated into ten-foot squares and 'allotted' to lawyers. When I first set eyes on the ones in Tees Hazari, they were like sabzi *mandi* stalls you still find across the country. At the time, the irony of lawyers' chambers looking like hawkers' stalls didn't strike me at all.

Getting the chamber built was effortless. Contractors prowled those platforms, offering an all-in deal for Rs 10,000. In four months flat, I had my chamber, inclusive of the electricity connection. Thus it was that in 1983, I cut the ribbon on my own full-fledged independent law practice! Which is not to say that the chamber brought me work: two people did. Yadav Sahib started to pass State Bank of India resettlement colony branch work to me regularly. I had walked out of his chamber, but he became my main professional lifeline. Even three years after I left, I still sourced 80 per cent of my work from his contacts. Somewhere in another life, Yadav Sahib must've had something he needed to give me. He picked this life to give it. If you are a lawyer and struggling as I was, I want you to know that you have a guardian angel waiting to take you under his wings, even if you don't know how to recognize him.

About the same time, State Bank of India Board member N.N. Mahajan sent me to see his Legal Head with a letter of recommendation. In weeks, I transformed into a State Bank of India Panel Lawyer. To me, the fortuitous magic of life is best illustrated by the fact that three people who owed me nothing— Uncle Syal, Yadav Sahib and N.N. Mahajan—got together and set me up as a lawyer out of nothing but the goodness of their hearts. This defined my fate for the next ten years.

It was not an enviable fate. Here's the deal: when High Court lawyers discuss their colleagues, they discuss the legal skills they bring to court. It doesn't work that way in the trial courts. When trial court lawyers discuss the work their colleagues do, the primary criterion is not the quality of their legal skills: it's the quality of their cash flow. I can understand this: three-quarters of all work in the trial court is soul-destroying: if someone is decently paid, he is truly envied. By any criterion anyone could conjure, I was at the bottom of the deepest drain and not going anywhere soon. Most of my work was low-end, low-paying and yielded low intellectual satisfaction. In comparison, the moonlighting I did as a journalist was magic. Regrettably, this wasn't an option. Before Vikram Seth, writing wasn't the road to making millions. It just made more sense to hang in there as a lawyer. Freedom really is another word for nothing left to lose.

Having nothing to lose did not mean that I enjoyed the drudgery of the next ten years. Every morning for a decade, I punctually left my Vasant Enclave flat at 8.45 in the morning and drove along the scenic road cutting through Delhi's forested 'ridge' past Buddha Jayanti Park. I then navigated the innards of Old Delhi to land at Tees Hazari by 9.30 a.m. You would probably need three hours to do it today! In the absence of mobile phones, the court clerk always waited for me in the parking lot. He collected my files and lunch basket and together we headed for the chamber. He was a snotty little fellow with a hyperventilating sinus. He didn't do handkerchiefs. He would wipe the dripping luminous bullfrog-green snot with the back of his hand and deposit it somewhere in the region of his right buttock. He was always trying to scam me out of a rupee or two.

Tees Hazari (translated into the Urdu as 30,000) used to be the only district-level court at the time in Delhi. The name came from the 30,000 Sikh soldiers who camped here under the leadership of Bhagail Singh in 1783 before attacking the walled city and occupying the Red Fort's Diwan-e-Aam during the reign of Shah Alam II in the closing years of the later Mughal empire. The place was a one-stop shop for all things legal when I started out as a lawyer. Delhi lived, loved and lost here: registering births, marriages and deaths. It also fought every class and style of court case here.

I once helped a friend get married to a lovely Christian girl under the Special Marriages Act within its walls. I remember her alighting from a black Fiat in a cherry-red sari looking radiant in her bridal finery and walking past a bus load from Tihar jail ejecting a long line of handcuffed undertrials with blood-splattered clothes; no doubt, they had settled some disagreement between themselves on the journey from Tihar. This kind of zebra-like yin-yang black-and-white totally polarized reality used to excite me a great deal in those days. When we got to the marriage officer, both bride and groom had to read aloud from a piece of paper a long statement solemnly affirming and declaring that they were above eighteen years of age and of sound mind, and voluntarily, with full knowledge of the consequences, without pressure from anyone, consenting to marry the other, or words to that effect. The statement ended with each of them further affirming on oath that if they had 'stated something that was untrue, knowing it to be untrue', they were aware that they would go to jail for one year with a fine of Rs 5000 or both! Who but the Indian justice machine could have thought up a marital vow like that?

The bride was in paroxysms of laughter before she was done but her old-school *fauji* dad was angrier about the perversity than he was about his beautiful daughter marrying a bania. Eventually, the two signed the register at the heart of what we call 'Registered Marriage' (no kidding about the register!). The ordeal wasn't over. Nearly out the door, the marriage officer wagged his finger at me, pointing to the groom. I yanked the groom back from the door whereupon the marriage officer smiled broadly, congratulated him, and handed him a gift 'on behalf of the Government of India'. It was a large carton of Nirodh contraceptives, all 144 of them!

But these memorable days were few and far between. On any other day, I had fifteen minutes before court time to split my daily list with the court clerk. By 9.45 a.m., each court had its own daily list posted at the door. We did one quick round at a trot before ten, noting case item numbers in each of the courts. We knew which judges were quick and which were slow. We knew which judges got to work sharp at 10 a.m. and which ones were perennially late. I had done this a long time and could predict when a case would be heard. At the end of the first round, we pretty much knew how the logistics of our day would pan out.

In India it takes four men to run a court, of which the judge is only the CEO. If you walk into almost any court, you will see three of these four people. The gentleman sitting in the middle on the high table is the judge. On either side of him, you will find the court reader and the stenographer. The court reader is the second in command here. He manages the court's files during hearings, calling out cases and handing over files to the judge. He also writes many standard form orders without reference to the judge! He is a powerful man. If you don't want your case heard, your court clerk can bribe him to lose the file for a day. If your opposite party paid him to lose your file but you need an important order from the judge, your court clerk can pay him to find your file quickly. Lawyers generally don't get caught up with bribing the court's staff but it's very difficult to run a successful trial-court practice without keeping a lot of court staff 'happy'. That makes the court clerk a key player. You need him to keep the court staff happy and he knows that you need him. This leads to expanding arrogance and capricious behaviour. Court clerks are never happy with their salaries, no matter how much you pay them. True happiness comes from scamming.

Court clerks scam all the time. They have countless ways to make money. They claim non-existent expenses, they pad up expenses, and they create self-inflicted problems and then claim expenses to fix them. The wealthier a lawyer, the wealthier his court clerk. There are many reasons for this. The court clerk of a successful lawyer gets a volume discount rate from the court's staff. This discount is never cycled back to the lawyer. Sometimes, the court clerk has court expenses reimbursed by both his employer and the client! Only genuine pricks become court clerks. Which I guess is just as well. I once had a retard for a court clerk who was asked to find out the next date of hearing in a case which was adjourned in my absence. Now you can't get that kind of valuable information without paying off the reader. The court clerk misunderstood. In five minutes, he was back shaking from a tongue-lashing from the judge. The judge demanded my immediate presence. I hastened to comply. The judge was seething with rage. He dressed me down mercilessly. It seems my court clerk had offered money directly to the judge while asking him for the next date of hearing!

The stenographer is the lowest in the court's power structure. It was his job to take down orders, and witness statements and judgments. Many did not know shorthand and typed directly 'on the fly' on ancient clattering typewriters. If the judge obtained the services of a second stenographer because he was behind on his work, the court sounded like something between a clattering steam locomotive and rapid gunshots: exactly the sound you had in the opening train-robbery sequence of *Sholay*. The steno was the least useful guy in the house, but if you needed an informal copy of anything he typed—a witness statement, an order or a judgment—he gave it to you while the file was still with him. His window of opportunity was short, because the reader grabbed the file as soon as he could, appropriating the revenue stream. Court records are cashable assets, and court staff fight mercilessly to control that revenue.

The final fourth leg of the judicial pillar is the court *ahlmed*, the guy who generally sits behind the lines of steel almirahs at the far end of the court. He is the storekeeper. He manages files between hearings, and that includes issuing summons to parties and witnesses. He is not visible at hearings but he is the man in the background, always in control of whatever happens in the case file. He is the guy your court clerk goes to when you want the record to look a certain way: like losing a document here or a pleading there or sticking in stuff you forgot to file the first time. In the rogues' gallery of solution providers in the justice machine, he is the last-stop shop because he has possession of the record for the longest time.

Lonely Planet never figured this out, but 10 a.m. sharp is the time to be a tourist in search of exotica in the Tees Hazari courts. Like a herd of rampaging elephants in the throes of a *mast*, a thousand lawyers scamper for the courts in a flurry of elbows, grunts, knees and chest bumps. This side of the Light Brigade's charge, where else in the world would you find such a dense concentration of alpha males in search of someone to bully, bluff, befuddle and bludgeon? Rush hour in the Delhi Metro has nothing on us. It's 'miscellaneous matters' in the first hour: meaning cases where the court supervises simple procedural stuff. Did you file the court fee and summon the other side? Have you filed your reply to the case or some application? Did you provide a copy of this document to that party? Do you admit the other side's documents or are you claiming he forged them? Seventy per cent of all cases on any given day fell into this category. This was always my neurotic nightmare hour. On average, I had sixty minutes and twenty courts to visit in a four-storey building 600 metres from end to end. On any given day, I negotiated the crush of the staircases and walked about three kilometres in that first hour. I even did this in a black coat on summer days when the temperature could hit 40 degrees C by 11 a.m. Bathed in sweat, eyes smarting from the salt trickling into them, having done this for twelve years I don't give a rat's sorry arse for acid rain, or global warming, for that matter. Humanity will overcome.

It was tough going though. If I didn't make the case when it was called, the court generously set the file aside for a second call in an hour. If I still didn't make the call, the court could set it aside to be heard at 2 p.m., but would likely dismiss the case for 'non-appearance'. That meant cost and time. Let me explain how. First, to restore the case to its 'live' status, I would have to file an application. This application would be 'put up' before the judge the next day. Very likely, he would have forgotten all about the cases he dismissed. He would then issue orders to the ahlmed (yes, the guy sitting behind the steel cupboards) asking him to produce the file in a week or so. The next week, the file would have travelled 15 feet from the ahlmed to the judge. The judge would now 'take up' the matter. Naturally, the law did not allow the judge to 'restore' the case unless he had heard both parties. He would then send a Court Notice to the opposite lawyer to come by and tell him why he should not be restoring the case. Since he had a busy calendar, he would adjourn the case by a couple of months for the next hearing. If the opposite lawyer didn't get the notice within this period, or did get it but fell sick, I could end up losing six months in just trying to get the opposite lawyer to show up. If he did show up, he could ask for an adjournment to contact his client, or he could say the client–lawyer relationship was over because the case had ended. More likely than not, the judge would send the notice to the client directly, which he did his best to avoid receiving. A dozen hearings down the road, when the opposite party did receive the notice, the same old lawyer would show up and demand that he be compensated with costs for the inconvenience caused!

When people talk to me about the law's delays, I talk to them about the attitude of the service providers. We are all part of it: lawyers, judges and court staff. We have set up a system that is designed for the producer, not the consumer. It can't move any faster. Where else in commercial life would you defer a decision on an important matter for three months because a service provider is 'on leave' or the lawyer is attending his distant uncle's funeral? Cases 'dismissed in default of appearance' were an extreme example of this attitude. More often than not, lawyers would complain, cases were dismissed in default en masse because the judge had probably not met his case disposal targets. When the deadline to show disposal loomed at the end of the month, they accused him of dismissing as many cases as he could. The cases wouldn't be restored for a year and by then, he would have been transferred.

Dismissed cases provided a great source of revenue for many service providers in the justice machine. You pay the stenographer and the oath commissioner (who stamps the affidavit) to prepare the application. You pay the government to file the application. You tip the court staff when you file the application. You pay the postal authorities to send the notice. Everyone makes money out of a dismissed case. The poor guy who filed the case seeking help from the justice machine is the only one who loses in the bargain.

It was worse if the opposing lawyer was a friend of the judge. Some lawyers at the time may have invested wisely in their relationships with judges. Is that why these lawyers received liberal court 'costs' from their opponents, sometimes for the smallest infractions of procedure? It was commonly alleged that some lawyers made more money collecting costs than they did collecting professional fees from their clients. You can never understand petty racketeering till you understand the conditions in which the subordinate judiciary functions in India. All that the majority of well-meaning judges could do to keep their heads above these murky waters was to see what they want to see and disregard the rest. Which I suppose is as it has always been with right-thinking people.

By 11.30 a.m., most courts had disposed of their long lists of 'miscellaneous cases'. The business now moved to 'evidence cases' and 'argument cases'. Evidence means statements of witnesses and it's nothing like the stuff you see those metrosexual mother-fixated shaven-chested heroes do in Bollywood movies. Witnesses in trial courts are obliged to be heavily tutored. They are judged on their ability to parrot whatever is written in the statement of claim or defence, depending on who they represent. If you ever find a witness who looks like he is telling the unadulterated truth as he experienced it, you should pause and carefully examine his lawyer. Why didn't the lawyer tutor this witness? Is he completely daft? Or is this lawyer the saint you have always needed to guide your spiritual growth?

In Tees Hazari, a busy court had twenty witness statements to record before lunch. The court would have to do it three at a time, the stenographer hammering away at the typewriter in one, the reader writing another in longhand, and the judge writing down a third in longhand. You had to admire the dedication even though the chaos was bewildering. The judge was generally too busy with his own statement to supervise the other two guys. Neither reader nor steno particularly wanted to record lengthy statements: they shortened sentences, distorted content and compromised the case, squabbled with lawyers and witnesses, demanded bribes to go on writing. These guys—unqualified, without a law degree—settled squabbles between lawyers on what was a 'leading question' or 'admissible evidence'.

It didn't help that the lawyers were trying to distort the statements too. If your witness stated two things, you expanded it to three. On the other hand, if the witness was produced by the opponent, it was your duty to object to every answer, rattle the witness, unsettle the other lawyer, lead the witness to places he doesn't want to go and generally add to the confusion. Getting a statement recorded without distortion was the ultimate test of grit in a very merciless world. It was a pathologically aggressive, homicidally hostile and nerve-wracking procedure. In that hour, your hard-pumping heart had bloated your face like a rotting pumpkin in a Jaisalmer summer. By lunch break, judge, stenographer, reader, lawyers and witness were all exhausted, their aromatic armpits speaking louder than words on an airless day.

The two hours after lunch were devoted largely to 'arguments' of all types. The 'arguments' period in a court was the picture-perfect form of spectator sport. This is when those who sat in the back saw the best legal skills come to the fore featuring thrust, feint, repartee, sarcasm, aggression, conciliation, drama, sentimentality, righteous outrage, mystery, suspense, disclosure, revelation and of course reconciliation all rolled up and scripted like an Ekta Kapoor serial! Trial lawyers are a highly skilled lot. A decade of effective trial experience in India is equal to a dozen incarnations in a superior court. Trial lawyers have the law at the tips of their fingers. It's a joy to see a pair of experienced pugilists perform over an evenly poised case even if the arena looks, and smells, like a gutter. Tees Hazari, at the time, operated like Tau Chandagi Ram's wrestling akhara.

Since I represented mainly SBI, my cases were boringly standardized. Final arguments were few and far between. Judges knew my case better than I knew it because a hundred lawyers had argued substantially the same case a thousand times before me. They knew which page of what documents to look at and most didn't want to see me at all. A case would get posted for final arguments, I would do the lawyers' equivalent of a formal

'Helloji, helloji' to the judge and he would reserve it for orders without a word from me. For this reason, I frequently found myself free after lunch, with time enough to have a relaxed meal and go over the next day's cases. Equally often, I would go home in the afternoon for a longish nap before I started work again for the next day in my office in the evening.

~

Whichever way you look at it, Tees Hazari was a brutal place to practise law. No one took any prisoners. You fought to kill and lived to fight. People who pulled their punches or hesitated before delivering the fatal blow basically lost. There were no prizes for second-best. Coming as I did from a privileged, protected environment, I was bewildered by the mercilessness of it all. This place was supposed to be about justice and fair play, but that did not extend to the way the lawyers treated each other, or the client. It was worse for women. Coming from a westernized cultural background, I could not understand the mindset which said all women were objects. They were watched with a very frank measured gaze, evaluated harshly with no empathy, and then treated as one of only three types. They were mothers, sisters and daughters to be protected, wives to be pushed around and reduced to servitude, or whores to be casually 'enjoyed'. There was no nuanced reality. Any newcomer was looked over and typecast in minutes, slotted by the way they carried themselves, or spoke. Rarely have I sat with a bunch of lawyers and not had one or the other raise an eyebrow at a passing girl and go wink, wink, nudge, nudge. It was truly weird.

From a woman's viewpoint, the environment was supremely intimidating. The glass ceiling was very real, and women had to work thrice as hard to be taken seriously. Worse, a fairly popular opinion of the time held that mothers, sisters, daughters and wives should all stay at home. Ergo, all women who came to court were whores. Women sensed this lingering hostility and many reacted to it by becoming hard-hearted. Others nursed a sharp tongue. Over a period of time, the 'feminine' women, if that is the correct way to put it, either left or transformed themselves into 'aggressive' women. To this day, I see this as a brutal example of people transforming themselves depending on the incentives provided by their environment. It's the same case in jail.

However, I am not suggesting that all women there were angels under siege. Even back then, I could see that in professional life, everyone made the best of the qualities they possessed. This was true everywhere, not just of lawyers. Men who were dashing and handsome pretended to hail from a blue-blooded lineage they did not descend from. Men who were suave and well-spoken projected intelligence they didn't possess. Girls who were pretty fluttered their eyelids and obtained favourable orders from judges. Those who saw the percentage in it slept their way up the ladder. I do suspect that two girls I knew were sleeping with their seniors. It's hard to be sure because there was just so much loose talk in this hyper-sexualized environment. I do know that the senior of one of these girls constructed a room above his chamber on the Criminal Side, converting it into a double-storey structure. He installed a bed there so that he could 'rest' between hearings. All too soon, he took to discussing upcoming cases with the girl up there every afternoon. In time, others were discouraged to go up the stairs while he rested. When the girl acquired leverage in that chamber disproportionate to her legal skill, sacking juniors and staff and lording it over everyone, everyone drew the obvious conclusion.

The other case was even clearer. This girl was a contemporary, attached to a criminal lawyer. I was trying to understand that branch of law, with little success, and learnt something from her description of the inside track. She was an amicable sort from a humble background, her father a clerk in some department. Her senior was reasonably successful, with a fair-sized office somewhere near Chandni Chowk. Like many criminal lawyers, he was supremely self-confident and extremely aggressive. I didn't think she would last, but last she did. There was a lot of non-platonic touching between the two in full public view when they were in court. She was comfortable with it. I thought the old guy was trying to say 'this here is my property so you guys keep off'—a preventive measure in Tees Hazari's predatory environment. It was only the beginning. Soon, she told me she had moved out of her parents' place and rented two rooms above her senior's office. She said she was inevitably late going home from the office and it was just more practical. In time, she stopped coming to the office. Years later, I was searching for some electronic component in Lajpat Rai Market off Chandni Chowk and stumbled into her. She invited me in for tea and went to her two-room set. She was comfortably off and she didn't mince words. She did not go to court any more but she did go down to the office for a couple of hours a day and help. She had not married and 'sahib' took good care of her.

Another lawyer I knew ended up as a mistress, though not to a lawyer. This is really Veena's story but I will tell it as best as I can remember. We both knew a girl, Kiran, who worked in a chamber nearby. She spent a year or two in Tees Hazari. Eventually she told us she had taken a job with a company in the Dariba Kalan area and invited us over. Veena decided to stop by the next time she was there shopping for jewellery. It was an amicable visit, but after lunch, as the afternoon progressed, Kiran's fat bania boss started to get restless. Clearly, he wanted Veena to leave but Veena was very good at not being told what to do. She kept up the banter with Kiran till he determinedly marched up to Veena and said, 'It's time for Kiran to rest so please come another time.' Back in the Daryaganj office, Veena couldn't stop laughing. 'Whatever he wanted to do, would he do it by resting,' she giggled.

Talking of 'rest', journalist Paran Balakrishnan, who helped kick-start my career as a freelance journalist, used to run the Sunday supplement *Economic Times Esquire* back in the late 1980s. In a maverick attempt to bring friendly neighbourhood excursions to the drawing rooms of the pink-paper reading classes, he sent me off to write a Weekend Getaway piece on the Sultanpur Lake. My wife and I decided to overnight it. We thought we'd arrived early but by noon the hotel car park was full and we were just in time to take the last of the available rooms. I filled in the hotel register. Every room was taken by Mr and Mrs Yadav, Mr and Mrs Hooda, Mr and Mrs Singh, Mr and Mrs Takhait and so on. No first names, no initials, and addresses shown merely as Old Bazaar Gurgaon, New Road Hissar and so forth. All of them also had the same 'purpose of visit'. It was 'rest'! We went back to the restaurant for lunch. It was Saturday and we were the only ones. Where was everyone? The waiter explained that hotel guests generally confined themselves to room service. I went off to photograph the birds after lunch. By the time I came back at dusk, all the cars but mine were gone. Which leads to the key question: with this much resting going on in Haryana, wouldn't you expect the Khap Panchayats to be upset?

Do female lawyers carry on with their male juniors? I doubt it. In the twelve years I spent in Tees Hazari, I only heard of one, and not a successful one at that. This boy was pretty rather than handsome, and his boss was an aggressive middle-aged woman who was very quarrelsome in court. She did criminal law and property disputes, mainly from one part of the countryside south of Delhi. Some months after he joined, it seems she started making overtures at him which he failed to spot. Eventually, he complained to a friend of his that she launched herself on to him one evening, grabbing his crotch before he could react. He quit her chamber right there and then, and law practice entirely soon after. I didn't believe the story at the time because the idea of sexually aggressive Indian women was still a bit off the usual curve. In any case, I would assume that middle-aged women would not risk their reputation on a young boy who was likely to brag about his conquest to his buddies the first chance he got.

What about lawyers and judges? I can tell you a couple of dozen stories of judges who slept with young women lawyers. Most of these stories were told by lawyers who had lost a case to the same woman lawyer. Such rumours are valueless. I did hear of one lady judge who reportedly romanced a subordinate clerk. She was the daughter of a presiding judge and Tees Hazari was all abuzz with her behaviour in her chamber behind the courtroom. They locked themselves in; she always ordered two cups of tea and asked not to be disturbed; she always went to the toilet immediately after he left her chamber. Who knows? Maybe she had an irritable bladder and tea didn't agree with her. I do know that months after we heard these stories, her exasperated father was compelled to marry her off to a gentleman said to be well 'beneath her station'.

～

Notwithstanding these entertaining diversions, trial court law practice was not for the faint-hearted. The hard part though was not in doing the work, it was in getting it. The chief difficulty with being a self-employed trial court lawyer even now is the multi-dimensionality of the role. You have to invest time in developing client relationships even as you invest time in acquiring legal skills. At the same time, you have to invest time building up an image with the subordinate judiciary even as you try to bring up a family. Inevitably, most lawyers are consummate jugglers, permanently on the edge of chaos. Since it is low-paying work, you have to do a lot of cases, which means long hours in the chair. Tees Hazari's foremost criminal lawyer at the time, the inimitable Dinesh Mathur, always said that the quality of a lawyer should be measured by the expansive width of his buttocks. If he really has put in long hours in a chair day after day for decades, why doesn't he look like he has boulders in his ass? It's a terrifying catch-22. Long hours of work mean little to spare for business development. If you haven't collected the work, you can't demonstrate your legal skills. But if you do circulate socially a great deal, you haven't the time to develop the legal skills.

That apart, we are talking about two entirely different skill sets here. Legal skill requires you to be incisive, introspective, analytical, obsessed with minute detail, and wildly ecstatic about spending humungous periods of time by yourself mentally masturbating over some obscure principle of jurisprudence. On the other hand, client development activities require you to be a pleasantly amicable sort of fellow, confident and dependable and none too threatening, ever available to your social contacts to hear a hard-luck sob story or attend a funeral. These are inconsistent roles, and many lawyers are never quite able to balance the two. Those who do, make it to the top.

As for me, like many of my contemporaries, I shot myself in the foot every week and determinedly made it to the bottom. My banker benefactor N.N. Mahajan once said to me that the secret of a successful life is not successful work, it is successful relationships. Being good at your work cannot give you what being bad with your relationships can take away from you. Trained to be hostile, aggressive and domineering, many lawyers all but chop their own professional crown jewels off. Others, who just don't have EQ or PR skills, never get the show on the road. Since I had all the vices and not many of the virtues, a decade passed with not a lot to show for the time. More often than you would think, I asked myself what I had been smoking when I decided to become a lawyer. It wasn't fair pessimism, because, as I eventually came to learn, this profession had room for people like me too. My luck was about to change.

4

Hard Choices

Every other kid I meet these days tells me he or she is studying to be a lawyer. I find this bewildering because as professions go, law is a particularly difficult one. Besides, many of these kids don't look tough or gritty to me. I can't help thinking that these kids have been seduced by the image people like Arun Jaitley, Kapil Sibal and Abhishek Manu Singhvi project on prime-time TV. They don't see the grunt work behind the glamour and the glitz, at least not till they get through law school and find themselves pitched right into the blood-splattered gladiator arena of Indian courts. Then they stagger about looking like shell-shocked survivors of an artillery barrage, their minds numb and their senses dulled. This is when they start to make mistakes and wreck their careers. They pick the wrong career path to follow, or at least one that leaves them an incomplete professional.

Any youngster entering the profession has hard choices to make. For example, one can be a litigation lawyer or a corporate commercial lawyer. Of course, one can also be just an intellectual property rights (IPR) lawyer, or just a competition lawyer, or just a shipping lawyer, but these are very narrow choices. Lawyers often make more money doing these narrow things. That is easy to understand. A narrow field is easy to master. The lawyer gets on his feet quicker. Then he can make money. But it's dumb to follow the money. Prince Paan outside Moti Mahal Deluxe makes more money than most lawyers. Why not open a paan shop instead? Chasing money is silly. The trick is to make money chase you. That happens because a lawyer has many skills, not because he can do only one thing. Think of the risk of having a narrow skill. If you find out a decade later that you don't like the job, or aren't very good at it, who is going to drive you home that night? Realistically, if a young lawyer wants to practise law, he has to either join a law firm to practise full-blown corporate commercial non-litigation law, or go to court and become a litigation lawyer. If his law firm has a litigation practice, so much the better.

So which is the better option: litigation or corporate commercial law practice? Frankly, in my view, it's a no-brainer. A lawyer may think he can write a fancy contract. How does he know it's fancy till he knows what a court is going to do to it if it gets its hands on it? It's difficult to be much of a corporate commercial lawyer till one has spent some years in the courts finding out how the courts view such manic-obsessive provisions as the force majeure, non-compete and hold-harmless clauses! Sure, it's great to be a corporate commercial dealmaker. That's what I became eventually, but I would not recommend that anyone should think about doing it till they've spent some time in court figuring out how the crap goes down in the real world where these things are evaluated, judged, violated and buried. Some of the country's best corporate lawyers have been great litigation lawyers: Zia Modi comes to mind before almost anyone else.

The angst of making a decision based on insufficient criteria does not end there! It's not enough to decide to be a litigation lawyer: the youngster then has to choose which court to practise in, and it comes down to one of three. He can go straight to the top, he can go to the middle, or he can go to the bottom. If he decides to go to the Supreme Court, he is playing footsie with appeals from cases he is incapable of fighting. This means he looks great arguing a pure point of law. When it comes to a meaty question on how cases get decided in Indian courts, he is in way over his head. Who is going to hire him to fight their cases when he knows nothing about what these cases have endured to get to the appeal stage? They might if his daddy is a great lawyer. They might if he is this great legal mind who flows like divine munificence from the hand of God (and the head of Maradona!). For the rest of us, mediocre as we are, the dice gets loaded against us. I have always believed in picking realistic goals and then working diligently to achieve them.

What of the middle option? High Courts are great to go to if they accept civil trials, but not all High Courts do. Civil trial cases are of the Tees Hazari type, like you see in the movies: where someone does someone wrong and you have witnesses and emotional arguments and the long-lost son reunites with his mother in the end. High Courts that have an 'original civil side' offer a great variety of experience. The young lawyer can then learn a little about how cases are tried, and he can learn a little about appeals and writs. If the High Court he joins doesn't accept new trial cases, it's like joining the Supreme Court at a lower level. What would be the point of that? With each passing year, starting up by joining a High Court is becoming a bad idea. Delhi High Court still accepts civil cases of all types but the cases get fewer and fewer as the minimum claim required to go there gets bigger and bigger.

This is why I remain a big believer in going down to the bottom of the ladder to pick up key legal skills. There are two benefits to this. In the short run, a young lawyer is more solvent because he picks up small cases with small fees soon enough. It's good for his ego too: beyond a point, asking his mother to pay the girlfriend's dinner bill isn't a big improvement over serenading her on shit creek in a leaky boat. More significantly, if a young lawyer does this, he has an end-to-end experience and he understands the entire production chain from raw material to after-sales customer service. In the long run, this is the best way to become a CEO.

Fancy consulting a managing partner of a law firm about your legal problems and finding that he is clueless about 90 per cent of them because he started in the Supreme Court! Either that or he is bullshitting his ass off. My law firm has cases in most High Courts, and I spend a lot of time hiring lawyers around the country. When I go looking for legal skill, I don't invite the dispensation of bullshit: I steer the topic under discussion till I understand what appointments this guy has been keeping.

This is a good time to sound a note of caution. Starting at the bottom in litigation is a great idea but it's also a great trap. For further information on the trap, ask me. Even better, to understand why an idealistic preppy from a snooty boarding school should be hanging about a place like Tees Hazari, ask me! Indeed, why become a lawyer at all? At a pinch, I would say three reasons: (i) the obsession with autonomy, (ii) the search for a mission and (iii) the need for diversity in life. An explanation is probably in order.

Start with autonomy. Which overgrown teenager doesn't want independence? Unfortunately, we live in a very interdependent world. The snooty top-class boarding school I was shipped to when I was ten was a crash course in existential absurdity! My first memory of it dates back to 1968: of being roused at dawn one icy January desert morn in an ethereal grey dorm where shadowy figures in white floated about like zombies with toothbrushes in their mouths. We herded into a bathing room full of boys jostling for position screaming 'next to you' at each other. In school, we did not form a physical queue. We yelled 'next to you' and that set up the order in which we would 'form up' to do anything. When my turn to bathe came, I was told that I was 'not allowed' to keep my underwear. Bathing in underwear it seems was forbidden by the rules. In an affront to everything that my small-town upbringing had taught me thus far, I learnt that immodesty was a virtue. Shivering in the dark on that cold winter day, I concluded that, in life, most rules are ridiculous: indeed, that rules depend on the ideological prejudices of the rule-maker.

Nearly fifty years later, the question whether one should or should not hang on to one's underwear continues to hover over the country. All around us, the dark and dirty deeds of rich, successful people are exposed in the newspapers, leaving them naked as if they have had the clothes ripped off their hips—but with no bad long-term effects. Others contract to take them off for cash, like Sunny Leone. Yet others take the cash knowing that sooner or later, their clothes will come off, like former telecom minister A. Raja and countless others. Shamelessness and adaptability may be synonyms in the India of today, but the lingering sense of absurdity is inescapable. Rarely are rules made because they are good for our collective well-being. Agendas are wrapped in hoopla and sold as eternal truths. Following rules that make sense to you seems reasonable. That is, other than rules you have to follow if you don't want your head lopped off, and there are plenty of those to go around.

Not long after, two events changed my perspective on my fellow men. As early as my first Sunday in school, I ran into a batch mate at the sandpit by that scrawny thorn tree near our dorm who promptly announced that God did not produce babies, some unspeakable activity between my parents did. This was an outrageous idea but my protests only brought jeers from everyone in the vicinity. I carried that humiliation with me for a long time. Even a ten-year-old could figure out that knowledge was power: a tool you can use to browbeat and dominate your peers. It followed that what held us together as a society was a bond of power, not companionship or love or even compassion. This is when I started to read books like a fiend, accumulating knowledge as nations accumulated weapons of mass destruction.

Some months later a scrawny kid, who didn't look like he could haul up the weight of his own shorts, picked a fight with me and beat me to a pulp for no reason that I can remember. All my friends at the time watched this dust-up with keen interest, one providing expert comments on my declining fortunes as I found my face progressively ground into the gritty dirt. Unable to believe that the downfall of a friend could be wildly entertaining to peers, this trivial incident led me to question group dynamics in any social structure. That is the day my mind broke free of social influences, and so it has remained.

While still less than eleven years old, it became apparent that our little boarding world was divided into a few leaders, a lot of groupies and the occasional oddball. One such was a genuine Bawajee eccentric who carried reptiles in his coat pocket and put other people's toes into his mouth on a dare. I began to understand that oddballs had their own place in the world. It was not necessary to either conform to anything or agree with anyone, nor become someone's groupie to be gratuitously gang-banged for fun. When you step beyond the pale and choose to follow the dictates of your own mind, a heightened sense of self-awareness is inevitable. This is a good quality for a lawyer to have.

Later that same year, I had an epiphany because a confident, talented kid decided to front a rock show. We borrowed guitars from the music department and raised Cain for an entire hour singing the best of the 1960s, even though we could only play three chords. The old Hawaiian classic 'Pearly Shells' was delivered as the pièce de résistance. The endearing memory of our house mistress's supportive smile as we embarrassingly banged away at the guitars and cymbals taught me that everyone has a benevolent angel somewhere, even if you don't know what you are doing. All you need to have is faith, a belief that when all is black and hopeless, someone will come along. This is a kind of liberation, allowing you to then do whatever you want with your life.

Subsequent events added to my sense of withdrawn independence and distrust of popular perception. This culminated at age fourteen with a permanent disrespect for authority. Pushing younger kids around and making them run chores was par for the course at school. I frequently found myself fetching ice for my seniors from a kindly teacher who lived a hundred yards away in a small bungalow. He had a heart of gold, but he wasn't married. He took a fancy to me. My memories of these events are very confusing: there were lips on my lips, then hands in my pants, then profuse apologies from his heart, then a mug full of ice in my hands, then more kisses, then more exploring hands, then more apologies. The guy was mauling me and hating himself all at once. It happened every time I went to get ice, and I went many times because he never said no. I learnt then that elders are just as perverted as the kids, and they know it. And just as often, nothing you get from them comes for free. I have never had reason to change my mind about this since. I have loathed hypocrisy and self-righteousness ever since.

By the time I was fifteen, I accepted the idea that the world was a loony bin. Kids crept about the dorms deep in the silent desert night cutting other people's pyjama *nara*s and drowning the characteristic smell of stinking stockings by squeezing tubes of toothpaste into each other's crotches. The teachers had all but removed themselves from the scene, leaving unsupervised monsters to terrorize others while the timid tried to negotiate their way through the jungle by becoming invisible. I learnt then that the world is not naturally rational, or fair, and it is incumbent upon each of us to find our stream of sanity in a world that truly has no method to its madness. Almost fifty years later, I couldn't agree with myself more.

Picking a profession isn't about what the job is: it's about who you are. If you are independent-minded, don't want to listen to anyone, have little respect for authority, have little faith in your fellow men, have an appetite too shallow to swallow crap, yet have great faith that things will work out for you in the end, then you might have what it takes to be a lawyer. Where else would you find a profession where you will get paid to disagree? In which profession are you going to be respected for iconoclasm, for your skill in coming down on the other side of the argument? Yeah, you could say this stuff was preordained. Only the legal profession, or perhaps journalism, has room for this kind of guy. As it turns out, I have done a bit of both!

This takes me to the search for a mission. What are you living for? Most people just want to have a good time. Just like the American Declaration of Independence, most young people consider it self-evident that men are endowed by their creator with certain 'unalienable rights, that among these are life, liberty and the pursuit of happiness'. It wasn't this way in 1980.

No doubt, some people back then thought money-grubbing and paper-chasing was a great idea: to me and many others, it seemed like a pretty crappy way to live. I mean not only does no one here get out alive: no one here gets his cash out either. Look around you: the dumbest, most pathetic monkeys have the most money. My father always said that the goddess Lakshmi often rides a donkey. I didn't want to be that donkey rider. The thing is, if you care to pursue the right goals, the law can be an intensely meaningful way to serve out your terrestrial time. For me, the fictional lawyer–detective Perry Mason had a great deal to do with it too. He ran a law office and saved distressed damsels accused of crimes they hadn't committed from the narrowing noose of the law. I must have read every Perry Mason mystery ever written. Indira Gandhi had even more to do with it. Living through the Emergency, it was clear that personal liberty was important, as was the rule of law and the quest for justice. Law practice would allow me to pursue entirely laudable goals while making a decent living, and it would give my life some meaning. Whether it turned out that way is another matter.

Which brings me to the third reason to become a lawyer: without a shadow of doubt, law is the one profession which allows you to be whoever you want for as long as you want, and then to change it when you want, as often as you want. Think of the lawyers you know. You find politicians, civil-rights activists, environmental activists, businessmen, corporate hotshots, real-estate tycoons, journalists, authors, bureaucrats, administrators, cops, diplomats, educationists, entrepreneurs, merchant bankers, property dealers, high-end speciality pimps facilitating government payoffs, even that peculiar breed of sanctimonious souls we call social workers. There are no boundaries to life here. You can practise for a bit, then decide to work for industry. Some years later, you can drop that and join a law firm. You can practise law in a law firm if you wish, or you can become a lobbyist. If you do anything interesting at all during these years, you can easily become the author of a fine memoir. In addition, you can sit on company boards and regale them with your invaluable insights, or you can become a Tom Hagen-like consigliere to a Godfather and help keep that rich crook out of jail. Truly, for the imaginative lawyer, the world is an oyster of which he is the gleaming artificial pearl. What's not to love about being a lawyer?

The best part is that you sit on top of the power food chain. You can use your greater knowledge, innate aggression and wide network of powerful contacts to manipulate people into giving you everything you want. You can use your knowledge of the law to invest wisely and, on a good day, rip some poor ignorant sod off. When you get bored of the moneymaking, you can entertain yourself in court all day watching political dramas play out in every sordid detail. In the evening, you can meet your clients, who likely as not will be a bunch of crooks, confidence tricksters and rascals. You get to hear sordid stories of scams, come-on schemes, sting operations and sex behind closed doors. It's a weird wonderful world, frequently unreal, where a cast of demented characters pursue their manic obsessions and quench the thirst in their souls with crazy cases that you should never have been paid to file. It's riotous good fun most of the time and, looking back, that is more or less how it has turned out for me.

Dad didn't agree when I told him, though. Contempt for lawyers was widespread at the time. Xenophobic 'respectable' small-town people saw the profession as the last happy hunting ground for confidence tricksters, sharpies, blackmailers, felons, rakes, losers, crooks and scallywags. Delhi University's law faculty was packed with Bihari graduates who enrolled for a law degree to give themselves time, space and a hostel room to write the UPSC exam and become IAS officers so that they could command hefty dowries. Nobody wanted to actually become a lawyer. As a Brahmin from Jammu with a nice Bihari-sounding name, everyone assumed I had the same ambitions. Heck, some of my closest friends were Biharis too! But I did really want to be a lawyer.

What do you do when your son wants to do something you consider unacceptable and you can't talk him out of it? Inevitably, you ask him to test his resolve with a bit of low-risk experience without committing himself to anything. That is how I ended up in Jammu's Mubarak Mandi Courts. The real world of small-town law was alien, and weird. Lawyers in Jammu at the time attended a few hearings but they sure as hell consumed a lot of tea and boiled eggs. There wasn't that much legal work going around, just as there still isn't in a great many towns in India. Then as now, provincial law practice offers some service law cases, a lot of criminal cases, and land disputes of all types.

People sat around waiting for clients and scheming up ways to become judges. Even now, the best lawyers Jammu ever produced—Raja Jaswant Singh and his son Anil Dev Singh, Dev Dutt Thakur and his son Tirath Singh Thakur and, of course, Dr A.S. Anand—have become judges. But I was not culturally a product of Jammu's small-town ethos, because I had grown up in Rajasthan and Delhi.

Jammu was an invaluable lesson in how not to become a lawyer. If you don't have a head start in life with a successful lawyer dad or a great and irresistible mind, your best bet is to make sure you practise law in the big Indian cities. This is where all the real work gets concentrated, and this is where the real opportunity is.

My own mess-up was not that I chose to work in Tees Hazari and learn the nuts and bolts of becoming a lawyer, nor that I chose to build a modest law practice from the ground up. The mess-up was that I did not focus on where I wanted to be ten years down the road. A clear intention is not the same thing as a clear objective. By 1996, I was well past the euphoria of professional independence and could see that I was stranded at the bottom of the ladder with no easy way up. I had dug myself into a hole and I couldn't find the shovel. Fortunately, I started to talk to people. That created the wave I was able to ride till I ended up in a decent-sized law firm. Coming up right away is the story of that wave.

Part II:
Dancing with Wolves

5

Break Out

Just the way a joke of a case became the beginning of my shining career as a divorce lawyer, a casual conversation with a friend became the catalyst of a great opportunity to escape the oblivion of Tees Hazari. Dhoot was that catalyst. Dhoot descended from a line of eminent bureaucrats. He was well-spoken, cultured and educated. He was tall and had penetrating eyes that saw everything. He also had all the self-assurance of the privileged Brown Sahib baba *log* with access to the inside track: Gymkhana memberships, plot allotment in snooty 'civil servants only' colonies, and the global exposure that comes with Daddy's plum foreign postings. He grew up on punk rock in the UK in the late 1980s. He was big on cynicism, mockery and idol-smashing. He was also condescending. He had a small office at home and no law practice to speak of, but he believed in the inevitability of his rise to the top of the legal food chain. He hadn't the walk, but he sure talked the big talk. He was very articulate, very amusing, and very urbane: an intelligent, good-looking mama's boy who could become somebody—if only someone could light a fire under his pretty bourgeois arse and flambé the phony superiority out of him. How could you not love his irresistible charm?

Frankly, there were a thousand other selfish motives to love him too. He was generous to a fault and always supportive of those who needed him. Eventually, as it turned out, he opened doors for me I could not have done on my own. The story of our short collaboration began when he asked me why we were not business partners. I was sceptical. He was approaching it from the factory end: if we set up shop, the customers will come. I was seeing it from the marketing end: if you have the clients, the service providers will crawl out of the gutters of Tees Hazari and throw themselves at your feet. I all but laughed away his proposal for collaboration, but I was willing to listen if he had a workable plan.

One week later, Dhoot was back. It had already been an extraordinary day. Old double-dating buddy Gurbinder Singh had come by my rented DDA flat in Vasant Enclave overlooking the Rao Tula Ram Marg Crossing on his ratty old Jawa, lugging a large backpack. Bhinderanwale was dead, Indira Gandhi had been assassinated, but Punjab was still under President's rule. Gurbinder, like many of my Sikh friends, had no idea on which side of the political divide he stood. But he did have a point to make. As we sat together, in the middle of his tirade against the government he pulled out a brand new airgun and shot at a grazing buffalo in the by-lane. The alarmed beast shivered, let out what I suppose is the bovine equivalent of a yelp and skittered off. Gurbinder turned to me with an evil glint over pearly white teeth sparkling behind a very black beard, 'You see the power of the gun? This is how you resolve problems! Mr Final Solution K.P.S. Gill would have been ecstatic.'

In the midst of this dramatic demonstration of realpolitik, in walked Dhoot with a partnership plan of action. The scene is irresistibly etched in my mind. We were sitting in the balcony of my second-floor flat drinking cheap gin from the army canteen with limes bought from the upwardly mobile paan shop down the road. The gin was pregnant with longing. In order to have access to the damn gin from the Army canteen I had tied a rakhi to a broad-hipped Asha Parekh type I would rather have seduced. If you can't bed 'em, bootleg 'em, I suppose! Dhoot flashed a two-page bullet-point list of issues at me. First and above all else, he wanted to know if the firm's name would be 'Dubey and Dhoot Associates' or 'Dhoot and Dubey Associates'! I was speechless. You can't make this stuff up. 'Can we toss for it?' I countered. 'No,' he said, 'names are fundamental.' 'So what is your next point?' I stalled. 'Point two,' he paused dramatically, 'is this: will we have regular desks in our office or coffee tables and lounge chairs to work from?' That's it, I told myself. This guy is demented: you cannot take him seriously! 'Do you want another gin?' I steered him off the minefield and we were fine after that. He gassed away, regaling me with lawyer gossip, letting our fundamental differences dissolve in the alcoholic haze of the boozy February night. I did however eventually manage to explain to him that we couldn't be partners till we could find a way to get customers.

That last piece fell into place when a famous corporate hotshot lawyer, Shanx, decided to step out into the jungle and start his own law firm. The plan seemed straightforward. Dhoot would set up a surrogate law firm and Shanx would route new business to it. When there were enough clients for Shanx to quit his current law firm, he would merge with the surrogate. Would I join his surrogate?

I had no idea. I didn't understand what being in a 'law firm' meant and I didn't think I was 'employable'. But here's the deal. If you are walking the thin line this side of solvency with a beautiful new baby girl, a rusty brown Maruti 800 and a dead-end law practice, would you like to remain marooned in the killing fields of India's Jurassic legal system for the rest of your life? Or, as an alternative, would you be willing to do anything, even wear purple pyjamas and hang upside down from the ceiling fan singing outrageously unfunny Shammi Kapoor hit songs, for a living? My baby girl consumed a lot of milk powder, and deserved a better future than I could give her at that time: I'd do pretty much anything so long as it was legal. The proposal seemed fair. Here's a successful lawyer who wanted to send me work and then pay me for the privilege of doing it. That's more than most clients had done for me thus far! If life works out for this guy, he would have his own law firm and I'll be his favourite apple-shiner. If it doesn't work out, there would still be the work he has sent. I could live with people laying their eggs in my nest. With nothing to lose, I went to see Shanx.

Like a giant eagle on a cliff planning a final swooping attack on its fear-paralysed victim, he stood in the centre of Delhi's Meridian Hotel lobby peering down his generous nose. He had a large boxy 'airline' briefcase in one hand, the other hand sunk deep into the pocket of his thick black overcoat. He was definitely a personality. 'Shanx,' he introduced himself as Dhoot and I stepped up to him. 'You're late.'

Dhoot mouthed the usual excuse about a traffic jam. Shanx turned to me: 'So you're stuck in the trial courts.' Man, he was direct! I suppose a man in his position could afford to be. He was the biggest billable head in Delhi's biggest law firm but he couldn't make partner. The three geriatric founder-partners had strung him along for four years and he was fed up. Amongst themselves, they thought his demand for partnership was ludicrous. I mean, you've been sleeping with this hooker on and off over the years and then one day, she leaps out of your bed and demands that you make an honest woman of her! In their world view, Shanx was a great billable head, as long as it lasted. After that, they would find someone else to screw. When Shanx figured this out, he decided to un-screw himself. He needed lawyers for his upcoming firm and Dhoot became his recruiter.

I saw Shanx as a strangely compelling personality. He had a commanding baritone voice, a deliberate way of expressing himself which was very controlled and very effective. He said a lot of things for effect. At the Meridian that day, he said things mainly to crush me. He asked what kind of work I did for my clients. All kinds of trial court work, I told him truthfully: help people collect debts, avoid paying debts, live in other people's houses forever without paying much rent, get married, get divorced, screw somebody for adultery, convict someone of rape . . . I trailed off, watching his distasteful expression. And what do I charge for these cases? Not a lot, I was truthful again: a few hundred rupees, maybe 500. For the entire case, he asked? Yes. And how long does each case last? Three to five years, I told him, and perhaps fifty hearings. His distaste turned to disgust. 'Five hundred for fifty hearings?' he spat. 'You fight for ten rupees a hearing?' But I do a lot of cases, I protested. How many? Up to thirty a day, I said. 'Every day?' he looked incredulous, 'Courts work six hours a day. Exactly how do you conduct a case in twelve minutes? I mean, do you have to wait between cases or do you take them back to back?' I wasn't feeling so cocky any more. Shanx completed his bomb run. 'I don't see how yours is a business. Any office you take will cost Rs 25 a square foot a month and you will need at least 500 square feet for yourself and your staff. If I take on your law practice, I will make a loss by acquiring a busy partner doing thirty cases a day and nothing else.'

I was stumped, which is always a good time to turn hostile-defensive. Do our lives need a 'business case'? Is law a business? Who are you to tell me I don't understand economics, or the legal profession? Like the deeply unpopular Ambassador cars of the time, I spluttered, started a couple of sentences, failed to find my transmission and tailed off into silence. Shanx waited, then questioned me some more on my skill sets. He was trying to figure out how to increase my 'rate of return'. 'Law firm managers are like traders,' he told me. 'I take your skill and I sell it to someone else. This is how you get paid for what you do and I get a commission.'

I left that meeting confused and a little angry. No one likes to look like the village idiot. He was right, but whoever admits to deserving decapitation? 'Bloody shopkeeper,' I thought, 'talking about rates of returns and rentals. What does he understand about a noble profession like ours?'

One thing about being poor: you always sleep well.

When Dhoot called me early in the morning one day to say that he would like to join me for lunch, I was more than delighted. Dhoot came in early, and without his tiffin box, compelling me to share mine. About the only hot food you got in Tees Hazari those days was aloo or chana with puris fried in large round-bottomed vessels of boiling oil in which a dozen of them sizzled and bobbed at a time. You will never understand the true genius of desi *jugaad* till you appreciate the finer points of cost economies and environmental consciousness built into cooking procedures in Indian dhabas. The wheat dough for the puris was kneaded by smooth-skinned Nepali boys, the sweat dripping off their chins directly into the dough, contributing considerably to the delicious, slightly salty taste of the puri, saving India's coastline in the bargain. If you were a squeamish Brown Sahib in a black coat, you could have a burger instead in the lawyers' canteen with blotting paper for buns and mincemeat patties made from what appeared to be roadkill. As the rains broke, when food rotted quickly, not even God could help you if you had neither wife nor mother to pack you lunch. I went years suffering from repeated annual bouts of stomach upsets every August.

Dhoot was ecstatic. 'The die is cast,' he announced with a sense of grandeur I did not share. 'We start our office as soon as possible.' Shanx was going to underwrite the cost of the office. I could join and keep the earnings from my own practice. I would get a share of the fees for all the work I did for the new law firm. We were to keep this going till Shanx was ready to move in. Dhoot asked me if I liked the offer. What was there not to like about getting access to a cornucopia for free? One month to the day later, I moved to the new office and my world changed. Years ago, my father said that fate and fortune always put three opportunities into every pair of hands. The successful guy was the one who spotted that opportunity and ran with it. Joining Shanx was the first of my three opportunities, even though I couldn't be sure of it at the time.

~

Not that the changes were immediately apparent. I still went to Tees Hazari every day and scurried about till lunch, stumbling from one court to the next, attending hearings without heart, living a life without commitment. I did a little work for the surrogate firm, which boosted my finances, allowing me to hire two junior lawyers. Then I started withdrawing slowly from everyday trial court work, letting the new recruits take the load, making myself available for the tsunami of economic opportunity to pick me up and carry me away to the land of endless gold, dripping honey.

The big break came two months into the new office when Shanx sent us a Danish client. They had a serious problem. They had won a great infrastructure project and now the Delhi High Court had shut them down. It was a strange case, quite outside my experience. Three years back, the Danes had started a joint venture with a local businessman called Sondhi. They bid for several projects together, none of which came their way. Activity ground to a halt and, in time, the parties tacitly agreed to move on. Eventually, the Danes made a fresh start, hired a managing director and successfully bid for this project. At this point, Sondhi came back out of nowhere and claimed to be a joint-venture partner. He persuaded the Delhi High Court to stop the Danes going it alone.

One quick look at the case and I knew that Sondhi was going nowhere with it. The joint-venture agreement wasn't an exclusive one: parties were free to work by themselves too. One of Sondhi's companies had also bid for the same project. Not all the attar in Chandni Chowk could mask the stink floating over this enormous castle of pure pig dung. I prepared a note on how to defend the case and sent it to the client with a copy to Shanx. Shanx went sonic. 'You've copied this note to the client,' he shouted down the phone, 'without first clearing it with me?' Isn't that what lawyers do? Render advice to clients? I told him he had not indicated any specific operating procedure. That made him madder. 'I don't have to specify procedure, damn it,' he ranted, 'it is understood that we need to confer first.' 'I am sorry I gave bad advice,' I tried to placate him. 'You can hang it on me and distance me from the file.'

'No, goddammit,' he was even angrier, 'you have not made an error. The advice is very good. I have no issues with it.' So what is the issue? I was really quite confused. Eventually, as he calmed down, I realized he had two big issues.

'First,' he thundered, 'you are not a solo performer any more. Law firms are a team game. You have to confer internally. This has nothing to do with being wrong or right. It has to do with group psychology and organizational culture.' Okay, got that, gurudev.

'But that is not the real problem,' he carried on. 'The real problem is that you have written this note within two days of the Danes referring the matter to you. You can't bill more than two days' work.' Why, did the Danes dislike quick replies? I could hear him over the phone fighting to conquer his impatience. 'Ranjeev, you have rendered 20,000 American dollars' worth of advice for a thousand dollars. Are you here to develop the law firm or bugger its revenue streams?' I freeze-dried.

'Do you have a passport?' he changed tack, suddenly softening. I said yes, though I had only travelled on it twice in a decade. 'Leave it with my secretary and let me see if I can retrieve this situation.'

~

Three days later, I had another call from Shanx. 'We are booked through to Copenhagen tonight. The ticket and passport will be with you in an hour.' This meant I had to reach the airport in six hours. The last time I travelled abroad, I took two months to prepare for it. 'You just make sure your bag has every legal paper and every law book we need.' I leapt to the task. When the tickets arrived, they were first class on Swissair. I'd only ever travelled coach.

You could say I was excited. In 1992, Delhi's district court lawyers did not travel first class to Copenhagen at six hours' notice to confer with clients; in fact they did not travel to meet clients at all. My wife was mystified. In her book, lawyers wore black coats and went to court every morning, drank copious quantities of coffee in the Bar room between hearings and leered at the 'lady lawyers'. They then returned at 5 p.m. and plunged immediately into their offices at home to emerge about 10 p.m. exhausted, with limp biz-kits, unable to perform their marital duties. 'Are you quite sure about what Shanx does for a living?' she asked.

In an almost irrepressible state of frenzy. I was at the airport three hours before departure with a fat bag full of books, another small bag full of clothes, not a cent of foreign exchange, and no Shanx to be seen anywhere. Indians didn't have international credit cards at the time and even if they did, no one was going to give me one. I sat in the first-class lounge and attacked the Drambuie with a vengeance; I was Genghis Khan invading the highly cultured Song Dynasty and there was something manic about the urgency with which I consumed something I could seize but not produce.

Forty minutes to the flight and Shanx was still nowhere to be seen. I decided to board the plane. He wasn't on the plane either. Twenty minutes later, as the gates closed, Shanx floated in with a small travel-bag, an overcoat and no check-in baggage. He sure walked the thin edge. Everything I had done in the first-class lounge of Swissair, I did again. While Shanx curled up and slept immediately, I attacked the red wine, then the caviar, then the food, and finally the cognac. When we hit Zurich to transfer to the Copenhagen flight, I had not had a shred of sleep. The next flight was déjà vu. Shanx slept while I had a full breakfast with wine, two kinds of sausages, eggs and croissants. As I finally prepared for sleep, the stewardesses asked us to fasten our seatbelts for landing!

I have hazy alcohol-sodden memories of the first day. Shanx took my written advice and tore it to bits, producing brilliant arguments to show that I was wrong. He never actually said I was wrong though. He converted legal issues into strategic commercial issues. He orchestrated a long debate on the approach that best met the Danes' commercial objectives in India. He then used those strategic choices to arrive at the same advice I had rendered in the first place. We closed the day agreeing that I would follow my own written advice and finalize a statement of defence the next day.

Looking back, Shanx had a standard operating procedure; he spun out a problem from thin air, let the debate rage, and then generated the solution which minimized the problem he had maximized in the first place. Between too much booze, too little sleep, too little understanding of strategic considerations and rank ignorance of this SWOT analysis they kept bringing up, I don't remember participating in the debate. I do remember what happened after the meeting though. We were in our hotel at 8 p.m. with bright sunshine in the Danish summer sky. Shanx spent the next four hours in a padmasana on my bed shepherding me through a succession of blue movies. I sat there squirming, not quite comfortable with a man who was older, smarter and not quite like anything I knew. I didn't come from India's video-player-owning classes and I had never seen a porn movie before. Shanx kept up a steady supply of derisive comments, laughing uproariously at the absurdity of it all.

Looking back, I am quite sure Shanx cared nothing for blue movies. In putting them on, he was 'training' me somehow, setting some sort of stage to reorder my mind. I can see that now. The biggest gift Shanx ever gave me was to teach me to evaluate what I see on its objective merit, without immediately subjecting it to a moral judgement. To him, everyone around him was an actor in a hilarious farce, some with and some without clothes. Sooner rather than later, he insinuated, the clothes always came off.

I also remember breakfast the next morning. I called for room service. The guy on the telephone was flummoxed. Why not come down to the dining room? So what if I hadn't taken a bath? It didn't strike me that it wasn't necessary to bathe daily in Denmark. He eventually delivered a mountain of food and refused to take any of it back, claiming that he had plenty more where this came from. I did not realize that the entire thirty-room hotel had six permanent employees and two working the kitchen. They didn't do room service either, but the guy was too polite, too, to tell me to take a hike. It was a society with too few people and too much money. I came from a society that was the opposite: people were cheap and expendable; the bread was everything.

The second day was more productive. I quickly prepared the statement of defence for the Delhi High Court, had it approved without material change and wrapped up the afternoon early, giving us time to check out the town before we boarded our flight back home. I was my usual tactless self on the flight. 'Do you realize that we could have prepared this document at home without these meetings?' Shanx was amused. 'No one here is working for the document,' he laughed. 'Everyone is working for the money. That's true of the company owner, employer and lawyer. As for our billing, it's not what the job is worth; it's what percentage it constitutes of the client's stake in the litigation!'

It was a valuable lesson in law firm management. We had prepared a six-page document that cost 10,000 dollars in travel, lodging and restaurant bills and twice as much again in professional charges. I could have done it at home for 1000 dollars and achieved the same quality.

Nowhere in the history of human endeavour to better itself, has so much been taught by so few in so brief a manner to one so undeserving with such devastating effect! I was sold on Shanx but there was a shock looming large in my immediate future.

6

A Gory Story

Soon after we returned from Copenhagen, Shanx sent his partner Raghubir Singh Deo to check us out. He looked like he came straight off a charpoy under the peepul tree of a south Haryana village with a name like an expletive from the anger-management vocabulary of a Jat village elder. He confused me immediately. He had the gravitas of a family elder and the gait of Raj Kapoor's character in *Mera Naam Joker*. He waddled more than walked; his baggy shirts tucked into ill-fitting pants that were way too loose at the waist. This incongruous sacking was held up by well-used leather belts that his pot belly was always eager to spill over. He spoke as politely as a Lucknowi nawab, but he also skillfully employed a wide range of Urdu expletives, often without discernable provocation. The incessant paan-chewing made his faux Lucknowi accent hard to understand. He was kind in his dealings, if somewhat spaced out. I instinctively knew he stood on the other side of a great cultural divide, and my long jump had always sucked.

As the days went by, we saw little of Shanx and a great deal of Deo. Deo supervised many of the small cases Shanx sent us, keeping a close watch on our activities without being intrusive. I didn't enjoy working with him. He was obtuse, unfocused and inattentive: he took off on a tangent without provocation and did not find his way back to the main road for prolonged periods. A ten-minute conversation expanded to an hour, destroying schedules, breeding impatience. I never quite saw where his skill lay. Dhoot was soothing. He frequently reminded me of Deo's enormous drafting skills, which equally frequently, I failed to see. Deo's drafting style was all 'heretofore' and 'pertaining thereto' and 'the selfsame said presents'. There was a lot of that going around in our profession, but it still didn't prevent me from rolling about helplessly with laughter every time I saw it. However, I could see he had an appetite for perfection. Unlike Shanx's hit-and-run professional philosophy, Deo was more thorough in his work than a Mother Superior was in her moral policing. By the time Deo was done with a document, you could be sure he hadn't missed a single louse in your dreadlocks.

There were other things to admire about him. Deo was a 'seasoned' individual, nine-tenths under the water and quick to see where other people were coming from. He had a soft compassionate side. If you ever got into a jam, he appeared to be the one to go to rather than Shanx, who appeared to be too much of a pragmatist.

Six months into our new law firm, Shanx summoned us to the Oberoi coffee shop. While Shanx looked grim, Deo looked like he had swallowed a tarantula and it was coming out the other end. Our secret surrogate law firm was now public knowledge. We were being bad-mouthed to our potential clients. Shanx wanted to launch a law firm immediately. We spent the rest of the afternoon discussing details. Shanx and Deo had arranged an office space.

They wanted me for their litigation work and Dhoot for their corporate practice. They said we would be partners. This sounded great, and as you would expect, Dhoot asked what partnership deal was on offer. Shanx was evasive. When the meeting ended, I had that feeling you get in the pit of your stomach when the girl asks you to come by for a drink and then excuses herself so that she can slip into something more comfortable.

That was not Dhoot's reaction. He was irritated. 'All this gung-ho, hail–fellow-well-met bonhomie is fine, man,' he complained 'but at the end of the day, what is the bloody partnership deal?' I wasn't bothered that the details of the deal hadn't been spelt out; I saw the opportunity and wanted in on it. Dhoot wasn't going to do it till he understood exactly what was in it for him. He said I was naive and asked me to step back till he'd had a chance to negotiate us a position in this new set-up. Sure, buddy, thought I: whatever greases your Irritable Bowel Syndrome.

Dhoot wasn't particularly visible the following week. He met up with Shanx and Deo every day, and came back grim and filled with determination. Meanwhile, Shanx took to calling me, seemingly in quest of small talk. He asked for inconsequential details of sundry cases, leaving the door open for me to start a conversation. I wasn't smart enough to figure what I needed to pursue. Dhoot watched me like a hawk when he was in, searching my eyes and trying to guess what I was thinking. As far as I was concerned, we were going to the new law firm and Dhoot was taking care of the details. It didn't strike me that the devil was in the detail.

Dhoot spent that entire week sorting out the details with Shanx and Deo. It didn't work out. Six meetings and some unpleasant words later, Dhoot opted out. He stormed in on a Friday evening, announced the deal was off and demolished my joyous weekend. 'They are not offering us a meaningful deal,' he said, 'and besides, I've looked at their case list and I don't think they are going to survive for long.' That was stupefying stuff. I protested. Dhoot persisted. 'These guys are lightweights. Shanx is all bluff and bluster; Deo is something out of a textbook on medieval history.' He said he had been to see the senior partner of their old law firm. Like those giant dinosaurs from Spielberg's *Jurassic Park* movies, they were going to wipe out Shanx and Deo.

I had no data, no means by which to judge the virtue of this conclusion. Dhoot wanted to know my future plans. I had none. He said the two of us should develop the surrogate law firm as our baby. He talked about the people we knew, the clients we had met, the judges who were well disposed towards us. He felt we had the basis of a beginning. He mixed charm, wit and dollops of optimism, and served it to me in a cocktail called 'Desire'.

I didn't think someone was a client merely because you knew him socially. I certainly didn't have the client base or the exposure to run a law firm. Till Shanx and Deo came along, I didn't know Dhoot had that client base either. He thought it was a budget issue. I said it was a survival issue. Dhoot had plunged head first into my low insecurity threshold. The difference clearly was that he still lived with his parents and I paid my own bills. I stubbornly resisted all his suggestions. I wasn't convinced about going to bed with this woolly-headed mama's boy with his Irish stories and dodgy work culture.

I went home thinking that I should close anything I could with Shanx and then convince Dhoot. But that is not how it worked out next day. It came down to loyalty and the right of first refusal. Dhoot had taken me to Shanx. If Dhoot had put himself up against Shanx, how could I go with Shanx? I needed to carry Dhoot with me, and I told him my plan. 'If you can give Shanx six months,' Dhoot said, 'can you give me six months?' It was an impossible argument to resist. Dumb moves often come from noble intentions, especially when they are grounded in a counterfeit sense of honour.

~

Dhoot didn't need six months. He needed a week. Out of the blue one morning, he produced a partnership deed and asked me to read it immediately. The document basically said that he had contributed all the capital to the office and paid for all the furniture. This was untrue. We had financed the office from the revenue stream that Shanx provided. It went on to state that Dhoot would be managing partner of the law firm and would be entitled to 'take all administrative/legal decisions'. I didn't like those slashes, nor did I understand what 'legal decisions' meant. It then went on to say that I would be entitled to a revenue share from the work I did. Finally it said that the firm would be called 'Dhoot and Associates'. He would own the name of the firm and whatever value that had in the market. The joker was offering me a job!

To Dhoot's credit and with the benefit of hindsight, I later realized I deserved the employment he was offering me. If there is a multiparty deal going down and you don't hedge your bets, talk to everyone, confuse everyone about your intentions—but instead pledge loyalty to the weakest beetle in the dung ball and present yourself as a willing whipping boy—you are going to get strapped across the buttocks with a cat-o'-nine-tails of sharkskin attached to billions of bibulous blue blistering barnacles at the tips. Only the naive could see it as betrayal. At the time, I was naive. I had tears in my eyes and my voice quivered as I looked at him overwhelmed with hurt. 'This is not right, Dhoot,' I practically sobbed, 'we are in it together and you are reducing me to nothing.' He laid out the whole shooting crap. I had a very important role in the office.

I would take care of the work and he would take care of me. He was patronizing. I was speechless with anguish at his perfidy. His easy sophistication was a knife in my back; it turned every time he justified something in the document. In ten minutes, I couldn't deal with it. I excused myself and charged out the door, driving home, my eyes swimming in tears of rage. I could have killed myself out of my powerlessness.

Hindsight always rips your guts out. What would have happened if I had told Dhoot right off the bat that we could either join Shanx or it was back to Tees Hazari for me? At the very least, we would still be friends. But we were young then. We both made mistakes. A naive kind of loyalty queered the pitch for me while a false perception of how business relationships get built queered the pitch for Dhoot.

As I now contemplate the business relationships I have successfully nurtured, it seems to me that at the heart of every sustainable relationship lies trust. Trust makes it possible for people to pull together as a team, to divide the job and focus on their part without worrying about who has the knife out for whom. Trust makes you strong. That is point one. Point two is that you can never make a sustainable deal that is not more or less an accurate reflection of the reality on the ground. If the partners pull equal weight, they can be equal partners, otherwise not. If you are both the legal brain and the marketing brain, why will you give me, a mere worker, more than a small share of the partnership? Even if an equal deal between unequal people gets written, how long will it last? Dhoot offered a job to the guy who had his own law practice. He gave ownership and control to the guy who had nothing but the office space, and the ability to talk himself into believing that he was the Amitabh Bachchan of law practice.

By evening I had the kind of cold rage that gets things done. I needed to explore the Shanx option. I chose to appeal to Deo's soft heart. Deo was conciliatory when I called up. We met early next morning outside his favourite paan shop at the Vasant Kunj D4 gate. His car was ragged and dirty and smelt vaguely of dead rats inside unwashed socks. He told me they couldn't close the deal with Dhoot because he wanted equality with Shanx and Deo. Dhoot told them I would settle for half the profit share they gave Dhoot. *That* was a revelation. Why would I take less than Dhoot? To cut a long and sordid story short, I told him I had walked away from Dhoot and was open to any reasonable position in their new law firm. Deo said he understood perfectly.

He wasn't kidding about perfectly. Now that I have run a law firm of my own for fifteen years, I can tell you that salary packages are never about what anyone is worth; they are all about what the next guy is getting. We raise salaries every April, and the apsaras rolling about at the feet of Indra in the great blue yonder are all my *bhabhi*s if it isn't all about 'but why are you paying that guy that much and me this much'. Everyone would be so much happier if I could get everyone in my law firm to write confidentiality clauses keeping all remuneration data secret on pain of ritual decapitation at high noon by the clock tower on Main Street.

But human insecurity drives everything, for everyone, every time. Even as I was talking to Deo, I was thinking that Shanx likes Dhoot more than he likes me so if Dhoot still makes a late comeback, then Dhoot will hit me back, etc. As I reasoned through this, it seemed to me that I needed to undermine Dhoot more than I needed the job. Undermining someone by bad-mouthing them to other people who are already upset is the easiest thing to do. And I did it, without the slightest hesitation. It was an object lesson in hate. Emperor Palpatine was right when he told Darth Vader, 'I can feel *your anger*, it gives you focus, *makes you* stronger.'

It enabled me to do things I could not to a friend, only because I believed he had betrayed me. The meeting with Shanx and

Deo went as planned. I quoted Dhoot's view of Shanx and Deo chapter and verse, then added salt, pepper and hot sauce. I told them Dhoot thought they were a bunch of bozos who wouldn't last six months. In half an hour I had them really pissed off with him. I also painted myself as the naive soul I had been all along without revealing that I had learnt very quickly. Within the hour, I had an unconditional offer to move immediately. I was offered an 'interim remuneration' that was 15 per cent greater than my current revenue stream. They said they could review that at the end of the year. Since there were seven other movers from their old firm, they said that they would wait for the new law firm to stabilize and determine everyone's partnership share by the end of the year.

I had my 'bye-bye love' meeting with Dhoot that evening. He acted as though it was a continuation of our previous meeting. He wanted to know if I had further concerns with the draft partnership deed. I told him I wanted no part of it and was moving on. He couldn't understand it: if I had a problem, why was I not discussing it with him? No dice on that, I told him. We came together as equals and if that was questioned, there was nothing left to discuss. He said if an equal share is all that bothered me, we could discuss that too. I told him that offering me an unequal share closed the door on all discussion: the dream was over. He wanted to know what I would do next. I told him it didn't matter: there is always another dream to find. His self-assurance slipped at that point. He genuinely could not understand what was so upsetting about his position. 'I was only negotiating,' he offered helplessly. I compounded my cruelty. 'It's a matter of honour, Dhoot,' I said. 'You don't negotiate with a friend. You keep the faith.'

What do you make of a group of people who sweat about their partnership shares at a new organization when they are clueless about their capability?

All around me, law firms are being formed and busted every day. I take it that they are being negotiated by lawyers who have nothing to negotiate about. Partnership deeds are being signed by youngsters with more client-grabbing skills than legal skill. Then six months later, the law firm is deader than Nehru's temples of modern India and the advance rent has been forfeited.

Delhi is probably the worst in this regard. We have a group of lawyers break away from a 'magic circle' law firm. Then they break up further and some partners go back to the parent firm. We have small law firms joining other small law firms to make slightly larger law firms, then splitting apart six months later because both sides came together only so that they could poach clients from each other. Not that anyone is admitting that. Of all the marble-glazed bovine excreta I have heard, the most appealing one yet was from a law firm that lasted three days. They said they split up because they realized they had too many conflicts of interests in their client lists!

Looking back over all these years, I will say this. There is no single dimension to any truth. There is no single viewpoint. All of us were young, inexperienced and cocky. I had the focus that flows from terrifying insecurity. Dhoot had the self-assurance of financial security. When the two collided, value destruction was inevitable. I see this in my law firm now with people applying for jobs. The rich daddy's kids with their sense of entitlement come by and ask about salaries and working conditions. The poor daddy's kids come by and tell me that money doesn't matter. They want to know what they will be doing. Deep inside, they fear their insignificance. All they really want is to matter. Inevitably, they win hands down and the preppies exit. As for the end of my collaboration with Dhoot, some of the regret still nags. The central truth simply comes down to this. I dumped the man who put the deal on the table after burning his boats for him. In a single stroke, I had learnt how to accompany rational self-serving commercial interest with a perfect kind of self-righteous claptrap. But then, isn't that how the corporate clientele I now serve functions all the time?

That doesn't make me feel any better.

At the time though, I did have the solace of knowing that I was going to a brand new law firm of which I was going to be the litigation partner. I would have been a lot less excited if I had known what actually awaited me.

7

Gypsies, Tramps and Thieves

She was tall and attractive, with creamy skin that glowed brighter than the moon on a magical Ladakhi *poornima* night. A Modern Indian Woman of the early 1990s, she made a lot of eye contact and never hid her bosom behind hunched shoulders. Like many Malayali women of the Nair community, she was supremely self-confident. When she pursed her perfectly formed lips in determination, I never could choose between running for cover or leaping at her with non-platonic intent. Pia Nair was the first person I met on my first day at work at City Law. She led me around the office and introduced me to everyone. It was a shock. The office consisted of fifteen cheap yellow wooden tables with matching chairs, one fax machine and two telephones in one room at the back of a building on Kasturba Gandhi Marg. In an era before laptops, when people still worked with physical paper, there were no books, no mountains of files, no pen stands, planners, whiteboard, court diaries, no nothing . . . The walls of the room were as blank as Manmohan Singh's face in Parliament during UPA2.

Pia was forthright about it. 'We left for reasons of principle,' she looked deep into my eyes, 'and we aren't going to do it by stealing cases and clients.' I looked right back into her eyes. Did she really not know about Dhoot's surrogate law firm? In that single moment, I fell terminally in love with her and decided I would always trust her because it was in virtue that she found her strength, even if it led to a no-way-back dump called Disaster. In time, I learnt she was Deo's right hand. He was the only senior she ever had, and she believed in his archaic philosophy and his sanctimonious posturing!

In a week, I realized that this law firm, like Delhi, sat on both sides of a river, and the garbage ran through it. Shanx had a small group of lawyers who were here because he was here. That included his talented assistant Pawan who served him every which way but badly: he managed his correspondence, his billing, and even communicated his beverage orders to the pantry. Deo had his own cheer group who followed his bidding. The pick of the pack was his neurotic Kumaoni court clerk Ravinder, who spent a lot of time engaging in pillow talk with Deo, whispering office gossip dredged up from the sewers. What he gained in data, Deo lost in authority. Ravinder spent most of his time heckling and jeering at the other lawyers, vitiating the atmosphere. The general staff attitude did not help at all. In this very politically sensitive organization, the partners continuously trashed their underlings. In turn, those in the middle treated juniors with disdain. In all this, the clerks—whose use-value to the firm put them somewhere in the middle of the political pecking order—kicked everyone that didn't have the direct backing of one of the partners. Middle-order lawyers responded by banding together and hitting back. I felt utterly alone.

Like many people who betray their inability to deal with power structures by ignoring them, I tried to immerse myself in work. Word got around that I was a slogger. My table filled fast with papers—court cases, opinions, claims, notices—things I knew already. I spent long hours in the office, quickly turned around work, keeping out of other people's way. This set off a curious chain reaction as I arrived at the receiving end of a kind of sulking non-cooperation movement. Snide remarks and suspicious glances followed me around like the stink of scandal. Were people jealous? I tried to share the work but no one wanted to help out. They were happy to attend meetings, but they didn't wish to park their fancy fannies on those ugly maroon chairs and deliver the grunt sweat. It was three months to the day that I received my first bit of support from another lawyer. I was stuck in court, desperate for case law. I called up the office and Neeru took the phone. In half an hour, she had sent me a bag full of well-judged relevant case law. I was surprised and delighted, because Neeru was not a girl the gods had created with *fursat* (leisure).

Truly, demeanours can be decisive of destiny. Neeru was a plump bania without looks or charm. She was short, fat and patchy-skinned with crinkly hair suggesting a recent electrocution. She had a cackling laugh most suited to a wicked witch unrolling a diabolical plan. The laughter never touched her eyes. She was tactless and could kill a promising conversation with a traffic-stopping comment. She came across as cussed and opinionated: an immodest girl with much to be modest about. Loyalty to Shanx appeared to be her main gateway to his law practice, and as his cheerleader, she guarded access to him jealously. Shanx relied on her for unquestioned support, and she in turn jumped a hoop if she was asked to skip a step. In time, I learnt that loyalty was not her only quality: she was fair if you played fair. If you didn't incite her hostile aggression, she could be remarkably amicable. She never meant badly, but she was very sensitive, and you could not needle her. She had a good heart, perched atop a dodgy emotional balance. But it was a decade before I figured any of this out, and by then it didn't matter.

Still, the fact remained that if I wanted to survive, I'd have to hitch my wagon to a star. With City Law, there were two Dragons to choose from. Deo offered a small law practice of the kind I knew, but he descended from an alien planet, speaking a language I frequently did not understand. He mixed emotion and thought in an eclectic churn much too obtuse for me to digest. I pretended warmth to him and he responded in kind, but deep down in my heart I knew this was a relationship with severe limitations. Shanx, on the other hand, was my kind of alpha male: charismatic, westernized, dynamic and utterly irreverent. He wasn't particularly accessible though. He travelled a lot, networked a lot and spent a lot of time rainmaking for the firm. With the whole firm to feed, he didn't have time to mollycoddle an unstable trial-court Johnny-come-lately like me. Unsure of how to advance my career, I ended up trying to reach the Dragons by cosying up to their cheerleaders.

This was a treacherous business. I thought Neeru was the quickest way to access Shanx, but she knew as little about social cues as me. She punched holes in my advances faster than I could retrieve my smile. I switched to Pia, mostly because I really liked her, but she was a good heart in the wrong camp. I remember Pia sidling up to me one day, complaining of hunger. I gallantly escorted her to the cafeteria next door and found myself lulled into an unguarded state of calmness, inhaling deeply the jasmine fragrance of her youthful body. I remember this feeding interlude mainly because Pia gossiped shamelessly about some of the lawyers. She even talked about unlawful carnal knowledge! This jarred because whatever the girl was, malice was no part of her make-up. She gossiped with me for the same reason that wives run down their husbands to their girlfriends. It's never about the husband at all; it's about the message, 'I'm telling you my innermost secret because I trust you completely.' I spent some time thinking about this. Succeeding weeks reinforced my feeling that I was being cultivated. Deo was extra kind, extra courteous. I had the distinct feeling that I was in Deo's camp without my consent and he was working to make sure I grew some roots.

In four months to a day, our idyllic Kasturba Gandhi world crumbled without warning: we lost our rented office. We had thirty days to find an alternative. Given the prejudices against lawyers in those rent-control days, we ended up in a seedy Business Centre in a small lane behind two chaat shops at the back end of Scindia House in Connaught Place. It was a fate worse than my chamber in Tees Hazari. We hired twelve small cabins—and small means just enough for one table, three chairs and no light at all. They looked like quickie rooms in a GB Road whorehouse and smelt like a garbage-recycling plant. We had hit rock bottom.

~

Curiously, at this time, Connaught Place itself was tasting a kind of rock bottom. When I came to study economics at Sriram College of Commerce in 1974, Delhi was still a cluster of mofussil townships with Connaught Place as its shining upscale heart. If you wanted a good suit, you didn't go to the market in Kamla Nagar or Model Town or even GK-1; you went to Sharma's or Vedi Tailors in CP. If you wanted to buy the latest Zeppelin or Sabbath album, Rhythm House, Berco's or Das Studios was about all the choice you had. If you wanted quality cold coffee, it was DePaul's or bust. It was the same with restaurants. Nothing matched liver-on-toast at Gaylords, unless it was the Mandarin Room at Janpath Hotel exploring the Paleolithic roots of modern

'Chinjabi' food. Hell, if you wanted a really good time, CP even had a couple of cabaret joints.

This is really my mother's story. Fresh from a trip to Europe that included Paris, when Mum happened to spot a 'nightclub' called Lido in CP's H block, she asked Uncle Syal if the domestic stuff was anything like the French version. Gallant to the last, Uncle Syal offered to take my parents there. Picture the scene. Uncle Syal was an ageing, balding, grey-haired, rather oily-skinned conservative businessman from Bungalow Road across the asphalt from Kamla Nagar Market. He oozed decency. His wife, my father's cousin, was a good-hearted small-town *sati-savitri* girl, totally middle class, totally Hindi-medium. My dad was a very conservative zamindar from Jammu. Mom was probably the most adaptable of the lot but still, she married into a family that didn't think women should go out to work. She filled her days with social work and kitty parties. When this incongruous quartet arrived at the cabaret, they were the only two women in the audience and the dancer went bananas. Being the 'safest' of the men in the room, the 'artist' focused all her attention on Uncle Syal, sliding her ample breast up and down his chest to 'Piya Tu Ab Toh Aaja', till regrettably, one of her heavy *thumka*s hit him squarely in the shoulder, sending him sprawling off his chair and to the floor. The four beat a hasty retreat.

Mom laughed about it for months afterwards. I asked her how far the dancer went. She didn't know because they lasted about three minutes into the performance. I just had to find out. When I got to Delhi, I looked for Lido in H-block but it was gone. Instead, I found another place in a small red building right at the foot of Minto Bridge. They said the cover charge was Rs 10. On my meagre student allowance, it took me two months to collect the money, but collect it I did. I arrived at the show one Friday evening. It was 9 p.m. and the show was not slotted till ten.

Every table was taken, the lights were dim and the waiters hustled drinks with a vengeance. I wasn't going to buy another drink over and above the cover charge so I sat on my one large Blue Riband gin and lime cordial for that entire hour. Everyone in the room maintained a guilty silence that entire hour, averting their eyes. No one ordered any food. Most of the clients looked like they had only just shut their shops in Mori Gate before showing up. Armpit aroma hung thick in the air. It wasn't sleazy, it was pathetic. Minutes before ten, the room filled with what I assume was the hired muscle. They leaned against the walls, glaring at everyone. They looked like cops moonlighting on the side. Then the cymbals clashed and the lady came on.

She was a wannabe Helen. She had lacy silk stockings and very frumpy panties adorned with rather second-hand-looking feathers of some indeterminate colour. Rows of multicoloured beads hung from her sagging Over-Shoulder Boulder-Holders, impairing the view. I was eighteen and still very obsessed with oral stimuli. I truly resented that the mid-on had extra cover. She started the grinding routine to a very evocative song by Lata Mangeshkar—'Aa Jaane Jaan'—I believe the only cabaret song the lady ever sang. She was as tasteless as the rendition of the original song in the movie. It did not titillate: it was a pantomime. For a super-sexed teenager from the deeply repressed 1970s, that was a damning indictment. I looked around me. The shopkeepers' faces were impassive masks, though some licked their lips from time to time. Finally, her routine came to its grand finale in a crescendo of frantic drumming and clashing cymbals as the strobe lights came on. At this point, the lady unhooked her Boulder-Holders and spilt the goodies for all of a fleeting second before the hall plunged into darkness and she disappeared. A deathly silence followed. Some chairs scraped in silent frustration. Other customers scribbled on chits and sent them in. I surmised these were cash offers for Act 2 with the same lady. This wasn't a cabaret dance. It was a footpath trader displaying wares, what lawyers would call an 'invitation to offer'. To cut a long story short, I waited for one more dance but it was no better. Then it was time to leave. The last DTC bus from Regal to the University left sharp at 11 p.m. I was on it.

By the late 1980s, even this pathetic relic of the cabaret era had left town. Meanwhile, suburban markets started to transform into the shopping–entertainment hubs they have now become. South Extension was the first, but then Lajpat Nagar was not far behind, nor was Sarojini Nagar. They were serving the same need, at different price points. CP became overcrowded, then run-down, then downmarket, till ultimately people sneered at it and said, yeah, they really didn't think it was more than a suburb of Paharganj's New Delhi Railway Station. Business turnovers started to decline and the sloth in the Municipal Corporation of Delhi accelerated the decay. Into this overcrowded, polluted, dirty CP, City Law arrived to launch its glorious super-high-end legal services.

About this time, my work took a dramatic turn. So far my law practice had consisted exclusively of cases I handled myself. I sold my services to potential clients, I drafted their cases and filed them, I examined my own witnesses, I did my own case research, and I argued cases myself. This worked fine for Tees Hazari. It didn't work so well for superior courts. City Law had its share of high-stakes cases, and that dramatically altered the way the business was run. I was now asked to do what all successful law firms did. Take a minute to understand this system, because this is how it has always worked.

Law firms in all the big cities follow the British 'Solicitor System'. This means that one guy finds the client and does the grunt work preparing the case, but he doesn't handle it in court. In Bombay, the guy who finds the client sometimes doesn't even do the grunt work preparing the case. What you get then is a *jugalbandi* between law firms, who are 'on record' as lawyers for the client, and court counsels, who carry the responsibility of fronting the court hearings. You don't have to be a law firm to be 'on record' of course: every individual *paidal* (foot-soldier) lawyer is naturally on record for his client.

The system works pretty well. Attracting clients is a business development function. It takes special skills. If you look at all the lawyers who run large law firms, they may be pretty good lawyers, but they are superb salesmen. Superb salesmanship and intense legal study don't go into the same box. Once the client is sold, someone has to prepare the case. Bombay law-firm managers push this job to court counsels. Pretty much everywhere else, law-firm managers push this job to their hired help. Consider the irony of this: you go to a well-regarded well-spoken law-firm manager for his legal acumen, but one part of your job gets done by some cheap labourer grinding away in the basement! Fortunately, whatever he produces does get reviewed by someone up the food chain. Then comes the fun part. Every law firm has an extensive menu of court counsels on offer. In City Law, we called them *ghora*s. Which ghora you rent depends on how much money you have to spend and what you want done. It's an expensive business, and if you haven't the budget, you can say goodbye to your plans for a devastating victory in court! It's not just law firms that hire court counsels. Often enough, savvy paidal lawyers do just the same if their clients are ready to pay for it. The higher the stakes, the bigger the court counsel you need. When the stakes get really big, you bring on the top-dog pride-of-Khajuraho Big-Dick Counsels! When it comes to court counsel, size matters.

Every High Court—and the Supreme Court—has its senior counsels. Delhi High Court at the time was a house divided between the Kayastha judges and the Punjabi judges. There were a bunch of neutral judges for sure, but most gravitated towards one or the other faction. If your case came up before a judge from one faction, you made sure your court counsel was from the same community. If your case came up before a partyless panchayat bench, you scrabbled around desperately looking for a son or a nephew of one of the judges deciding your case, and if none was to be found, you brought in a top-banana senior counsel from the Supreme Court.

The theory behind this practice makes perfect sense. A court counsel argues to a brief, 'case file' if you prefer. He is an officer of the court, here to assist a court. He knows neither client nor the client's case. His job is the pursuit of justice for the party he represents. All he knows about the case is what is stated in the case files presented to the court. He presents the case to the judge as it is given to him, impartially, with perfect detachment. The court counsels are masters of the law and it's their job to be on good terms with the judges.

Law firms, on the other hand, play doctor-doctor with their clients, and I mean that quite literally. They are a client's first port of call, and there is a fair bit of confidential conversation between them. Like any family doctor, the role can far exceed the narrow legal one. A client may come in to discuss a legal issue, but he can also discuss something sensitive, like his apprehension that his friend is his wife's lover. Even within the hard-core legal ambit, the law firm prepares and manages the case, determines and implements legal strategy, briefs senior counsels and plays general dog's body, absorbing all of the client's stress and neurosis while taking attitude from movie-star court counsels. Back in the 1980s, before the monopolies of the superstar senior counsels was broken and true competition appeared on the scene, top-flight court counsels treated both law firms and paidal lawyers like trash. In turn, since the client saw the law firm as a low-end service provider, they got the same treatment from the client. It was a terrible career choice because every direction entailed humiliation. When I'd had it up to my neck, Deo patiently explained to me that I must not lament my fate which surely even I knew was about the same as the one befalling a prostitute in GB Road when hung up to dry between a disgruntled hypersexual customer and a greedy sadistic pimp!

I remember feeling this way when we represented a senior British journalist of a global news agency. He had hired an attractive secretary and was rewarded with the kind of soul-satisfying flirtation that only those with great ambition but limited performance can experience. He failed to see that the lady's close attentiveness was mere courtesy to the boss. I don't know how far he got with his amorous plans. He claimed that over a period of time, she demanded more and more perks, benefits, days off and pay hikes. When he couldn't deal with her demands any more, they had a terrible row in the office at which point he sacked her. That was a big mistake. Whatever their relationship was, she never claimed it was sexual, because in no time she had slapped a case of wrongful termination on him. She made a simple case. The man was pursuing her for sexual gratification and when she failed to succumb, he sacked her. She now wanted damages, big fat damages.

For those with an abiding interest in illicit sex in office cabins, here is a bit of gratuitous advice. If you are compromised and unable to deliver on the quid pro quo you promised your amorous interest, project yourself as powerless, professionally diminished and unable to meet the lady's demands. Take the humiliation, grovel and roll about in the slime. Encourage the lady to leave for greener pastures, even help her with contacts, but never—repeat never—end it in a row. Hell hath no fury like a lady seduced and then ripped off.

As far as I know, this was the first sexual harassment case in the Delhi High Court and the judge's principal response was embarrassment. The lady wanted immediate reinstatement pending adjudication of her money claim. What's more, she wanted the English journalist's passport seized to prevent him from skipping the country. He wet his pants in horror. Deo thought we should hire Ashok Sen, undoubtedly one of India's top lawyers, because there really were no budgetary constraints. Sen accepted the brief.

Ashok Sen was quite a personality. My favourite Sen story is the time he showed up at a trial court to argue a case while it was in session. The poor magistrate took one look at him and jumped to his feet. Sen was sardonic as sin as he addressed the judge in his most clipped Oxbridge accent: 'it is not the custom of the law for the Bench to rise for the Bar, my lord.' Trust Sen to chuck a wicked 'my lord' at the bottom of the pecking order of judges! The judge shifted from foot to foot for a moment, and then sat down in confusion. In time, his confusion changed to pleasure. I mean, here was the great Ashok Sen, appearing in his court. When Sen's case was called for hearing, the judge extended a friendly welcome and told him he was happy to hear his arguments. Sen was unmoved. 'We are but lawyers, my lord, and appear everywhere. For the price of my professional fees, I will address a lamp post,' he said. The guy who told me this story was convinced the judge never quite cut through the Queen's English or the case would not have been won.

Naturally, I made my first trip to Sen's chamber with great apprehension. I had never been in the presence of such eminence, let alone briefed such a senior lawyer. I knew neither the game, nor its rules and pitfalls. No one in City Law wanted to help. Sen was charming to a fault. He 'settled' the brief, meaning he read the written statement of defence I had made and meticulously corrected it with a red pencil. It was a typical British-era, UK-educated top lawyer's draft: restrained, minimal, limited to the hard facts without flourishes. I then went to my office, typed it up and sent it back to the client. This is where things started to go wrong. The client went and obtained another opinion from another paidal lawyer who hacked Sen's draft to bits. He then sent this hatchet job back to me. This 'client version' wasn't so much legal draft as a propaganda pamphlet, complete with extensive quotations from communications between boss and amorous interest, emotional excess and simulated tantrums. Clearly, the two drafts represented the mother of all cultural clashes. The client started to pressure me to file this Bollywood-screenplay version. I tried to contact Ashok Sen but he was out of the country. On the principle that the client was king, I filed the client's extended edition . . . and invited myself to my own funeral.

When Sen heard I had changed his 'settled draft', he refused to appear. I called up the journalist and was told it had to be Sen or nothing. Sen sat on his ego, the journalist sat on his 'client's prerogative' and I got it from both ends. This was my first experience of independently briefing a truly all-time-great counsel and as the great sages who meditated in the Himalayas for a thousand years would have put it, it was a case of *Pratham Chumbanaan, Danth Bhajnam,* translated from the Sanskrit roughly as 'First kiss, broke teeth'! Ultimately, it came down to how low I would bend and how much humiliation I would take from Sen before his anger subsided and he agreed to appear. Running litigation for a law firm was a brutal life. And this was no isolated case.

Here's another typical story from about the same month.

Amongst the kettle of fish slithering in the pot at City Law was this balding sleazeball, iconic in his capacity for mischief. He was short, fat, and had the magical gift of using his pinkie to find all manner of miniscule gems inside his nostrils. This is difficult to do unless you stick your elbow well out into the world with the palm of your hand facing outwards. If one was walking down a narrow corridor and overtook Dutta when his elbow was sticking out, one ran the risk of perforating his sinuses. Most people agreed Dutta was a low life-form. Deo delighted in his gutter sniping ways, the way others enjoy slapstick slipped-on-a-banana-peel humour. Deo used him to ruffle the feathers of those he did not like, treating him like a yapping guard dog and running to his defence every time Dutta messed something up. He also used Dutta as a messenger boy to push screwed-up cases to me. Naturally, I never knew whether Deo only pushed butchered cases at me or whether all City Law cases had been hacked to death. Either way, I went to court mainly to be mauled by judges.

One late evening, Dutta handed me a file and asked me to attend a briefing meeting with one of India's all-time greats, the Supreme Court counsel Pestonjee. At that time Pestonjee was at the top of his game and largely seen as a really sweet guy. He enjoyed jazz and women, and reportedly had remarkable success with both. I had the night to read up the file, which I did, but no sooner was I ushered into his presence next morning than he asked me for several critical documents of which I knew nothing. Pestonjee flew into a rage. My ignorance compounded his anger. He spat venom at me in a room full of sniggering paidals. He then threw me out of his chamber. Naturally, I had the jitters when court started; would he show up at all? Not that I could blame him. He had a stressful hearing coming up and he could not win without documents his law firm wouldn't supply. Pestonjee however was no ditcher. Always the perfect gentleman, he was faithfully in court well in time for the hearing. He was conciliatory and warm. He also had the skill and stature to survive the court hearing without the documents. No great damage was done. It all ended quite amicably but I was in a black mood that day.

Dutta was faffing about the office laughing when I got back. Was he aware that Pestonjee had asked for some documents? Sure, he leered back. 'Why didn't you tell me?' 'Because if I had,' he laughed, 'you would have refused to handle the case.' 'Do you realize you could have screwed the case up?' 'Yeah,' he shrugged, 'but that would be your problem since you were handling the case.'

I was incensed, and charged into Deo's room. Deo couldn't see what the fuss was about. 'We all know what Dutta is, Ranjeev,' he dismissed my anger. 'It is for you to see how to protect the client.' 'But how do I protect a client if Dutta won't tell me what is expected in a case I have never handled before?' 'This is a law firm, Ranjeev,' he shrugged, 'you have to figure out for yourself how you are going to achieve that objective.'

I couldn't shake off the trauma of this callousness. I barged into Shanx's room. How could he have a law firm full of such half-witted perverse bastards? Shanx disapproved of my moralizing.

'You are ascribing to Dutta motives he may be too dumb to formulate,' he retorted, 'he is just a lame duck playing true to type—that is all.'

'But how can we run a law practice with such bad resources?'

Shanx waved me away. 'Anyone can win a derby race if he owns the best thoroughbred, Ranjeev,' he said, 'but if you do, all the prize money you ever earn will only go to paying off the price of the thoroughbred. The trick is to win the race with a donkey.'

~

With the benefit of hindsight, I should have thanked the two Dragons for their insightful guidance. They explained to me a most basic truth about law firms. I had so far believed that we were coming together as a team to provide a better service to the market. I now understood that law firms exist to serve the agendas of their members. Keeping up the pretence of 'protecting the clients' interests' was just another way of saying that we had to preserve the firm's goodwill so that we were able to pursue our agendas better. That did not mean that the firm's goodwill took priority over the individual lawyer's personal agendas. If one lawyer wanted to mess with another, he would happily compromise 'the client's interest' to discredit his colleague. This is true not just of law firms but of pretty much every piece of the service industry. Law firms, investment advisers, merchant bankers, stockbrokers, and other 'advisory service' entities are all only brands, a mere name board under the shelter of which individuals drive their private ambitions. These service providers owe their primary allegiances not to their organizations—their brands—but to their markets, i.e. customers. Individuals within law firms have no long-term stake in the fate of their law firm. If the place blows up, they are fine only as long as they can bail out with some customers. This simple fact explains every mystery you may ever encounter about the way in which these entities function. When members of law firms big and small behave like brats fighting over the last morsel of pudding, they are acting perfectly rationally. Each lawyer is here to protect his piece of the customer base. When lawyers in a law firm undermine each other even though they are working for the same firm, they are doing what every sensible person would. To get ahead in life, they have to extend their influence over the client pool while destroying their rivals' influence over the same client pool. The 'client's interest' is the least of their problems.

This is why members of law firms compete viciously with each other. More often than not, they compete to a point where the client's interest is jeopardized without a thought. Upwardly mobile lawyers push clients in directions they should not be going, knowing fully well it's not good for the client. They do this because it is good for them. We see the same dynamic play out between rival lawyers on either side of a line of skirmish. There are no permanent clients. Your rival's client could become your client in the future. Much of the acrimony we see in negotiations over corporate commercial deals flow from this opportunity. The lawyers aren't fighting to protect the client: they are fighting to retain or extend influence. This is why much of what lawyers fight about is marginal stuff: unlikely events which will never come to pass, and if they do, will have only so much financial impact. The tragedy for the client is not that its advisers are fighting over nothing; it is that they are fighting over the right to tell him to go to places he need not go. The irony is that frequently, the client is paying the lawyer by the hour to carry on this brutal internal warfare repackaged to appear to be the protection of the client's interest.

We may come to these painful conclusions with a flashing flick of the wrist but the consequences of these conclusions may take a long time to work out. Not everyone who tops the theory paper does so well in the practical examinations. I heard what I was being told but I didn't want to accept it. Instead, I denounced the Dragons in my mind as bad leaders and worse human beings. It took me years to accept the central self-evident truth about law firms. I yo-yoed in an emotional roller-coaster ride, swinging wildly between cynicism and the need to believe. In the meantime, since this process had only just begun, I sank slowly into depression. We had a terrible gloomy office, ugly colleagues, unsupportive staff, a doubtful future and no way forward.

When my wife came to Connaught Place to see me one day with our eighteen-month-old girl in tow, I welcomed them into my little chamber and gathered up my child into my arms, seeking the warmth of innocence in this ugly place. This was new to both of us because she was always asleep when I left home early in the morning and asleep when I got back home late at night. No doubt, the alien environment with its harsh incandescent lights and long dark shadows accentuated her fears. As I held her in my arms, she started to cry hysterically. My wife was the paragon of managerial efficiency. She quickly pecked my cheek goodbye and took her back home while I sat stunned in my seat. I started to cry, the silent tears rolling down my cheeks as I slumped helpless in the dark recesses of my anguish. I cared nothing about the harsh reality of my life. I cared nothing about the lack of money, the constant work pressure, the stress of being at the bottom of the power pie, the frustration of failure. I cried for the dying hope of a better day and, when I got home, I drank myself to sleep on rotgut whisky. I started a whole new career of substance abuse.

As it turned out, I need not have pitied myself quite as much as I did. Deo had already planned a move to a new office, and better times were going to be advancing upon me shortly. Not without some ugly surprises though.

8

Legal Morality

The winter of 1993 was a cold one. Even without an office of its own, City Law sliced through the foggy freeze with startlingly little loss of revenue or manpower. There was no attrition. At the time, it seemed that the intrinsic Indian loyalty to caste and tribe had won the day. After all, the Dragons and their groupies had left the old firm together and it seemed logical for them to sink or swim together. In time, I came to realize that the followers had nowhere to go. They were all in it together because they needed Shanx just to keep breathing: if he let go, like the victims in the *Jaws* movies, they would all be lost in a frothy mess of thrashing decapitated limbs, swirling waters and gurgling bubbles escaping finally from lungs rapidly filling with water. City Law wasn't a US-style carrier command group; it was one aircraft carrier and lots of porous rubber dinghies strung out on tow ropes!

It was Deo who finally found an office for us. It was nice: a spacious penthouse with ample parking in a well-managed building in a quiet part of town not far from Bengali Market. It even had a small 300-foot cubbyhole appendage on the third floor which we could use as a store. As it turned out, this nondescript piece of real estate became my central reality for many years, but let me not get ahead of the story.

We moved into empty rooms just as we had when I first joined City Law. We coughed our lungs out as the interior decorators went room by room, painting walls, installing bookshelves and polishing woodwork. This put a terminal end to any ambition I may ever have had to add paint-thinners to my list of potential substances to abuse!

It wasn't all black though: City Law finally had its own office. My own brightly lit office room, complete with a private loo, greatly added to my increasing optimism. When I didn't get lunch from home, a helpful flunky quickly ran down to Bengali Market and got me a box of aloo–puri trumpeting itself on the cover as 'an irresistible selection of India delights, bite by bite'.

One March morning I had a call from Shanx at 5 a.m. He was customarily short. 'Ranjeev,' he barked, 'do you know the Asha Deep building on Barakhamba Road?' I did.

'Be there at noon, go to DS Construction's office on the third floor and ask for Rick Wilson. I will join you there.' He rang off. No explanation, no background. That was vintage fast-bowling Shanx at his inimitable best. I was bang on time, perhaps a few minutes early. Shanx was an hour late. That too was his style. He believed that punctuality is for the unemployed and the unimportant: flunkies wait, powerful men are waited for.

Rick Wilson was DS Construction's CEO. He was a worried man. The company was building a 400-MW hydroelectric project in the Himalayas and work had ground to a halt. The roots of the problem lay in the imprecise English the National Hydro Power Corporation (NHPC) had used when it put out a global tender for the construction of a tunnel beneath a high plateau around which a river curved. The project aimed to pick up water at the north end of the plateau, bore a tunnel under the plateau and expel the surging water through the turbines of a power house on the other side. The Notice Inviting Tender suggested that the owner—NHPC—had tested the soil and confidently predicted that the earth under the plateau was solid and stable. Relying on these representations, our client—the DS Construction consortium—bid for and won the tender.

Work proceeded quickly after the award of the tender because the client imported a 75-metre-long Tunnel Boring Machine—or TBM—which basically chewed away the earth like a scary mud-eating science-fiction monster. Not all the way though. Four kilometres into the boring process, DS Construction hit a fossil valley. A sea of mud gushed over the TBM, filling up a kilometre of tunnel, killing four workers. Now if you are not a geology fanatic, I need to explain this.

Fossil valleys are buried areas of the earth which at some point of time were at the surface. Over aeons, these fill with mud and then get buried under rock and rubble. In time, solid earth seals in the mud so you get a real solid crust of earth on top, but if you dig deep, what you have down there is still a sea of underground mud. Now, if you want to bore a tunnel through this mud, you have to order yourself a special purpose TBM: one that can dig and line the tunnel with steel plates to hold out the mud at the same time. The Himalayas have a great many fossil valleys so it's not that this was an utterly unimaginable mega surprise. DS Construction relied on NHPC's soil tests and ordered a rock-chewing TBM, not a mud-managing one. Now it had a mud-filled tunnel to excavate by hand. How many years was that going to take and at what cost?

To get the project built in time, DS Construction needed a new TBM with steel-cladding capability, unsustainably deep pockets to buy the TBM, and several years more to complete the project. What was to be done?

'Okay, situation understood,' Shanx perked up, 'tell us who is to bear this project risk.'

Rick was uncertain. 'If you look at the notice inviting tender,' he said, 'you will see that under soil conditions, the government has stated that they have tested the soil and the annexure specifies it as hard rock.'

'Is the notice inviting tender a part of the contract?' asked Shanx.

'Unfortunately no,' Rick revealed, 'we signed a comprehensive contract after that.' And what did that say? Rick dug out an encyclopedia-sized tome. In less than half an hour, it was clear that NHPC had washed its hands of all its tests. The contract said that DS should do its own tests and should satisfy itself about all 'local conditions'. The client was in deep trouble.

'If we excavate this tunnel again and pull out this TBM,' Rick pondered, 'we are still going to have to order a new TBM with cladding capability. This is going to delay the project by two years. Even if the government does not claim damages for delays, the added cost of the project is six times our projected profits over the whole project.'

'Do you have insurance?' Shanx asked.

'We have a short-period business interruption insurance, that's all. In fact, given our worldwide condition, this project could push us into bankruptcy.'

Shanx raised an eyebrow. 'Are you saying that you cannot perform under this contract unless the government pays you for all the damage?' he asked. Rick nodded.

'And the government is certainly not paying you when the contract clearly says that this is your problem,' Shanx added.

Rick protested. 'Given the special circumstances, why would the government not take a commercial view and make an exception? After all, this is an important project in a disturbed state: there are larger strategic realities involved.' He really wanted to believe in his hypothetical model of a benevolent government doling out tax-payers' money to foreign contractors who dispense with soil tests to save another lousy buck.

'This will not happen because that is not how the Indian government functions,' Shanx retorted. 'First, the national interest is not something that concerns our government. Second, your contract puts the responsibility squarely on you; why should the government bail you out of your misery?' He then paused dramatically, 'And finally, regardless of the merits of your case, no government servant will ever rule in your favour.'

'Regardless of whether we are right or wrong?' Rick looked incredulous.

'Absolutely. Any government servant who decides this case in your favour is going to be accused of taking a bribe.'

'We don't pay bribes!' Rick was quick to protest.

'It doesn't matter what you do or don't do. The allegation will come.'

'But we can disprove such an accusation!' Rick was pleading.

'To whom?' Shanx barked, 'To Parliament? To Opposition parties?' Rick was silenced. He looked like a man out of his depth.

'So what are my options?' Rick looked grim.

'If you want the government to pay,' Shanx was forthright, 'you will have to prove to an arbitrator that the contract puts this risk on the government and, frankly, I don't rate your chances high.'

'Are you suggesting that we are facing bankruptcy?'

'Certainly not,' Shanx was enjoying this. 'The problem is you are asking the wrong question.' Rick was getting really confused. Shanx moved to rescue him.

'Since the contract clearly states that this is your risk, to seek legal opinion on this point is a waste of time. The only question you can ask is how you can get out without paying a whole lot of damages.'

'We can't get out of this contract, can we?' Rick looked unconvinced.

'You can always get out of any contract if you have the imagination,' Shanx was being wicked. 'Give me something to shoot the government with.' Shanx started to go through a mental checklist with Rick. Has the government defaulted on any of its obligations? Is it late in making payment? Has it failed to supply something it should have? Do you have any other grievances you can capitalize on? The session went into the contract with a fine toothcomb. By late evening, it was clear that NHPC had done an impeccable job. Rick looked defeated. Shanx didn't.

'Okay, if NHPC is not at fault,' he seemed to start afresh, 'give us another reason why you can't perform.' Rick didn't get the drift any more than I did.

'There must be other reasons you can't perform!' Shanx was strident. 'Is there a critical approval you don't have? Is the local government imposing unfair conditions you can't meet? Is there a public road unable to carry your materials that the government has failed to repair? Are locally procured materials not appropriate to dam construction?' Rick had no such grievance. It irritated Shanx.

'How can this be?' Shanx shouted. 'In this terrorist-ridden region, are you telling me that all roads are functioning, labour is freely available, and your subcontractors are lulling themselves to sleep night after night singing lullabies?'

'We don't have a serious problem.' Rick was quite clear-headed. 'We get the odd firing in the hills around the project and our contractors sometimes have to lie low when things get too hot, but it is not too much of a problem.' Shanx didn't like that.

'Then view it as a problem,' he advised. 'You have guns going off in the night, you have scared contractors, you have roads that are impassable from time to time, you have curfew from time to time, and you probably get extortion threats from militants . . . are you telling me you don't have a problem?'

'I am not saying I don't have a problem,' Rick protested. 'I am saying it's not a serious problem.'

'But the seriousness of a problem is in its perception, isn't it?' Shanx was adamant. 'Who is to judge what constitutes a serious problem? I don't think you should mix perception and reality.' He paused dramatically. 'I am a successful middle-aged businessman operating a profitable business in a country with a severely impaired justice delivery system, great poverty, a dysfunctional police force and a corrupt bureaucracy which is always extorting money from me, but curiously, I am afraid mostly of my wife. Who is the final arbitrator of who I should be more afraid of? A bomb going off fifty miles away scares me. My mind goes blank and I can't work. My staff is threatening to run off. If you want to get out of this project, you can persuade yourself to be a little petrified, can't you?'

Rick remained unconvinced. 'Okay, even if we stop work from time to time because of shooting and so forth, this will only delay resolution of the problem; it doesn't solve it.'

'That is not true,' Shanx was clear. 'If the other side can see that you are capable of sitting there and doing nothing for long periods of time, they will pay you to go away and do the job themselves.' The penny was beginning to drop for Rick.

'You can sit there forever,' Shanx continued, 'work one day, halt work for ten days because of all your multifarious problems, then resume for one day, stop again . . .' Rick finally got it.

The idea was to declare force majeure one day at a time. This is completely legal. Most contracts have a clause which allows a party to extend the time to perform a contract if an 'act of God' prevents it from doing so immediately. The force majeure menu is large: natural calamities like floods and earthquakes, hurricanes and epidemics; mechanical accidents like explosions and road crashes and equipment breakdown and broken roads; political risks such as terrorism and mass political agitations and nasty governments nationalizing industries . . . etc., etc., etc. Militancy in a region, especially in a contract with a government-owned entity, would inevitably be covered under force majeure. Even if a contract didn't have a force majeure clause, the law of contract provided for one.

~

Rick accepted the proposal. Shanx laughed all the way to the car park.

'Shanx, you know that this militancy argument is not sustainable,' I complained. He nodded.

'That depends on what you mean by sustainable. If you are asking me whether I can justify it every time I declare force majeure, the answer is maybe or maybe not. But I don't think NHPC is going to go to court and try to prove that we can build a dam in the middle of a proxy war.' He paused. 'However, that is completely beside the point. The point is that when you declare force majeure, the government doesn't know your intention. You chop the goat an inch at a time. It frustrates the government but each individual provocation is not worth a fight. The government will scream but it will not precipitate.'

'No, but at some point they will get pissed off,' I said.

Shanx chuckled. 'True. At some point they will get pissed off. Then the real fun starts. They will want to fight, we will have some billing, but equally, the political troublemakers will move in accusing government of non-performance and so forth. Government will be embarrassed and, in time, all they will want is that we get out of the project on any terms so that they can get someone else to do it.'

'This is the beauty of litigation in India,' he concluded. 'The system is so convoluted the defendant can stall and defeat a very good case. There is no sin quite as great as aspiring to be a plaintiff in an Indian court!'

The client was faithful to Shanx's script. DS Construction flooded NHPC with reports of firings, extortion letters received by mail, kidnapping threats pasted at night on the company stockyards, panicking workmen who broke bonds and hotfooted it back to Bihar without permission after a particularly noisy night of Kalashnikov gunfire, etc.

NHPC was surprised. Another contractor was developing a large hydro project much deeper in the mountainous wilderness close by with 200 foreigners and 4000 Indians at about the same time and they weren't being difficult. Two of their expatriate engineers had been kidnapped in 1991, which had led to a long negotiation with the militants culminating in an 'escape' ninety-seven days later. They had even faced shelling from across the border but all this only led to an eighteen-month delay. Why was DS Construction so antsy?

The argument dragged on, but dragging the argument on wasn't going to get the project built. After all that had long gone on in the North-East, and later even Punjab, NHPC knew that even on the most optimistic estimate, militancy could last forever, or twice as long. DS had effectively buried the project. To cut a long story short, the project moved very slowly, if at all, over the next two years.

NHPC tried to cajole DS Construction, failed, then threatened DS with dire consequences, and failed again. It mulled the option of suing DS for damages but management took the view that throwing good money after bad wouldn't get the project complete. Not to put too fine a point on it, NHPC succumbed to the tactics and DS bailed out. The parties terminated the contract without cost to either side, DS Construction cut its losses and exited India.

Pondering over what had gone on, I felt myself filled with angst. 'This just isn't right,' I told Shanx one day. 'Whatever the Notice Inviting Tender may have said, the truth is that DS Construction did sign a comprehensive contract and DS should have paid the bill for an obligation they assumed.'

Shanx was not impressed. 'Any contract is capable of multiple constructions, Ranjeev. You can write what arcane legalese you want, but if you can't make it stick, it's worthless. What matters is what a party is capable of doing on the ground.'

'Yes, but we made Indian taxpayers pay for the fossil valley disaster because NHPC claimed to do a subsoil test they didn't do and DS Construction refused to pay for a risk they had agreed to undertake.' Shanx looked bored. 'You'd better decide what you want out of your life, Ranjeev. Corporate commercial law practice and a hyperventilating conscience don't sleep on the same bed!' Then he softened.

'We all practise law. To us, that is the right and wrong of what we can, could, should, would, can't, shouldn't, wouldn't do. If something is illegal, you shouldn't be doing it. If it's legal, it's the right thing to do: forget the morality claptrap.'

In that moment, I knew that Shanx had revealed to me the very heart of the ethical void. I stopped and stared.

~

I was deeply grateful to Shanx for the exposure he was giving me. I was delighted with the work, and gratified at the insight. But I don't recall specifically going up to him and thanking him for the invaluable life lesson in professionalism he gave me.

Here's the deal. You may think you are greater than what you do. You may think you have an inner core, a character, a central personality, something that rises above the slime you wallow in. You are lying to yourself. If you wallow in muck, no matter what you do, a lot of it will stick. This is why stockbrokers lie effortlessly. It's very simple. The stockbroking business is nothing but financial prediction. These predictions hang on the occurrence of mainly non-financial events. These guys are not trained to predict the future. No one is, or can be. They don't know which party will form the next government. They don't know if the price of oil will rise or fall. They don't know whether a devastating flood will totally destroy a profitable pharmaceutical factory in Kashmir. Still, they tell you what to buy and what to sell. Where do they get their easy self-assurance from? They get it because they know that stockbroking is a confidence-trick business. They know they are bullshitting you. In time, they can't tell the truth from lies any more. When they are asked to express an opinion, they base what they say on what is in their interest to say. Not too far in the future, the moral compass becomes a complete philosophical abstraction to them. This is inevitable.

Lawyers pay a similar kind of price. The legal profession moulds your character. If you are going to spend years and years listening to sordid stories of brothers castrating brothers, of brothers trying to gyp their sisters out of their share of the family estate, then sooner or later, the landslide of cynicism will bury you. I don't know any successful lawyer who is also naive. I know plenty who posture a great deal of pseudo-humanistic piety but none who live those values when they are on their legs in a court, or negotiating for their clients. To choose to be a lawyer is to explore the sewers of human perversity. When you pass daily through a sewer, some of the excreta will become you.

So how do we live with ourselves? Lawyers who continue to hang on to old-world notions of dignity and honour train themselves to live their private lives in a separate compartment from their professional careers. Men find this easy. The male of the species is adept at creating chambers in his heart: he then stores his compassion for his infant son in one compartment and his murderous rage at his enemies in an entirely different chamber. He is a doting dad at home and a vicious bastard in court. Women find this harder to do. I am not saying they can't: I'm just saying women seem to live more holistically. Their emotional realities are more integrated. The glass ceiling is not the only reason women find it harder to progress in the legal profession.

Curiously, the essential brutality of being a lawyer doesn't seem to bother youngsters these days. From being quite the pariah profession in the eyes of small-town Jammu in the 1960s when I grew up, law is today the unanimous flavour of the month. Many wannabe lawyers are still young enough to be rather idealistic. There is a great irony here. The last decade has been witness to a steep decline in the public's perception of the quality of the judiciary in India. Thirty years back, it was not the general belief that all politicians are crooks, that more than a few courts are corrupt, or that the legal system is failing to deliver on its promise.

Has this led to youngsters walking away from the law in droves, choosing other professions instead? Of course not! Law colleges are proliferating like maggots on ripped flesh. Why does everyone want to be a lawyer today? Is it because the fires of crusading reform burn in the breasts of young students who want to seize this historic moment and snatch our innately good legal system out of the hands of the corrupted older generation and transform India into a utopia?

Don't let me distract you as I split my sides with mirth. The truth is that all of us, not just youngsters, are highly vulnerable to the incentives of our environment. Success today is equated with the amoral pursuit of economic self-interest, and law is as good a field as any to pursue it.

So does the environment mould lawyers into amoral creatures? Or are those ready to be moulded subconsciously throwing themselves into this profession? Are lawyers making a choice or are they the victims of a subconscious self-fulfilment? I have no doubt in my mind. Unwitting, unspoken, youngsters make subconscious choices and mould their characters in a way that brings them closer to their financial goals. Somewhere along the way, youngsters seamlessly drop their scruples. Not that it matters very much anyway. If you are an idealistic young man who thinks he is going out to change the world, I'm afraid I don't have good news. Indeed, if I was a betting man, I would guess that the world is more likely to change you!

9

Kashmiri Double-cross

If I was a romantic sculptor, he would be pathos. He had the quintessentially Kashmiri hooked nose with deep ruts running down his sunken cheeks. If you said anything to him at all, he inevitably shrugged his shoulders in sad resignation, sighed slowly and launched into an unsolicited homily. His refugee status did nothing to alleviate his genetic unhappiness. Beneath that dejection lurked an emotionally unstable personality with an appetite for self-destruction. Khazanchi was a smooth-talking middle-aged loser with a confidence trickster's air of evasive bragging. He interrupted every conversation to lead it back to himself, switched topics by the minute, and inevitably left the ugly aftertaste of a man who had lied to your face knowing that he was lying and knowing that you knew. If he didn't keep bumming cigarettes off me, at least I would have had the privilege of disliking him without there being a money angle in it somewhere. When Deo announced that he was creating a new Jammu and Kashmir by putting me in the same room as Khazanchi, I didn't go bouncing off the walls in excitement. Instinctively, I feared that his lean and hungry look had all the menace of Brutus holding a knife behind his back. That is exactly how it prophetically turned out for me.

Our early interactions were pleasant enough. Deo wanted him in on whatever I did for Deo, which meant that he—like every other work-shirker in City Law—wanted to attend the client conferences and avoid the grunt work. This I learnt to live with, but when he began to feel he was entitled to being in on whatever I did for Shanx, my antenna started to thrum. City Law was big on politics, so was this Deo's way of keeping tabs on what Shanx was doing with me?

To begin with, Deo got what he wanted because Shanx's favourite client—let's call them Climtrol—got hit by an excise duty Show Cause Notice. Of all the *sarkari* lunatics it has been my privilege to experience in my three decades of law practice, there are no lunatics quite as perverse as some taxmen, and the excise-duty boys have inevitably been the crème de la crème. I am deeply in their debt though, because their monumental stupidity allowed me to kick-start a great career leap!

The facts of this case came straight out of Ripley's Believe It or Not. Climtrol's claim to Indian fame lay in its range of white goods, and that meant washing machines, microwave ovens, air-conditioners, refrigerators and whatever other overpriced gadget your wife talks you into stuffing into the space you don't have at home, simply because the Kapoors next door have one. When Climtrol came to do business in the new liberalized India, it had sold its products mainly in cold-climate countries: it wasn't sure how its products would survive India's varied conditions. Climtrol planned on selling machines everywhere in India: from the icy cold of Kashmir to the dry heat of Rajasthan, from the soggy wet of Assam to the heat and humidity of Kerala. It needed to track the performance of each machine and to do that, it had to be able to tell one machine from another. Now how do you do that? You identify white goods the same way you identify cars: you give them a number plate!

Climtrol started to give unique serial numbers to each of their machines. This had all kinds of spin-off benefits. Climtrol started a new series every month, so everyone knew how much Climtrol manufactured each month. As you can imagine, a lot of machines failed in the early years. With an eye to the long term, Climtrol was very good about replacing them free of cost, even when they were out of warranty. Failed machines were sent back to the company's R&D department, dissected like frogs in school biology labs, repaired and then sent back as replacements for the next lot of failed machines. Like any large global bureaucracy, while doing this research on its own machines, Climtrol made sure machine numbers were carefully written down with every 'movement' document that ever got created. If you were bored enough to troll through Climtrol's warranty and repair records, you could write the travelogue of every machine that Climtrol ever manufactured from its very date of birth. You could tell who bought the thing, where it went, when it failed, when it came back for repair, what was wrong, when it was repaired, where it went next, and so forth. There was nothing wrong with what Climtrol was doing. So long as it paid tax on every machine it manufactured, it is nobody's business that Climtrol wanted to write machine biographies in its corporate records.

That's not how the excise department saw it. Everyone evades taxes in India, if they can. The tax boys can't catch anyone easily because no one maintains any records. When there is no evidence, there is no case. In this black-marketing cash-dealing little-black-book-accounting country with a peculiar love for world-beating tax dodges, the anti-evasion wing of the tax department had precious little to do at the best of times. What little investigation it does get to do, a well-aimed bribe somewhere up the food chain kills before it gets too far! Now, in this empty void where tax investigators have no records at all to investigate, when they suddenly found out that a crazy foreign company was generating masses of production and sales data tracking everything they ever sold, they started to froth at the mouth like rabid dogs. They stumbled on this information because a sacked Climtrol distributor decided to get even with the company by whistle-blowing its affairs to the excise department! Climtrol had chucked out this dealer and he was really upset. He decided to get even by whistle-blowing a baseless smoke-and-mirrors story of tax dodging to the anti-evasion department. The excise boys fell for the story, believing that they were on to something really big. That's when everything started to spin out of control.

It wasn't just a retribution story though, or a great love for India. If the ex-dealer was proved right, he got 10 per cent of the tax demanded as his reward. Some of this money came his way when the Show Cause Notice was served, the rest when the department actually collected the tax. Think about it: if you can make a bullshit case with enough in it to have a Show Cause Notice issued, you can make serious money no matter what the final fate of the case. Indeed, it's in your interest to exaggerate the claim as much as possible because your reward would increase proportionately. The whistle-blower managed to persuade the anti-evasion excise wing that Climtrol was engaging in a colossal tax fraud.

One sunny evening, a bunch of anti-evasion sleuths showed up at the door of all nineteen of Climtrol's factories and depots across the country. Over the next twenty-four hours, they seized ten tin trunks of documents and twenty-four rusting machines. There the matter stood for a year because, in truth, Climtrol had done nothing wrong. Climtrol employees made countless pointless visits to the department and recorded dozens of redundant statements. Everyone understood that the anti-evasion unit had egg on its face. Not that it mattered. A bureaucratic procedure, once started, must plod on tirelessly through mud and snow, till everyone forgets who ordered the march, or why. Climtrol thought this is what would happen to this case as well. It was not to be. The government had spent a lot of money on the raid. What was the result? Questions were raised within the department. To justify the cost, when the matter could be stalled no longer, a thirty-page Show Cause Notice showed up at Climtrol's door demanding a couple of hundred crores as unpaid excise duty (plus penalty and interest).

For the young and the blessed, I can reveal that excise duty is a tax on manufacture. Every time a factory manufactures something, the company pays tax on it. It doesn't pay tax when the goods come off the production line though. It pays tax when the goods leave the factory on their way to the shops. This makes perfect sense. A company can manufacture something and decide it is not worth selling. Maybe it's rubbish quality and unsaleable. Maybe there is no buyer. Or maybe, like the whisky guys, they need to mature the brew for twelve years before they bottle and sell it. If Scotch whisky manufacturers selling those spiritually therapeutic eighteen-year-old malts had to pay tax the moment they made the whisky, all of them would be bankrupt and we would be drinking something else! Tax is paid when there is a sale to be made. The way it works in practice, when Maruti sends out twenty cars, the factory-gate guys note twenty chassis numbers and engine numbers and the factory pays excise duty on twenty cars.

This brings us to the key point here. If the excise sleuths were able to identify the date of manufacture of a machine from its serial number, any error in noting that number will lead them to believe that the machine was manufactured in some month other than what Climtrol claimed. For example, if Climtrol paid excise duty on 250 machines in March last year, but the sleuths found a serial number that suggested Climtrol had manufactured 400 machines that month, Climtrol was in trouble. How did the excise sleuths know? Because they found a reference to a failed machine number 400 manufactured in March last year in a repair-related document! So didn't that prove that 400 minus 250 = 150 machines had been sold without paying excise duty? They had such machine numbers in repair records for every month that Climtrol had been in India. They added up the numbers and concluded that Climtrol had produced three times more machines than it had paid tax on. They even said they could prove it because they had twenty-four machines carrying serial numbers on which no excise duty had been paid. It was impressive stuff.

Climtrol went crazy. It didn't have the installed capacity—or the funding, or the capital—to manufacture at that scale. Where on earth were these numbers coming from? The Show Cause Notice relied on several hundred repair-related documents. Climtrol asked the excise sleuths to show them the documents. The excise sleuths jeered derisively and refused. 'File your reply in thirty days,' they laughed, 'and when the case is heard by the adjudicating authority, you can look at the documents.' 'But we can't answer these allegations unless we understand where these documents are coming from,' Climtrol pleaded. 'Too bad, suckers' was the unspoken shrug, 'we can't give you documents before you file your reply.' Catch 22!

Thinking about the problem, it came down to this. The case was based on twenty-four actual machines bearing serial numbers on which no tax was supposedly paid. The rest was paper trails of machines long after they had been sold. Climtrol could easily argue that it could write whatever it wanted in its records about failed machines in the field. Would the authorities buy that? This is a country where you assume the smoke and then scream 'Fire!' A case based on irrelevant documents had been created and now Climtrol had to deal with it.

Climtrol talked to its employee and dealers. It learnt that these paper trails were created from one document to another: no one ever checked if the machine being sent with the document actually had the number. So if one guy made a mistake in noting down the number, the next guy faithfully reproduced the error. So you could end up with all sorts of fanciful numbers. It really came down to 126 errors in noting down serial numbers. That transformed into a tax claim of 150,000 secretly manufactured machines! Now you see why we are the only nation to have mastered the Great Indian Rope Trick?

What about the twenty-four seized machines? Climtrol wasn't worrying. Punched number plates deteriorate quickly in the heat and the humidity; a *0* can be read as a *9*, an *8* or even a *6*. Clearly, the department was conveniently misreading serial numbers to suit its purpose.

All this enlightenment didn't mean that the problem disappeared. You can't defend a case till you refer to a document and say: this number should be that number because it was copied from another document that had that number and not this number. Climtrol had to get its hands on the repair record. The authority wouldn't hand over the documents till the reply was filed. Climtrol had to go to court. That thirty-day deadline was key, leaving Climtrol no choice. Before the time was up, it approached the High Court and demanded access to these documents before it was required to file its reply. This really made the department see red. In a clear case of teaching a company a lesson, the department issued a notice directing the entire board of directors of the company to present itself for questioning at the anti-evasion department in RK Puram at 5 p.m. one Friday evening.

It was an outrageous move. The department had completed its investigation. The Show Cause Notice had been issued. Why did they now need to question the directors? The significance of the 5 p.m. reporting time did not escape Climtrol either. If a man is arrested on a Friday evening, the law does not require him to be presented to a court before Monday. If you ever get called on a Friday evening to visit the police, take your toothbrush and undies along because as God is my witness and Tarun Tejpal is his prophet, you are going to the slammer. Three blissful days in jail is more than your average director in a multinational company is prepared to have as an authentic transformational eastern spiritual experience. They knew that if they complied with these summons, they were in the slammer for at least the weekend! The directors had temper tantrums and the management scampered about in frenzied confusion. Shanx scurried about administering legal tranquillizers, first to the directors, then the shareholders, then the MD, and then every underling who had received a death threat from any of the above. It was educative, funny, yet completely nerve-racking. Shanx couldn't stop laughing between phone calls. 'How will you ever make money if the client never gets buggered,' he asked.

That wasn't the worst of it. It was June. The High Court was shut. The vacation bench of the High Court sat once a week in a mood that was, well . . . vacational! How did I rate my chances of getting a vacation court to issue a stay order in an incomprehensible case about excise duty and tax evasion which went on and on about this document and that document and some convoluted story about serial number errors? Judges are human too. Few judges understood tax laws, fewer cared, and no one was going to go out on a limb to help a multinational who may have evaded crores in taxes. If I had been Emperor Nero, 'quo vadis' was the question to ask!

Khazanchi jumped to the rescue. Khazanchi said he knew an all-purpose fix-it-God called Sat Bhagwan in Chandigarh who could deliver anything. Khazanchi was very persuasive. Shanx laughed the loudest. 'Oye Deo, this prematurely ejaculated Kashmiri Pandit is telling us that Sat Bhagwan, the true God, is going to deliver a stay order to us?' Deo smiled his soothingly patronizing smirk. '*Aisa hai*, Shanx,' he patiently explained, his lips pursed, 'even the beggar who knows nothing knows somebody who knows something.' For lack of alternatives, Shanx decided not to exclude options. In no time, I whisked off Khazanchi to Chandigarh.

~

Khazanchi was as good as his word. Sat Bhagwan was a laconic man in the twilight of his career, oozing gravitas and introspection. He lived in what appeared to be a small farmhouse on the edge of the Leisure Valley in a single-digit sector in the swankiest part of the swankiest neighbourhood of the sleepiest town in north India. He was a career lawyer of forty-five years' experience and he looked like he had kept every lawyerly appointment ever known to mankind. He did a lot of silent deliberating between sentences. He is what the Punjabis call *doonga*, meaning deep: deep as in a bottomless well into which you may yell and wait indefinitely for an echo. For me, talking to him was a superb exercise in teeth-gnashing impatience-management self-development. Once he understood the case, he asked for a day to suggest a solution. I spent that day drumming my fingers on the depressing bar of the Mount View Hotel listening to vile *tota–maina* stories about the loves and lives of Khazanchi in the Kashmir valley before the recent mass migration.

It was worth it though, because when we went back to see Sat Bhagwan next day, he said he could deliver a stay order by Friday morning in time for the 5 p.m. deadline. He asked for a humungous sum of upfront professional fees: humungous as in ten times the professional fees any top-gun Chandigarh senior lawyer would charge to file a writ petition and argue a stay application. Shanx blew a gasket when I called him, then called Climtrol and confirmed that a company guy would deliver the money by that evening. While we waited for the Shatabdi Express to arrive, we loitered about Sat Bhagwan's office as he drafted a super-simplified case presenting a crude picture of the legal issues in asking for a stay order. I made an attempt to fill some detail into the draft. Sat Bhagwan shook his head in disapproval. 'Dubey Sahib, please keep it very simple. Too many facts confuse judges because it forces them to think.'

Sat Bhagwan was as good as his word. The Shatabdi arrived at 8.15 p.m.; the money arrived in his office by 9 p.m., the case papers were transmitted to somebody's house by 9.30 p.m. and we were asked to go back to the hotel and await news. We spent all of the next day swatting at house flies in the Mount View Hotel. I didn't mind. The pool was cool in the dry June air and no matter how hot the day, the 'Fitness Trail' next door was the best place to lech at curvaceous ladies in tight clothes doing wet and sweaty versions of Katrina Kaif–style item numbers. Khazanchi kept in touch with Sat Bhagwan on the phone and sure enough, as he had promised, he delivered the order to us on Friday morning at 11 a.m. The order restrained the department completely from further investigating the same case or summoning company officials. Shanx was ecstatic. 'This *dukki* Khazanchi is a *yakka* yaar!'

Every now and then, people talk to me about corruption in the judiciary. I tell them that in my thirty-four years of high-stakes litigation, I have never bribed a judge. Literally speaking, this is completely true. It is also true that I have never bribed an income-tax officer or a politician or pretty much anyone more important than a traffic cop, if not asking for a receipt for an on-the-spot fine is corruption. I don't need to bribe judges, or income-tax guys, or anyone else. We are a country of outsourcers. Since I run a law firm, and have an office administrator, I'm even better off. When I get an inflated electricity bill, I don't have to deal with it. The office administrator does. That explains why mainly street vendors and scooter rickshaw drivers vote for AAP—they don't have an office administrator. Even if you don't have a secretary, you just need to know people who have a reputation for providing quality management services. If I need to get an order from a court in Jhumri Telaiya, I ask a contact for the name of the mover and shaker there. There are several variations to the theme. Some lawyers excel in dealing with some judges; others excel in finding the judge to deal with once they understand the 'deliverables'. I deal exclusively with the local lawyer so the only fee I ever pay is the lawyer's professional fee, generally by cheque. What happens on the other side of the payment is where I have my eyes wide shut.

Do I believe that no dirty dealing is done because I'm not looking? Nope. I read the newspapers. In 2008, a bag containing Rs 15 lakh in cash was delivered at the residence of an alarmed Justice Nirmaljit Kaur of the Punjab and Haryana High Court by a lawyer's court clerk. As it turned out, the court clerk had royally messed up because the money was actually meant for Nirmal Yadav of the same High Court! The case drags on. In September 2013, the High Court suspended the former special CBI Judge of Patiala, Hemant Gopal, after a preliminary inquiry 'found substance in complaints of corruption charges' against this judge.

I refer to Chandigarh only because my story is a Chandigarh one. Isn't it fair to assume these are not isolated cases?

That said, you can get by in this profession quite easily without ever engaging in dirty dealings. You only need to make one moral compromise: you must be willing to deal with people who may be dirty-dealing. A great many of us do that. We choose not to see so long as results are delivered. We probably argue that if we were obliged to deal only with clean people, we couldn't possibly pay our taxes! I mean, we don't know what pragmatic compromises our government has been compelled to make dealing with some dubious guy in some distant land, only to protect our national interest! Morality is a sliding scale, many of us would argue—never mind the elevated moralistic soapbox oratory. Call this the Manmohan Singh solution . . . and don't cast the first stone, as Jesus advised us.

This Chandigarh story had a great sting in the tail. Stay order in pocket, we rushed to catch the 12.40 p.m. Shatabdi out of Chandigarh. As soon as we settled comfortably in our seats, Khazanchi thrust an envelope into my hands with Rs 10,000 in it. 'From Sat Bhagwan,' he said. I didn't want it. 'Arré, this is the norm, Ranjeev,' he pushed back my outstretched hand clutching the kickback envelope, 'it is insulting not to make this offering when you send business.' 'How about you?' I asked. 'I have one too.' I began to lose my nerve. I mean, after twelve years of perching timorously on rickety Tees Hazari chairs, I had seized an opportunity to join the major league. I wasn't going to jeopardize it for ten thousand lousy bucks. I went and spilled the beans to Shanx the next day. He was amused. 'You can't return the money now,' he laughed while dispensing with any ethical judgement, leaving me hanging in the air with no solution. The disquiet wouldn't leave me. As it turned out, I was off to Europe soon to confer with another client. On my way back, I converted exactly half the money into dollars and bought a nice perfume for Shanx, which he accepted with bemused if somewhat surprised good grace.

The weeks that followed became a curious circus of Khazanchi exhibiting a greater and greater sense of entitlement. My business was his business and he had the right to tell me what to do in every brief. He started to use my cigarettes like they were pencils. I'm not kidding. He even cleaned his ears with my cigarettes. Enraged, I eventually told him that he could not participate in any of my briefs unless the senior partners said so. Khazanchi's eyes spat fire, and he stormed out of the room muttering, 'I'll show you.'

An hour later, I was summoned to Shanx's room as Deo exited it, eyes bulging and mouth frothing with paan-stained spittle. 'In thirty years of law practice,' Deo hissed as he went by, 'I have never heard of a partner of a law firm taking kickbacks.' Clearly, Khazanchi had gone squealing to Deo and Deo had carried the kickback story to Shanx. Shanx feigned mock-serious disapproval even as he suppressed his amusement. 'You can't be doing this again, Ranjeev,' he sternly commanded me. I nodded my dumb agreement, eyes downcast. We both knew that he was engaging in a ritual, like the mounting of a subordinate male by the alpha baboon. I didn't mind at all so long as I continued to get the exposure to good-quality work. The moral of the story surely was that if you want to engage in dirty tricks, make sure the alpha baboon has his hand in the same till.

As it turned out, this was a totally false moment of triumph for me. I thought I had the partners all sorted out. I was wrong. Very soon thereafter, and to my great surprise, the Dragons got together and royally screwed me into the ground.

10

Partnership Déjà Vu

Nothing breeds quite like excess success. If you win cases, deliver results, shine at work, more work will chase you. The reverse is equally true. As the days went by, the work I did for City Law increased. This put me in touch with the fast-rising stars of the legal world, many of whom are the hottest shots today. They came in all shapes, sizes and standards of avarice. Not a great many that I recall put the quest for justice above the quest for personal revenue stream. I soaked in the dominant mood of the environment, transforming myself into a moneymaking machine. It didn't enrich me personally, but it was selfish and exploitative nevertheless. Justice was the bullock cart we all rode on our way to material paradise.

Some of the antics of this profession's leaders made for extreme stuff. An association of small manufacturers once hired one of the Supreme Court's leading counsels of the time to argue a writ petition in Jammu. He quoted a fee too heavy for small-town businessmen to bear. They agonized. They had too much

riding on this case. Scraping their savings off the bottom of their
secret biscuit tins, they collected every last paisa and came to
Delhi. We briefed this top Supreme Court counsel. Two days
before the hearing, this eminent lawyer's trusted court clerk
showed up in Jammu and contacted the president of the local
Bar association. 'The Big Man is coming to town and would
anyone else want his case argued?' It was our air ticket, our hotel
bill and our brief, but the flunky collected four other cases for
this Supreme Court counsel. He also collected four air tickets
and cash in lieu of the hotel bill. Naturally, the Big Man wasn't
going to spend the day waiting for our case to come up. He
flitted from court to court while the clients started to experience
the onsets of terrifying nervous breakdowns. Finally, when our
case got called, the Big Man was in another court, leaving one of
a battery of local lawyers to argue our case. Luckily, he showed
up in time to catch the last bit of our action, but till he did, the
wooden floors of the court visibly sagged under the weight of the
clients' sinking hearts.

This is why I am always cynical when lawyers get emotional
in court and ask judges to have mercy on their clients. Lawyers
can be ruthless about their own fees. We are perfectly happy to
argue that our client shouldn't be forced to pay the other party,
or the government, because he is a poor man, but that courtesy
doesn't always extend to our own professional charges! I am happy
to extend that criticism to the judiciary. When you have mercy
on a client and do more for him than the law prescribes, you are
being merciless to his opponent in court. Robbing one man to
help the other is not justice.

It is for this reason that I am especially sceptical of lawyers in
politics. Watch the best of us in a TV debate and you can't help
but be impressed. But we are only arguing a case, and our client
is a political party. We are trained to convince a judge, who is

trained to be sceptical of us. When we take the same skill to the common man, the general public can't see the sophisticated way in which we nuance facts, introduce slants and persuade others. But a lawyer's ability to persuade voters is not the same thing as his determination to deliver his promises. It does not help that, more often than not, long years of legal practice have made us into amoral creatures. We promise the moon but do we seriously intend to deliver on it? That apart, the amorality leads us to behave in a way that is quite the opposite of what we project. Nothing illustrates this better than the irony of lawyers—who are supposed to be the upholders of the rule of law—leading movements to paralyse Parliament and thus undermining the basic structure of our Constitution.

Avarice is by no means the greatest of sins. I once briefed a very eminent counsel to argue an arbitration matter for me. We had filed the arbitration request before the wrong desk and were one day delayed in filing it at the right counter. It wasn't that big a deal but this hotshot spent 90 per cent of his time in the conference telling me how messed up City Law was. I absorbed the tongue-lashing while his young lawyer son wandered in and sat about sniggering. The next thing I know, he's commanding my client to let his son contribute the argument notes and the case law. I was by now so totally diminished in the client's eyes that he was nothing if not relieved. A week later, the client moved the brief to the son. Today, when I hear the same lawyer wax eloquent about probity in public life, waves of nausea rise from the pit of my stomach. Another irritating quality is that a few lawyers will make others pay for things they would never buy if they were themselves paying for them. For example, they order fancy overpriced wines in pretentious restaurants when hired to argue out-of-town cases, make demands for ever more luxurious cars to transport them to court, demand the booking of alternate business-class tickets every half-hour in different airlines just to be sure. Conspicuous consumption on another's account is not just exploitative: it is callous and dare I say . . . unjust. How can my generation ever complain about the ride quality of any car when we have all grown up touring in Ambassadors and never known an air-conditioner in a car till 1986 ushered in the Maruti 800? By then, we were thirty years old and entering midlife.

The saving grace, though, is the brilliant performances we sometimes get to see in court. It's a delight to watch these performances which as often as not are sharp, engaging, witty and brilliant at repartee. It's a pleasure to be in the company of a great counsel. Every paidal has his share of tales to tell. Like the time a counsel thundered and fumed for half a day, finally closing his arguments with a triumphant flourish. The court was mightily impressed. How was his opposing counsel going to counter his sheer impact? He stood up with a patient dismissive look on his face. 'My lord,' he began, 'my learned friend has generated a great deal of heat, but I am afraid he has failed to throw any light on the subject!' The court was in splits. 'My learned friend' is a common enough way to refer to the opposing lawyer, though more often than not, it's a particular way of expressing contempt for his intellect! I remember another counter that improved on the one above. In response to a particularly effective hour of argument, the replying counsel began thus. 'My lord,' he spread his hands in exasperation, 'my learned friend has perfected the art of the Japanese Fan Dancer.' The entire court held its breath. 'He has drawn attention to the subject but he hasn't revealed anything!'

Some of this caustic humour carries through to the relationship between lawyers outside court. Delhi's most successful law firm in the 1970s and 1980s was undoubtedly DNM and Company. Many nationally known counsels of the time owed at least part of their reputation to DNM's patronage. More than one found their invoices falling progressively into arrears. One was particularly upset and stopped accepting briefs when his outstanding bills crossed Rs 30 lakh, an awful lot of money at the time. DNM realized that they needed to pay something so they sent an on-account payment of Rs 1 lakh. I was told this story by the lawyer who carried the cheque to him. The counsel looked at the cheque, then at this lawyer, then again at the cheque, then sat thoughtfully silent for a while. Finally making up his mind, the counsel folded the cheque four times along its length, then rolled it tight into a tube and dismissed the lawyer with this parting short in explicit Punjabi: 'Tell DNM partners to use this the next time they get constipated!'

There were times when the service that a law firm had to provide bordered on surreal. The craziest time I remember is when we went to Chandigarh to argue Climtrol's excise duty writ. You will remember this case from a previous chapter. After Sat Bhagwan procured a stay order for us restraining the anti-evasion boys from summoning our director, we filed a writ petition raising fundamental legal issues. We argued that the case was smoke and mirrors: the facts didn't support the conclusion. We asked that all other legal proceedings should be stayed while we argued these heavy legal issues. That prayer was way over the top. If the income-tax guys think you have evaded taxes and send you a notice, can you ask a court to stop the notice dead in its tracks, as if you are above the law? We didn't expect too much but stonewalling is often a good legal tactic. The senior counsel in that case was a brilliant UK-trained barrister. I was much in awe of him and to my surprise he treated me with great courtesy. At the time, that was pretty extraordinary too, especially since I wasn't that good at briefing him. Given the amount of work I was running through on an average day, where was the time to prepare briefs?

We landed up in Chandigarh the evening before the critical hearing, and my teetotaller counsel started his shock therapy by ordering two rounds of Drambuie. I spent the evening fearing for the next day. It went downhill from there. The next morning, he called up my local lawyer Manish Jain and said he could not argue the case because his spectacles had come apart. Now Manish is as good a networker as you will find in Chandigarh, but to get an optician to open at 7.30 a.m. was more than what India's sleepiest town was going to suffer. Hand it to Manish: he used up some of his accumulated goodwill and by 8 a.m., the spectacles were as good as new. I can add that my counsel was brilliant that day: brilliant as a bulldog who wouldn't let go even after the judge told him he'd had enough and thrown the file back to the court reader. 'Just one more citation, my lord,' my counsel pleaded and moved on to the next case. The file went back and forth half a dozen times before, in sheer exhaustion, battered by a relentless counsel, the judge caved in and said, 'All right, admit, notice, stay.'

It didn't end there. Back from Chandigarh, my counsel was on the phone with me. He had forgotten his favourite chappal in Mount View Hotel and wanted it back. I called Manish. He was alarmed. 'You want me to ask the General Manager for a chappal?' 'Thank your stars it's not his unwashed underwear, Manish,' I quipped. That put Manish in a good mood and off he went, successfully completing the mission. 'Can I deliver the chappal myself and bill the client?' Manish was laughing down the phone. We dispatched the court clerk by the next Shatabdi and sure enough, losing nothing of his humour, Manish had gift-wrapped it in blue neon paper! I couldn't resist a peek at the retrieved footwear, expecting diamond studs. What I got though was a third-rate Kolhapuri chappal at the end of its useful life, the straps unravelling at the edges, the soles all but ground down to holes. I could have bought the guy six pairs of new Kolhapuris and it would have been cheaper than the bill I paid for the court clerk's travel, boarding and lodging.

~

Mercifully, no counsel ever asked me to supply him with sex in exchange for a court appearance. I guess counsels never need that: like alpha males in all spheres of life, they get plenty. Much of this is rumour, but the logic is inexorable. Success is all about fame, fortune and fucks. Some women are proud to give it to them as an act of admiration, like paying a great compliment. Others offer it in order to advance their own careers. Everyone is fighting to get ahead. You make the best of what the gods have given you. You can marry power, you can sleep with power, or you can demand sex in exchange for power. Here in these lofty amoral heights, there are no principles, only primal instincts and the efforts to achieve ambitions. There are plenty of stories though, and lawyers entertain themselves in the canteen by passing those around.

What do lawyers think of stuff like this? It depends on which lawyer you talk to. A few older ones are very conservative and shake their heads sadly. A great many are hyperventilating types looking for someone to denounce. A lot of the successful ones react very differently. Most are very entertained, and not a lot else. Such stories improve with each telling, but nobody seriously thinks the worse of the participants of the story. Someone said harsh judgement is only a cover for jealousy! This tells you everything you can ever want to know about sex at the Bar.

That leaves open the question whether top counsel ask briefing lawyers for sex. The answer is 'maybe sometimes'! I am serious. After I had published *Winning Legal Wars* in 2003, I started to receive requests from different people to teach litigation strategy in a workshop format. By the kind of osmosis that only those totally out of touch with reality can experience, I had the brainwave of starting an institute of legal knowledge. I went about it in the traditional way, setting up a respectable board of directors before trying to establish a knowledge pool. Many eminent personalities were generous and forthcoming. One particularly eminent top-of-the-line Supreme Court counsel did more: he demonstrated why women get so uptight about sexual harassment at the workplace. Up until that point, my attitude to propositioning ladies had been, 'Look, I am making you an offer. If you don't like it, I am the one dealing with rejection, right?' I changed my attitude completely after I got propositioned myself.

He was a batch mate from law faculty. The first time I went to see him on this subject, he asked his secretary to seat me in his inner office and before I knew it, he was telling me how sexy I was back in law school. In time, we were discussing who was sexy in our batch and who was not. I was amused and kept up the banter. This guy had always been pretty effeminate, limp wrists and all, and spoke in a particularly effete way. Up until that time, I'd had the usual Public School student's prejudices about homosexuals and found his antics hilarious. I didn't quite get that he was hitting on me. When I told him about my plans, he said he'd think about it and to come back later, which I did. The second time around, I was back in his inner office and this time he pulled no punches. Not to put too fine a point on it, he insinuated that if I wanted him on the board, I would have to give him something. I got the drift and told him I was terminally heterosexual. He said 'Yes, but you know, Ranjeev, the sexual urge is a very powerful instinct.' It was my turn to tell him I'd think about it and get out of there alive.

I was livid. My butt in exchange for accepting a seat on the board of my institute was a humiliating offer. I carried my anger around for a long time. I even talked about it to a common friend I had been close to since college. He was dismissive in a cruel sort of way. He startled me enough to examine the psychology of propositioning! It comes down to this: a contemptible lecher is simply someone you wouldn't like to sleep with; the one you'd like to sleep with is a sexy person. Some good came out of it: I got over my anger and I got over my deep prejudices about gays. But mainly, I slowed down my propositioning of women considerably! As I see it now, he offered me a good-faith trade and I rejected it. Your trade currency may be my moral boundary, but that does not give me the right to claim moral superiority. It's not as if I have lived a particularly 'moral' life. Quite the contrary, I must confess.

So was there a lot of sex in the legal profession in the 1990s? No more and no less than anywhere else, I guess. That is the same thing as saying there was a lot more than anyone was admitting! Much depends on who we are talking about. The permissive age had not yet arrived in India though it was knocking on the door. Sex in movies was still mainly voyeuristic: the starlet Mandakini doing a peek-a-boob wet-sari song for Raj Kapoor. Sex between young lawyers was then beyond the borderline of the socially acceptable. One young lawyer I knew said that westernized upper-crust Indians were not where the action was at. He was a boarding-school snob himself, and he said he scored the greatest success with girls from middle-class backgrounds. He regretted only that he had to compromise on the quality of conversation. Was he concerned about being ensnared and compromised by a gold-digger? Not at all, he argued. He had many reasons. For the kind of girls he seduced, guilt and excitement in these dangerous liaisons was still a big part of the heady experience. Besides, if their families found out, the girls were likely to be lynched long before the family showed up at the Romeo's door.

What about affairs between older people? I'd say there was rather less than there would be now. Older lawyers are very busy people, but the reasons were mainly cultural. It was too complicated and risky. Indian families were very controlling at the time. If you were 'happily' married, you had to call up your spouse several times a day in the era before mobile phones to clock in and explain what you were doing. And if that wasn't enough, you probably called up your mother every day too. Misrepresentation is hard to sustain when multiple agencies monitor the assets! Besides, income levels were lower, so hotel rendezvous were not practical. A friend of mine once had a rollicking affair with another friend's wife only to have his friend show up at his door unannounced while he was mid-romp with the girl. Paralysed by fear, he locked himself in the house while his friend all but broke it down. It got uglier and uglier. To cut a long, sordid story short, the lovers fled to the hills, destroying two marriages in the bargain. It didn't end so badly for my friend though. He migrated to Delhi, set up a successful law firm and made quite a good life for himself. Years later, I had a youngster from his office apply for a job. Why was she leaving? The girl was very forthright. The boss had too much of a roving eye. He wasn't forcing himself on her, was he? Not at all, she said, but the atmosphere was 'uncomfortable'. In what way, I asked. He was carrying on with the receptionist and locked himself in with her far too often. That vitiated the office atmosphere. It also did not stop him from propositioning his junior lawyers when he went out of town with them! She said the receptionist didn't have a view on that because he really 'spoilt' her with a fancy salary and gifts.

When it comes to sex for work, the gossip was everywhere. You never knew what to believe. For years together, we heard stories of a successful Supreme Court advocate-on-record bedding anyone who would send her a certain amount of work.

We even had 'authoritative' lists of everyone who sent her work but didn't want the perk. It was a short list. We heard other stories of dramatic professional progress based exclusively on chamber practice! I preferred to disbelieve such stories. The gender bias was palpable. It was commonly assumed that every man who sent work to a woman, or otherwise promoted her, got something back from her. I could send work to another man but no one would assume I was gay!

Of the credible stories I have heard of older men and younger women, a lot of them were really a kind of tragedy. I will buy into the proposition that most men will take a shot if they get it. I will also buy into the proposition that men are genetically programmed to 'spread their seed' in an attempt to achieve genetic immortality. That said, the results of these affairs are rarely good for either party. I have seen this play out in the legal community, and I have seen it play out in my client pool. More often than not, I've advised my client's key employee on what to do after the story becomes public. It's a boringly familiar story. The guy is pushing fifty years of age. His wife of twenty-five years thinks he's an ass; she knows him well and sees the warts all too clearly. He works too long and is never at home. When he's at home, he tries to be 'relevant' by interfering in how she runs the home. She doesn't like that. She tells him off a lot. She also doesn't like it that he invests no time in the kids. She runs a great home and doesn't want to hear his ill-informed wisdom of how that's done. She can brood on all this because she doesn't have a lot to do. She does not have a job. She doesn't need to. All the work the husband does translates into plenty of spending money. She fills her days with hen parties, lunches and clubs. All her friends are married to similar asses.

About this dysfunctional marriage, the husband has a very different narrative. His wife is controlling and manipulative. She bosses him around, as many middle-aged women do. She wants him to shut his trap and open his wallet wider. That apart, she hasn't taken care of herself. How did that delectable young girl he married turn into this cantankerous hag? The tragedy of her sagging bosom drives him to distraction. Besides, she is so bloody ungrateful. He has worked all his life. Everything they have he has put on the table for her. She is taking it all and is still bitching. Why is no one pinning a medal on him for the life he has provided her? She complains that she feels victimized and discriminated against. She bangs a drum for women's liberation. How on earth can a woman who has two maids, a driver, unlimited spending money and no job to have to slog at feel aggrieved about the discrimination she suffers because she is a woman? Bottom line: he resents it that she takes his money and gives him attitude.

Lurking somewhere beneath all this is another great regret. A great many Indian men have split their wealth between themselves and their wife over a misconceived perception of tax efficiency. If the marriage falls apart, the guy's goose is truly cooked because she will take the half that she has in her name and still demand maintenance for herself and the kids. The courts will support her too. Women-centric laws have truly liberated educated Indian women but, in the bargain, they have bred a generation of insecure middle-aged men. That's a lot of loose cannons, no pun intended!

The kids in the marriage aren't necessarily much of a consolation either. By the time they are teenagers, they think him rather an embarrassment. He tries to share their interests, but they don't think it's cool for an old fart to pretend to be their friend. They too want his money, but they don't want his *gyan.* He tries to compensate by pushing people around at work, but it's not enough. His faltering self-confidence adds to the cauldron of confusion. He looks at his paunch and he begins to ask himself if he is still attractive. Does he still have it in him? Is it too late? This kind of guy is ripe for an affair. He builds up his fantasies till there is no stopping him. He explores the mysteries of the firm youthful body, as opposed to the flab and flatulence at home. He yearns for the magic of life, the thrill of sharing an intense emotion.

Into this boiling cauldron comes a young lady. Bear in mind that this lady is vulnerable too. She is young and impressionable. She is deeply impressed with this powerful, persuasive man, this living example of male success. In this intellectual profession, he is sharp and powerful and on top of his game. He has credit cards, cars and cash. Maybe he asks her to discuss a legal case over a 'working lunch' at the local Michelin-starred restaurant. Maybe they need to travel out of town for work and meet up in the evening over dinner. He knows wine, he orders off the menu, he can tell the difference between rockfish and red snapper. She is totally wowed. Then he jumps right into it. How can she resist?

Not that she may want to resist. I mean, what is the competition looking like? Her boyfriend, who doesn't make nearly enough money and is getting ill-treated by his boss? She wants the world and she wants it now. What she ends up getting is a poorly performing old fool who's sleeping with her in order to address issues that lie elsewhere. Besides, he isn't going to commit to her anyway, or leave his wife and children. That's when she begins to wise up. When she figures that out, it ends in tears and recrimination. As far as I know, the only time it does not end in tears and recrimination is when the girl is perfectly clear why she is in this relationship. In that case, there are demands for money and career advancement. Either way, the old fool pays a disproportionately large price.

I am not making this pop psychology stuff up. I've been in this business a long time and I've heard this story far too often, generally with regrettably few variations. For sure, a lot of older men understand all this and still try to seduce the girls. They know it will end and have all manner of strategies to deal with it. One client, whose seduction technique I particularly admired, had a simple formula. 'I sleep with them thrice,' he said, 'and then I am out.' How do you get out, I asked. 'I have several variations,' he explained, 'but they are all variations of venereal disease.' Another said he ends affairs by deliberately failing to perform and then claiming impotence! Clearly, the secret is voluntary anticipatory humiliation.

That leaves only the business of vulnerable old men and young ambitious girls. It's quite the flavour of the month these days to project men as predators and women as universal prey. It's a half-truth. I don't claim not to be predatory in my instincts but as a managing partner of a law firm, I am more vulnerable than you would believe. In the last ten years, I can think of at least three occasions when a girl who works for me has propositioned me. I have always assumed her reasons were professional rather than personal. This is entirely understandable. Hundreds of lawyers come to work in the city. Most don't get too far. It seems like a fair option. Of the thirty or forty girls who have worked for me in fifteen years, three isn't much of a percentage. It's always been very dignified. My ego has always been tickled pink but, alas, I have no need that needs addressing, and besides, I have too much to lose! The risk distribution between a managing partner and a young lawyer is always too asymmetric.

~

But I have got far ahead of my story. Back in City Law, I progressed up the sludge-shoveller's ladder. You could say life was fun in those days. The firm had stabilized. The two Dragons ruled it and five followers lived off their crumbs. Neeru and Pia did a lot better than the rest, working for Shanx and Deo respectively. Neither

Dragon allowed the other's junior to get a sniff of his work. Dutta spent most of his time faffing around when he was not disrupting someone else. If I hadn't been so paranoid, I would say he could have died one morning and it wouldn't have mattered.

The only City Law follower I have not introduced so far is the Professor, but then there isn't that much to introduce. Tall, soft-spoken, good-looking and articulate, he oozed decency and good breeding. He appeared to have all the raw ingredients of a good lawyer, but they never came to fruition. Every legal issue paralysed him. He couldn't ever lay his finger on the pulse of a legal problem, let alone offer a solution. He wasn't dumb; but like many college professors at Delhi University, he had analysis paralysis. In my nine years with City Law, the only time I had anything to do with him, he went complaining about me to Deo. Deo was always a tantrum in search of provocation, and rogered me royally as a result, leaving me bent and bleeding. Not long after I left City Law (with all the revenue I contributed to it), Deo was forced to squeeze him out.

Meanwhile, unknown to me, the storm clouds were gathering at City Law. Once the firm had stabilized, partnership aspirations began to rear their ugly heads. I had come in from the cold but others had been made promises when they were brought in. This takes us back to a question that every ambitious lawyer in a law firm always asks when he wants to branch out on his own. In order to start a law firm, the Dragons needed at least ten experienced lawyers. Where were such lawyers to be found? On the principle that it is best to deal with the known devil, they targeted second-rung lawyers within their old firm. In a concerted attack on the chosen elects, they spoke of a rosy future in a new law firm, in which they will have partnership, the moon and, like a good jihadi bomber, sixty-four virgins per head in paradise. They made them highly lucrative and highly vague offers. When Shanx set up City

Law, the monkey circus went with him. Now, they wanted a piece of the action. It was the chickens coming home to roost.

~

I wasn't particularly a part of anything. I shared neither history nor an unholy alliance with these guys, which is not to say I didn't want a partnership share. I just didn't know what I was entitled to and so didn't bring it up at all. Others presumably did. As their confabulations went on, the environment in the office started to deteriorate. The Dragons reacted by screaming and ranting up and down the corridors of City Law. The followers pushed for me to join the battle. Were they using my work to get a partnership share? I didn't have the EQ to figure this out but, unaware, I became the symbol whose rise and fall would determine the fate of the whole simian army. The Dragons reacted to this development the only way they could. They started to cut me down to size.

It was easy to do. Nothing I turned out was good enough. Every client meeting had one Dragon or the other trash me publicly. I was assigned no new work and some that I was already doing was withdrawn. It was bewildering, and the way I saw it then, and now, utterly unnecessary. Eventually, the Dragons decided my expectations had been managed enough. Shanx ushered me into his room. Deo sat smirking distastefully as the paan-stained dribble ran down the corner of his mouth. What did I expect as a partnership share? I tried to play it as smart as I could. I needed to position myself or, for all times, I would get screwed by being equated with the followers. I took my gamble.

'Look, I am not the equal of both of you and never will be,' I opened, 'but I don't want to be screwed because I am not demanding.' Deo chewed the cud of that vile maroon stuff in his cavernous mouth and nodded grudgingly. Shanx was businesslike.

Bullshit artistry didn't appeal to him when he was serious. They had decided to keep half the equity between themselves. What did I want? I replied that I had a running law practice, however crazy it is, and that that should be recognized. Sure, Shanx shrugged. I was the trial litigation expert in this law firm, I added. Shanx didn't like that, but he appreciated straight-talking. 'How much smarter are you than the others?' he shot back. 'Twice as smart as the girls and half again as smart as the guys,' I shot back. 'I want to retain 5 per cent for a retirement fund,' he disclosed. I did the mental maths. Dividing 45 per cent amongst five people took me to a 12.75 per cent share, or thereabouts. 'From a purely arithmetical standpoint,' Deo asked, 'Will you settle for 12 per cent?' I readily agreed. I knew that I wasn't here to protect the partnership share. I was here to guarantee that the work flow from City Law to my desk started up again. I did not know then that in this negotiation, I had reaffirmed an eternal truth about people. This is how it goes.

When it comes to granting salaries in my office, everybody wants to be paid what their friends are paid in India's top law firm Amarchand Mangaldas. When I tell them they should work for Amarchand if they want Amarchand salaries, they then switch tack and talk about market price. When I tell them the market doesn't work for me because I can only monetize a part of what they earn for me from my clients and give it to them, they slump in frustration and finally say they will take whatever, but not less than the guy on the next chair. In all this, there is no talk about competence, skill sets, billing, money earned or career graphs. It's all about what Amar earns in Amarchand or Mani in the market or just Pappu on the next desk. When you run a law firm, you should know that everyone always has one eye on the computer screen, but the other on Pappu, or Pumpi, whatever . . . That is HR, desi style for you.

I was out of the loop on the partnership for the next month or so, refusing to be drawn into the confabulations of the followers. Eventually, we had the anxiously awaited partnership meeting one afternoon. Shanx was forthright. 'If you want to be equity partners,' he declared, 'you should be ready to assume the liabilities of the law firm. We have substantial bank overdrafts and we would like everyone to sign these loan papers.' It was a jaw-splitting punch in the face. The followers actually thought there was going to be substantial profit-sharing when they became partners. They had not contributed clients, capital, logistics or substantial legal expertise to the firm, yet they wanted to be partners. Now these two were asking them to put their money where their mouths were.

I was the first to sign, being the eldest of the rest. I figured I had nothing to lose. Besides, no bank could ever recover what I did not have to give. Neeru played to her master's voice, her face unreadable. She signed quickly. Pia, with her Nair fortune, signed without a furrow creasing her brow. The rest got the runs. Dutta started to shake. The Professor ran out of the room and had to be hauled back in by the scruff of his neck. Elation in the room had long given way to apprehension. Pia picked up on the outstanding partnership story. 'Who gets what?' Shanx asked. 'Do senior partners get a majority?' Everyone nodded. This angered Shanx. 'Are you telling me I am working this law firm for 25.01 per cent? Where are all the clients coming from? Who is doing the billing?'

His rhetoric slammed into a wall of sulking silence. A long pregnant pause later, he continued. 'Ok, I will be generous and settle for 30 per cent. I can't take more than Deo, who is my senior, so even if I give him the same, 60 per cent is gone.' Still not a murmur. 'So how do you wish us to divide 40 per cent amongst six people? Equally?' Shanx smirked.

Dutta pleaded, 'I have twelve years in the profession, man! Are you going to make me equal to someone half my seniority?'

Shanx lightened up. 'Since none of you have a client base or bring in much revenue, should we do it according to years of practice?'

Uneasy glances flitted about the room. Pia said she had seven years and Neeru said she had eight. The Professor said he had ten. How do you divide 40 per cent in three categories between five people? No sooner had we started on the arithmetic than Shanx wanted to know if we were retaining a share in trust for future partners. That broke the followers' backs. To cut to the chase, we agreed that the ladies would get 5.5 per cent each, the guys would get 8.5 per cent each, and I would get 12 per cent. We would dilute when we inducted more partners. Dutta wanted to know the terms. 'Don't you trust Deo to make proper terms?' Shanx snapped. That ended that.

The loop on the sordid drama ended a couple of weeks later in a final signing meeting. Deo read out key clauses. The senior partners retained the name, the goodwill and the right to hire and fire. The rest participated in the equity but could not ask for accounts. Senior partners would allocate the surplus between distribution of profit and reserves at their discretion, which would be final. We were invited to sign the document without being allowed to read it in detail. The deed would be kept in the office and no copies would be provided. We could sign now or miss the bus. We trooped up and signed. I had a quick look at the language of the draft: it was harsh and one-sided. We were worth nothing, we had signed nothing and we had achieved nothing.

I felt utterly humiliated. I had not asked for a partnership deed, or a share. Putting me through this charade was to my mind a naked show of brute force. My world so far in the trial courts had been merely demeaning. On an angry day, I felt like the drainpipe of the civilized world. My role as a lawyer was to push the sludge along downhill but mainly off my own client's legs. Not any more. City Law brought home to me the meaning of moral compromise in the legal world. Justice is what our profession promised to deliver, but not unto each other. I joined the law firm to pull together as a team but we manipulated and hurt each other, feeding off the negativity, demeaning our partners. My accumulated resentment against the destructive power play, the manipulation, and the dehumanizing assault on our values now found new focus. I swore never to forget this humiliation, and I never did.

The world I had come from was already closed to me. The door to the world I had to go to was not yet open. Like those gritty heroes in Hollywood disaster films, I constructed a typical survival narrative around my experience of City Law. I told myself that if I grit my teeth and pick up the skills, one day I will have payback. It was ridiculously filmy but, like any good comedy, a great truth ran through it. This resolve never wavered. Like the Count of Monte Cristo, I counted the years to judgement day. I didn't know that I was going to a fate worse than the one I had already suffered. That I found out in the months to follow.

11

Squashed Bananas

Law firms have only one real asset: people. That makes them easy to set up. Even better, the value of this asset increases with time. If you set up a law firm and manage it half decently, the years to come get progressively kinder. The agony is of course all in the setting up, something that my old buddy Dhoot may not have quite understood. The problem is that the jokers who come together to set up a law firm want it all: a piggy bank of expectations which bears no relationship to the jungle out there. They want to fix whatever is wrong with their life without losing any of the good stuff they already have. Managing that expectation is a nightmare. It doesn't help that lawyers are generally independent-minded and aggressive. How can you possibly set up a law firm unless you know how to integrate a bunch of high-kicking mavericks into cart donkeys?

Shanx knew the answer to this one. To bring together his law firm, he sold the most ridiculous dreams. That wasn't such a big deal. If you think about it, every lawyer, especially every court lawyer, is ultimately a storyteller. If you want to win a case for a client in court, you take a random set of sometimes connected facts and weave it into a great legal story. You then sell it to the judge so that he gives you a favourable judgment. Shanx wasn't just a great lawyer; he was the mother of all marketing gurus. He spared no excess in selling his story. He talked about a City Law building with a squash court in the basement and a jacuzzi in the penthouse. He talked about offices in half a dozen countries in five years. He talked about being so busy we would meet only in airport lounges, spinning tales of pretty much everything this side of floozies in the penthouse jacuzzis! It was such dreams that allowed all the followers to follow the Dragons without debate or dissent.

It was easy because the suckers who lapped up all this claptrap were clueless about the world Shanx inhabited. He was a board member of a dozen companies, had an enviable list of American and European clients, had cash that he could wipe his ass with every morning, and a travel itinerary that took him overseas pretty much every week: week on week, year after year. He was a movie star and if you were a budding starlet with ambition, you would spread just about anything you had to have one shot to be with him. Two years on, the firm was up, but no one's life was any better. That's when the seams started to come apart. A partnership deed had been signed, but where was the reward?

This forced Shanx to address the fundamental issue: once people start to really soar in the stratosphere with the bozo's dream you sold them, how do you bring them back to earth? How do you integrate these wannabe movie stars and demote them back to the extras who dance behind a shirtless Salman Khan in group songs, which is what they really are? What do you say to the budding ramp model to avoid hiring him after you've done your thing on the casting couch? Shanx had it all figured out. In a nutshell: acquire, diminish, deconstruct and integrate. What this means is build up the guy while hiring him, then slowly grind him into dust. After the joker's self-esteem is really low, deconstruct him and make him rebuild himself into the guy you need for your law firm. Now, when he finally becomes the custom-designed pig who needs no education, you can integrate him into your firm.

This is what Shanx did after signing our partnership document. He unleashed the process of diminishing us all. At the heart of the process was a small 400-square-foot space used as a store on the third floor of the building. The sin wasn't that it was two floors down: it was that this store could only be accessed through the fire escape at the back of the building. Weeks after we signed the deed, Deo announced that Dutta, the Professor and I were third floor bound together with the court clerks and the stenographers. Naturally, Neeru and Pia were not included. It was humiliating. I tried to talk my way out of it but Shanx wouldn't shift. 'If I am to put all these non-performers in their place, Ranjeev,' he explained, 'I have to make sure you go down first. If you don't go, they will not. All I can say is that if all goes well, I will get you back up.' Looking back, I ask myself what kind of absurd logic was that? Perhaps I did have a case of Stockholm syndrome already. I certainly had no choice, considering that much of my work still originated from Shanx.

The simian sanctuary on the third floor was nothing if it was not proof that in any law firm, 20 per cent of the lawyers bring 80 per cent of the revenue. Lawyers did damn-all there. The Professor sat around for hours staring at his files sifting pages, his brows furrowed in intense concentration. I never saw him dictate anything and I don't think he had more than ten files to process in any given year. Did he stare at the files in incomprehension or was he a Zen Buddhist? Dutta was the circulating bad penny of the piece. He went from desk to desk, hassling someone or the other between delicate nose-picks, gossiping here, gassing there and gurgling with a jeering laugh everywhere else. No one ever assigned a file to him and said, 'This case is yours to do'. Like plaster of Paris, he filled any gap we found in the wall, and like plaster of Paris, he didn't last long there. We sat around along one wall in tiny 5 x 7 plywood and glass cabins that didn't quite reach the ceiling. On the other side of this incomplete glass wall sat a dozen sweaty staff members who cleaned their ears with rolled-up newspapers, snorted into their shirt cuffs, scratched their arses and giggled invectives while talking trash about the lawyers. So much so that the place reeked of that unmistakable combination of too much armpit aroma stuffed into too many synthetic clothes garnished with too much coconut oil. It was truly disgusting.

Even if you take the subjectivity out of it, the numbers told their own story. The third floor had three 'partners', three young associates and six non-revenue support staffers: twelve people in a space with cubicles so small you couldn't stretch out your arms as you yawned without hitting something. As opposed to that, the main office had eight lawyers and six support staff in 5000 square feet, ten times more space than we had. We were the dregs and we were made to know it. In Delhi's status-obsessed culture, it didn't take me long to experience the ill effects. Clients who came to see me immediately drew all the right conclusions: I was trash, and I sat in it.

Within six months, my expectations were perfectly aligned with my situation. That was true of Dutta and the Professor too, with one material difference: I wasn't defeated. Not being defeated meant hammering away at the briefs that still came my way, trying to do what I could with my small trial-court practice. To progress, I was working long hours and cosying up to the clerical staff so that they would push my work along. I even flirted with aromatic stenographers to get them to prioritize my work, till Deo put an end to that with a well-aimed jibe about roadside Romeos masquerading as lawyers. He was right of course, but I was getting no cooperation and I couldn't progress without boosting my efficiency level. I tried to entice a succession of juniors to work for me, but Deo systematically undermined them till they got the message. The handsome halfwit we all called Doodh was probably the worst case of them all.

Doodh came fresh out of Daryaganj. The son of a lowly bureaucrat, he was very bhai-sahib-turned-mod, desperate to make his way. It seems Doodh didn't like tea or coffee and demanded hot milk three times a day; it all came to a head when the pantry head started buying endless tins of milk powder, decimating the office budget. I roped him into working on my Tees Hazari briefs while I tried to kick myself up the ladder, but Dutta worked equally hard to drag me back down. There was nothing subtle about it. Dutta told Doodh that working for me was not a good survival strategy in City Law. He sent Doodh off to run errands exactly when I had cases listed in the trial court. When Doodh kept his appointments for the trial court hearings, Dutta went complaining to Deo, who screamed at Doodh for disobeying orders. Clearly, Deo was trying to kill off my trial-court practice, or run me out of the firm, the end result of which would have been the same.

Deo front ended the misery equally. Every time Doodh messed something up, Deo called me in for a ticking off. Perhaps all of it was not planned; he was an underwhelming school bully who needed a whipping boy whenever he'd had a hard day. Yelling at a junior struck him as an entirely reasonable stress-buster. Deo could be very small-minded, as you would expect from a patriarchal village elder. I thought about quitting at least twice a week. But there was nothing to quit to. If you have no choice, there is nothing to decide. Inevitably, Doodh started to crack up. One late Saturday night, behind on his work and under pressure from Deo, he had a nervous breakdown. He went and lay down on top of Shanx's office-topped table and slept through till Sunday morning. When he woke up, he started tearing at his clothes and screaming profanities. Finally he passed out. The frantic chowkidar rang Doodh's home number. The frothing thrashing Doodh was carted out by his father at midday on Sunday.

On Monday morning, the father was complaining to Shanx that one Mr Dubey had tried to kill his son. Shanx was livid. 'If you can't take care of your juniors,' he spat at me, 'you have no business to have any.' Deo didn't need to echo that: he just went about spitting *maa–behen* curses every time he passed me in the corridor. Isolated, without juniors, overworked, rejected, hassled by dogsbodies, I had hit bottom. Did I look like a wolverine in a bear trap? Nah! I'm aggrandizing my situation. I was just another pathetic loser of the type commonly found in every other law firm.

With no youngsters to work with and no support in the law firm, it looked like I would be in the dungeon for a very long time. Then came a turning point: computers. If you were born too late to experience the transformational experience of IT, you will never know how computers empowered people like me. In a flash, I was liberated from infrastructure bottlenecks. I did not need office staff any longer and I could work anywhere. In those days before Windows, I struggled through life at the 'C Prompt' of Microsoft 3.2, till I could navigate into and out of drives, open and close programs and type up my own documents in Word Star 4. This was still the time before Hotmail, or the Internet, but

I could print up my stuff, fax it, receive faxes and process more work. I could even carry my work around in those crazy five-and-a-quarter-inch floppy discs. Eventually I purchased my own 'assembled' 286 computer from a cut-price barsati operation in Lajpat Nagar for home use. I used to work on it from home and on Sundays. I was now able to take on more work.

Does good fortune come in pairs? I don't know, but my stars changed quite suddenly. Arvind happened. In fairness, I should say that what Khazanchi tried to take away, another Kashmiri Pandit gave to me. Arvind was an unusual guy. He was super-intelligent in the way he could read people and he was a great salesman. He was also very focused, so focused that he only owned six navy blue trousers with three matching coats and twelve white shirts; he couldn't be bothered matching clothes, he said. He worked like a dog and drank like a fish. He had a consultancy agreement with Busando for getting financial closure of a 1000-MW coal-fired private power project in central India. This was worth a very large sum of money. Busando was amongst the largest Korean business houses at the time, keeping company with Hyundai, LG and Samsung. Lawyers who had such clients were coveted by many law firms.

Shanx was ecstatic when he heard that negotiation of the Busando Power Purchase Agreement was within Arvind's scope of work. Arvind didn't really care whom he hired: at the time, no Indian lawyer understood the private power project business anyway. Shanx put me to the task, mainly because he had no one else. Deo didn't agree; he wanted the business for himself. Shanx had to work on him a bit. Did he see himself turning around drafts overnight? Did he see himself being screwed over by consultants and dealmakers? Did he really, really want to work like a dogsbody paidal lawyer? Deo grumbled but subsided. At the end of the day, he could push his case only so far. Shanx affirmed my assignment, pumped me up with sunshine and good words, and sent me to the slaughter.

Of course it was slaughter. I didn't understand the power business. I didn't understand what the government was trying to do. I didn't understand what the client was trying to do. I didn't know how to draft anything. I was the last man for the job and I fooled nobody. To Arvind's credit, he was most encouraging. He hired a knowledgeable retired bureaucrat, and an American technical expert, to guide him through the process, and with these resources, he launched out on a wing and a prayer in search of financial closure. I am eternally grateful that these gentlemen carried me along because, by the time the deal got done, I could write a legal contract as well as anybody. I am not saying that I understood how to distribute business risk in a legal contract just yet: I am saying if you told me what you wanted, I could capture your intention very clearly on a piece of paper. You can fool a lot of people if you dress up well, and my drafting progressively became very pretty!

You must not think poorly of these guys for carrying me. Infrastructure contracts are about risk distribution, and that is a political decision. It is an easy decision for any politician to make. Thanks to what the papers call 'anti-incumbency', very few governments last long enough to face the consequences of the contracts they have signed. Arvind knew that the Power Purchase Agreement we got ultimately depended on the deal Busando would do with the political process within the state government. Any lawyer who knew the basics and could learn to write cleanly was good enough for him.

The Busando deal catapulted me to the life of the sexy 24/7 lawyer. I managed my trial-court practice in the morning, City Law's High Court practice in the afternoon, and wrote power-sector-related legal opinions in the evenings. I spent many days in the conference rooms of the lakeside hotel in the state capital butting heads with officials and lawyers from the state electricity board. Sure I continued to make a fool of myself—no one goes from zero to hero in the legal business in a day. But I had a learning curve that any self-respecting mountaineer would be proud to climb even in good weather. It was heady stuff.

It took us a year and a half to negotiate the Power Purchase Agreement. This entailed innumerable visits to the state capital. A greasy fixer type joined our negotiations somewhere along the way. Busando had asked for his presence and the fixer reported only to Busando. No one admitted to why he was there. He was candid about his mission. He was a chela of the head of the state electricity board, or the SEB. He was here to 'get the work done'. You didn't need a PhD to understand what that meant.

The fixer's presence was a great help. Many sticking points in the negotiation started to get resolved after a backroom powwow between some SEB officials and the chela. It was a rollercoaster ride. The SEB would be flexible one day and stubbornly sit on some issue the next. When I asked naive questions about it, Arvind asked me to be patient. 'Perhaps a payment got delayed,' he smirked. Inevitably, a hard day and heavy *khus-phus* later, everything would be fine the next day.

After one particularly hard day on one of our innumerable trips to the lakeside state capital, we all went to meet the concerned executive head of the state. It was, as I have later learnt, the way it always is. You meet the boss. You both smile. He says nothing directly. He indicates that the chela—who is also in the room—is known to him. It's very subtle: just a hello and a familiar question about something unconnected indicating that the two have a history together. Obliquely, you have been told that this chela has the boss's ear. Then you part amicably. The next day, you fix a deal with the chela. Not long after, the big boss signs the file you want signed. Credible deniability strikes back!

In all this, Busando's project manager was clearly taking huge pressure from home. He didn't speak to minions like me much but received many phone calls that left him drained. I could tell because his body language turned very submissive as he muttered into the mouthpiece. I could tell that his tone would then become pleading, even though he was speaking Korean. He also took to drinking himself to sleep when negotiations did not progress, enough to pass out, though he was always very alert the next morning. This is a very Korean thing. Korean office parties, even in India, in those days, were a riot. They drank each other under the table and most were incoherent before it was over. Just before staggering out to the car, you could be sure the CEO would announce that the work would start early the next morning for some contrived reason. This was done deliberately—Korean-style machismo.

As the negotiations progressed, or more often didn't, the Busando manager started to lose his nerve. Arvind reacted to that by 'managing' the amount of information he told him. The Busando manager and I did a lot of swimming at the end of every working day. Because of this, he tried to open a channel of communication with me. I did not cooperate. That was ethical but stupid. My reasons were simple: I was too dumb to know how to handle it, and too scared to start something I could not manage.

The sheer prolixity of the negotiation was enough to drive the Busando manager into a mistake. At some point, he hustled the process and managed to persuade SEB officials to close the document. Out of the blue, the SEB's lawyer had a tantrum shortly before the signing ceremony. He objected to the manner in which the final draft had been approved, made a speech about not providing a certificate, and walked out on his client. We thought him very unprofessional at the time, but was it just that? Come to think of it, the guy did look vaguely like Arvind Kejriwal! The

SEB lawyer got sacked and replaced by a brilliant British power expert. This extended the negotiation by another nine months.

Here's the deal. Lawyers bill by the hour. While you pay for time, they have a sense of what they need to earn before they feel adequately compensated for the value they are delivering. You can either agree to a fancy fixed price charge regardless of time spent, or you can agree to pay by the hour and then have the lawyer prolong the negotiation till he has earned enough! Sure you can overrule him and close prematurely, but to do that you have to understand the issues. Besides, you then have to take responsibility for assuming the business risk. If you are an SEB manager, that is a potential CBI inquiry you really don't want to come back to haunt your retirement years. Then again, if you are an SEB manager, you can't close the deal till you get a political nod. That depends on the other deal going along on a parallel track. So the British law firm renegotiated everything, but still ended up pretty much where we had been before. The final close-out negotiation of the deal took all of a fortnight.

It was gruelling work in the state capital, sometimes stretching forty-plus hours without break. We argued back and forth all day, a lawyer on either side, supported by teams of technical and commercial professionals. Eventually, between the negotiation team, Busando and the chela, the SEB agreed to sign an agreement we could be justly proud of.

I have vivid memories of my journey back on the Shatabdi. I had slept so little for so long that I staggered about in a daze. A close relative was travelling on the same train but I failed to recognize him. Even when I did, I could not switch modes from lawyer to nephew, leaving him very confused. I had yet to learn how to keep a dispassionate distance from the work I did. My elation did not end after I returned to the office. Shanx totted up my hours and it ran to a tidy sum. His body language changed and, with it, changed my own perception of my worth. Self-confidence allowed a different man to come to the surface.

~

The weeks that followed the Busando contract were heady. My new-found self-belief encouraged me to plan for the future. I now set about reinventing my image with cold deliberation. First up, a proper car! This had long been on my list. One of the wisest clients I ever had was Mr S.D. Salwan who took it upon himself to educate me on the ways of the world, but with zero success, I may add. He was in a dispute with his brother over their shared business. I had been recommended to him by Mr K.P. Verma, a kindly district judge. Salwan Sahib took me under his wing when he hired me.

'My father came from Pakistan with nothing, *kaka*,' Salwan Sahib was forthright with me. 'The first thing he did was borrow money from a friend and buy a car. He then took the car to the bank. The bank manager assumed he was a wealthy man and gave him a loan to rent a large shop and start a furniture business in Connaught Place.' He paused, nodding imperceptibly as he let this sink in. 'When you borrow money to buy a car, you have a successful business before you start. Just make sure it's the biggest flashiest car in the market.' 'What if I can't afford the car?' I asked. He was the picture of flabbergasted patience. '*Kaké*, don't be *bhola*,' he had the expression of a father fondling his son's hair, 'the car brings the money to pay back the loan!'

I went to Shanx and asked him for a raise, enough to buy the just launched Maruti Esteem. Shanx was evasive and bumped me off to Deo. Deo hedged, and offered me a raise equal to half the car's instalment. I started to argue. 'Ranjeev, *apni aukat main raho*,' he muttered ('know your place, you twit'), words which,

even twenty years later, I never allow myself to forget. It was 'take
it or leave it'. On a salary that just about paid the bills, I elected
to go with the Salwan School of Business Development. Thus,
one Monday morning in 2004, I went down to Saya Automobiles
in Connaught Place and booked a car whose instalments would
be half my total income for the next five years. It was a great
leap forward. In the eyes of those who saw me driving it about in
Delhi's increasing life-after-Maruti-800 traffic, I had arrived.

I shouldn't end this chapter without telling you what
eventually happened to Busando. We got the Power Purchase
Agreement the way we wanted it, but we couldn't get the fuel
linkage. Still short of financial closure, Arvind died. He cut
himself on a broken whisky glass and the bleeding didn't stop.
Busando lost its primary consultant. Naturally, Arvind's sub-
consultants banded together and asked to see Shanx. Shanx was
particularly arrogant at the meeting. They had come to ask City
Law to join them in approaching Busando for a solution. Shanx
rubbished me, patronized them and left everyone confused about
his intentions. I guess it really was about me. Shanx had given me
the client, but he would have appreciated being treated like the
queen bee. Instead, the client had relied on me, and cut him out
of the data loop. Shanx was only looking for an opportunity to
reassert himself in a relationship he was out of, but they got the
message that he didn't want to join them. They went to Busando
without us. Busando fairly paid whatever was owed up to that
point to Arvind's widow and moved the remaining contract to
them. Arvind's widow paid them their share of what she received
for the job already done. City Law lost the assignment, the money
and the client, and got nothing.

Not long after, the Power Purchase Agreement we had signed
was challenged in the High Court. It was exotic stuff about who
would be paid first out of the SEB's income if things went wrong.

This bitterly fought battle ended with the arrangement being overturned. Busando went back to the drawing board to find another way to secure payment and the project went backwards. Eventually, when the financial crisis hurtled the Asian Tigers into a tailspin in 1997, Busando went belly-up. The Korean government broke up the group and sold its assets in 1999.

The conclusion? Arvind died, the project died, Busando died, City Law's revenue from the deal died, but I came out, for what it was worth, an infrastructure lawyer with a Maruti Esteem and the swagger of a man striding forward confidently to meet his rosy future. My party had only just begun. A lot more action was coming up very soon.

12

Crossroad Capers

If you land up in a law firm and find yourself encouraged to get business and work autonomously, you are already on to a great thing. If on top of that, the law firm also helps you grow into a substantial legal 'personality', you must be the child of a much greater god than I was. Better than me for sure. After the dust of the partnership debacle died down and the followers were relegated to the dungeons, ideological fault lines between the Dragons began to rip the firm in two. It came down to what they wanted from their law firm.

Let me try and explain the issue. If the Dragons wanted to see the law firm grow, they needed to create departments, encourage their middle-order batsmen to increase interaction with clients, pitch for new clients, create teams of juniors who worked for them and generally grow into substantial billable heads. On the other hand, if they wanted to be a niche boutique law firm, personally fronting a limited amount of good-quality work, they needed a flock of supporting lawyers who could execute the work, but only so far. City Law's main problem was that Shanx wanted a large law firm—which meant teams of lawyers working in groups within departments—while Deo wanted Shanx to route all his work through Deo. So while Shanx tried to encourage the team to upscale their skills, Deo worked to undermine them. It seemed to me at the time that Deo firmly believed that his salvation lay in ruling over a bunch of moronic gamma-minuses with no legal skills. These mixed-message antics tripped me up completely.

This kind of disconnect between a brilliant rainmaker and a competent worker with no business development skills is not exceptional. I have seen this scenario recreate itself in many law firms. The world is full of very good lawyers whose marketing sucks. Addressing this bottleneck is not rocket science, but somehow, Shanx failed to address Deo's disconnect.

I am none too sure Shanx successfully addressed his own disconnect either. The Dragons were severely damaged by their experience of the time when they were themselves juniors. They judged the present through the prism of their shared past. My progress alternately elated and worried Shanx. He regularly introduced me to new clients, whom I increasingly managed independently. This worked well because he travelled out of the country a lot and wasn't available to the client much of the time. I filled this gap, which pleased him, but when he found he was out of the loop, he turned resentful. He wanted me to develop my skills, but he did not want me to develop a client list. That's not what he said to me of course but when I tried to grow a little, I was discouraged, even when it was really small-ticket growth from a very low level. A few feeble attempts I made to introduce clients to the firm also failed: he declined to meet the client, rubbished me to the client or trashed the client and sent him packing. When I sat back confused and did nothing for a bit, he lost no opportunity to trash me for being a flunky. Damned if you do, damned if you don't, and bullied in either event.

I guess the key to this repetitive behaviour pattern was in the bullying. Most organizations fail because they have no vision. This was never City Law's problem. Shanx had a very clear vision, but he excelled at shooting himself in the foot. Deo fed him back-stabbing conspiracy stories as often as he could. From where I was sitting at the bottom of the well looking up, neither Shanx nor Deo trusted anyone, because deep inside they did not trust themselves, or each other. In this I passionately believe: if you trust yourself fundamentally to do the right thing at the end of the day, you will trust other people to do the same unless you have specific reason to believe otherwise. Then the guy you trust will sense your goodwill and will trust you back. These guys trusted no one, so no one trusted them. In this, they proved that most prophecies are self-fulfilling. Looking back, I see it as a kind of tragedy. If you are totally consumed by your insecurities, how will you ever develop reliable working relationships with your colleagues that will carry you to the end of your working life?

By my third year in City Law, I had a clear conception of my main challenge. I had to find a way to develop a client list without feeding the insecurities of the Dragons. Winning Deo's trust was the logical way to do it but this was impossible. Deo did not want to see me in a corporate commercial advisory role. He certainly didn't want to see me as a third player in a two-Dragon law firm. While Deo was undoubtedly a much better human being than I ever gave him credit for, he appeared to have severe self-awareness issues. He simply could not see that Shanx would have been happy to send Deo more work if Deo was capable of delivering on it. Shanx wasn't in love with me: he was coming to me from compulsion. If Deo had recognized that he was not the delivery end of the service spectrum, he could have developed a working relationship with me and 'taken me in'. Instead, he chose to cut me down to size, and when that failed, he ran out of options.

That same compulsion—to get someone to deliver the service—also propelled Shanx to protect me from Deo when the heat became unbearable. To be fair, I made his job harder by frequently aggravating Deo with my tactlessness. We are all prisoners of our personalities, condemned to live out our behaviour patterns repeatedly. I offended Deo more than I needed to, but only because he was trying to crush me. Retaliation was heaped on retaliation. It was crude stuff, and totally unnecessary. Most personality battles are really so very tragically unnecessary, but who has the self-discipline? All I had going for me was desperation.

Fortunately, fate soon put an end to this destructive game. Shanx opened an office in London and Deo went off to man it. It seemed impossibly exotic and sophisticated when viewed from India. In truth, it was exactly the kind of dump most loudmouth lawyers have today when they tell you they have opened an office in London, or New York or the Gobi Desert. These are rarely proper offices. Most lawyers simply negotiate to hang their boards outside another local lawyer's office. They entice a local lawyer with a promise of sending work, which never materializes. Those with more self-respect actually rent a place and start out small. Shanx did the respectable thing but it was still a cut-price operation. I later had the good fortune to visit it while it lasted. Neeru joined Deo, and the two ran the office out of a small flat in Cheapside, with an English secretary. Deo looked comically out of place in London, a paan-chewing village elder in a checked overcoat dictating letters about legal gibberish in an unrecognizable accent to a bewildered cockney girl. He could not get over the fact that she cheerfully left mid-sentence if it were 5.30 p.m., decimating his turnaround time and leaving him to complete his letters the following day. He couldn't bring himself to learn typing and Neeru didn't go to London to become his part-time stenographer.

For me, this was a godsend. With Deo and Neeru gone, I lost my vampire bat and Shanx lost his main support on the corporate side. Slowly but surely, corporate commercial advisory work started to come my way. Yet again, I started to travel overseas with Shanx. Life looked up and I started to learn new things.

~

The Nordic telecom company Telsta jumped into my life at 6 a.m. one morning in January 1995 with a well-aimed audio kick. 'Hilton, 9 a.m.,' Shanx barked down the phone. 'Meet a guy called Mathur from Telsta there at Club Privé.' He rang off. In the years since, I have learnt to take these things in my stride but I was thrown totally out of whack when I arrived there to find true and utter bedlam: teams of three or more people representing each of five joint-venture partners and teams of six or more representing four different bidders. The bidders were making initial presentations on network equipment supply contracts for the upcoming GSM-based mobile telephony tenders. Over lunch, Mathur introduced himself as Telsta's India representative and described the five partners of this new joint venture, Global Mobile Telecom Pvt. Limited, or GMT. As far as I could make out, the Nordic company Telsta and the Thai company Lotus Telecom were the two main players in the game. They had one respectable Indian partner—Suntel—with a minor stake, and two other dubious Indian players: Ray and Kathuria. The last two were there as a peculiar result of India's new telecom policy.

This was amongst the late prime minister Narasimha Rao's greatest gifts to the people of India. Late in 1994, the government floated global tenders to award contracts to run mobile and paging services in well-defined 'telecom circles'. Foreigners could hold up to 49 per cent of the equity capital of the operating company. Few Indians had the money to build mobile networks at the time and fewer still had the technical expertise. Foreign telecom companies jumped into the fray, desperately scrounging around for desi majority partners, who were not to be found for love or money. They eventually ended up finding big-talking small fry who pitched themselves as corporations but did not have the money to buy the equity. The result was a bunch of under-leveraged foreigners in a permanent state of nervousness over their minority stakes, tied to a pack of over-leveraged desis with no financial stakes in their majority-owned companies. These desis ran amok harassing their foreign partners, extracting all manner of concessions and pay-offs for delivery of no particular value. At these preliminary presentations, they sat in the front row asking idiotic questions, trying to dominate the discourse.

Mathur introduced me to an attractive Nordic lawyer from Telsta's legal department. She produced a minimalist Nordic-style equipment supply contract: the kind you would love if you were a fan of Ikea's design philosophy. Would this work in India? At the time, I thought it came out of the homework of a first-year law student. I said as much, so we spent most of the night butting heads in the conference centre. I tried to decimate her version and she tried to retain the integrity of the original. I had my way but, now that I think of it, why didn't we simply sign the damn thing under Nordic law and be done with it? After all, if it was good enough for a Nordic lawyer, it was good enough for a Nordic court. Was it a combination of youthful exuberance, unearned arrogance and north Indian chauvinism? I had a giant north Indian ego and she was a woman: so where would that have left my manhood? Or perhaps, it's just that I had two kids at home who needed to be fed, and I needed to log up the billable hours!

I look back at my first year with Telsta with great amusement. These Nordic people had the most incredible corporate culture. First and foremost, they simply did not do cynicism. If you told them that the moon was made of green cheese, they would believe it, till they received information to the contrary. Their work culture was quite the opposite of how we did business in India. Here, we distrusted everyone till proven otherwise. The Scandinavians also had assumptions: they assumed that everyone would behave responsibly and would do their job in a mature fashion. They had no concept of micromanagement or supervision. Again, this was the opposite of how we operated here. As I worked with them, I found myself advising individual managers who operated more or less alone. They knew nothing about committee decision-making. This led to bad decision-making in a business culture where everyone was happy to cheat and lie to everyone else.

But that was still in the future. Thanks to the support I provided Telsta's attractive lawyer at short notice, Mathur sent me off to finalize a similar contract for another venture in Chandigarh. Telsta had a 51–49 joint venture with the pride of Punjab's public sector, a government-owned company everyone called P-Tech. In time, the joint venture came to be known as PPSL. P-Tech at the time was run by the ultra-dignified super-stiff Harjeet Singh. His behaviour was drowned in affectation. Even a half-ass newbie like me could see that he had a thing or two to teach Libya's Gaddafi. I learnt in Chandigarh that P-Tech was both majority partner and equipment supplier to their paging service joint venture. I couldn't get my head around the conflict of interest.

PPSL was housed within the P-Tech complex but Harjeet projected a very arm's-length attitude towards PPSL. He didn't want to contribute to the negotiation because he sat on the boards of both parties to the contract. He asked me to negotiate directly with a super-smart P-Tech hotshot called Raval. When I went way over the top with harsh terms, Harjeet magnanimously registered his protest, smiled indulgently and conceded everything. I was impressed, for no good reason as I later learnt. Basically, P-Tech was no supplier at all. They had done a back-to-back with Israel's Aviran, marked it up, and signed a contract with PPSL. No one in Telsta considered checking whether P-Tech manufactured the equipment or just distributed it. No one asked for three competitive quotes from similar suppliers. No one even asked Aviran directly for a price quote for a supply directly from Israel.

I saw it as gross dereliction of duty, but that was hardly the worst of it. As part of the joint-venture deal, Telsta nominated a man called Jan Ulrich to head finance. He was a kindly man with six kids and a logistics problem you could slash your own throat over. One kid had to come from school and the other had to go to a tennis lesson and a third needed to catch up on her horse riding. He spent his whole day managing car movements and bumming favours from Harjeet: a club membership here, an introduction to a school principal there. I spent many evenings at his home. I have seen him patiently eating his dinner while his toddlers crawled all over the dining table and up his back with a pizza in one hand and gobs of tomato sauce in the other. Such a man could never confront Harjeet over P-Tech shafting Telsta. As the months went by, he increasingly lost touch with the finance function. P-Tech sent him bank statements by way of reporting but he had no idea if P-Tech had supplied the equipment he was paying for. Inescapably, Telsta finished paying for the network years before it was scheduled to be built. Worst, Telsta completed contributing capital long before the money was required and years before P-Tech even planned to pay in their share of the capital. P-Tech milked the joint venture to an early financial death simply because Telsta had no culture of distrusting or supervising anyone.

The same script ran again in GM Telecom, Telsta's mobile joint venture down south. This company was managed by the matronly, kindly, soft-spoken and utterly unthreatening Adela. Adela specialized in conflict evasion. If you spoke aggressively to her, she looked the other way, nodded absently and skipped out. If you locked the door before she could skip out, she agreed with you, skipped out and then pretended nothing had happened. That's more or less what she did during GMT's board meetings. This encouraged the venture partners to push her around. As time went by, GMT's board meetings became increasingly animated. The Thai partner Lotus Telecom ganged up with one of the dodgy Indian partners Ray to push their private agendas aggressively, leaving Telsta and the respectable Indian business house Suntel on the receiving end. Kathuria, the other dodgy Indian partner, started out playing swingman but in time he edged closer and closer to Ray. It all came to a head when Telsta received notice of a new case from the Delhi High Court. A total stranger to their joint venture—one Palanpuria—claimed he was the real shareholder and he was now being excluded from the venture. Adela was clueless: who was Palanpuria? She asked Ray and he said Kathuria had nominated Palanpuria to hold Kathuria's shares because Kathuria was a UK-based NRI, meaning that he would be treated as foreign equity. This tells you everything you would ever want to know about Telsta's corporate processes. Adela hadn't reviewed the company record. She had no idea who had signed the joint-venture agreement, let alone who had subscribed to GMT's shares! In this Pandava Katha of five partners, who was real and who was fake?

Adela shared this body blow with her management at home, and they put Mathur to the task of helping her find a solution. He talked to Shanx. Shanx took a very what-you-see-is-what-it-is view of the whole thing. Who had signed the shareholders' agreement? Who was recognized as the subscriber to the company's organic documents? Who had subscribed to the shares? Who had received the share certificates? In each case, it was Palanpuria! So where was the controversy to resolve? Clearly, Kathuria was no one. Adela didn't buy that. Never mind the paperwork, she said; I made a deal with a group including Kathuria and we have to honour our word. That sounded like 'we must all ignore the law when it comes to private words between contracting parties'! Curiouser and curiouser, we thought. Stuck with a stalemate, Telsta sent down the Swedish lawyer Björn Högström to meet up with Ray and sort out the mess.

He need not have bothered though. The moment we entered our meeting, Ray announced that we were here to write a new joint-venture agreement because the old one was 'non est'. In legal parlance, this meant that the signature on contract was signed by mistake and without knowledge of its meaning. In other words, it was horse shit. Our eyebrows kissed the sky. Högström wanted to know why it was non est. 'Because it has not been acted upon,' explained Kathuria. 'And who has not acted on it?' asked Högström. 'I have not acted on it,' said Kathuria. 'So does that mean Palanpuria is a shareholder because there is no shareholder contract and you are nowhere in any record?' 'No,' Ray shot back, 'we will write a new joint-venture agreement.' Högström was aghast! 'I am here to resolve a share ownership issue,' he protested without success. 'Besides,' I added, 'why should we write a new joint venture?' 'Because your client has breached the contract,' the Ray guy spat out. And how has our client breached the contract? 'Because your client privately offered to buy us out!'

I didn't get it. 'So claim breach and terminate then,' I shot back. 'There is no need to terminate a document that has not been acted upon,' he retorted. This was getting really crazy. 'I'm sorry,' I said, 'your knowledge of the law is at variance with mine. We were sent here to find a solution but this is hardly a solution.' 'It is too late for objection,' Ray cut in. 'Adela has agreed to a new draft and it must incorporate our new agreement.' 'I am not aware that this is why we are here,' I was very green at the gills. Ray fished out a paper. 'This document has been signed by Adela and you are to make a new agreement.'

We looked at the new paper. It said Telsta recognized Kathuria as promoter shareholder. It said Telsta gave up management control in favour of Ray. It said Ray would be CEO and Telsta would nominate a professional external managing director. I was livid. 'You are now in management control because you were made an offer by one shareholder, which you reported to another?' He couldn't see that he was profiting from his deviousness. 'Yes,' he was very smug. 'And why would you benefit by double dealing?' I was getting angry. 'You should be asking your client, not me.' The possibilities of that meeting had exhausted themselves. We looked at each other, and we ended the meeting.

Outside, we immediately burst out into neurotic laughter. 'Did she tell you about this document before she sent you to India?' I asked Björn. She hadn't. I could make no sense of it. 'So what is your client's agenda, Björn?' 'I don't think she has one.' 'Really?' I exclaimed. 'I think she does not understand what she has signed.' This, in the Nordic scheme of things, made it all right.

Getting out of this piece of paper wasn't that much of a stretch, if one wanted to. You can't amend an agreement without signing another agreement and that takes a lot of procedure: stuff like board resolutions, power of attorney to sign such an agreement, etc. We drafted a letter to Lotus letting them know that Adela had no authority to give up management control. Högström carried the letter back with him but Adela refused to issue it. Telsta had no system in place to review what Adela was doing in India. They trusted her and that was that. I wouldn't swear to it but, very likely, she trusted Ray and Kathuria and that was that!

It drove Shanx nuts. He made sure it drove Mathur nuts. Could Mathur stop Adela? He said no. 'She is in charge of GMT and she decides what happens in that company.' Shanx called up Suntel and they confirmed a Bangkok meeting to prepare a new joint-venture agreement. Björn Högström later called me up. 'I've recommended your name to Adela to help with the joint-venture negotiations.' Shanx was not pleased. Being upstaged by your half-baked M&A sidekick is not a nice feeling to have. To cut a long and boring story full of tantrums short, I arrived one early morning at the Sheraton Grande on Sukhamvit in Bangkok with a small airbag, a return ticket and 100 dollars in cash. I had no credit card to my name because no bank would give a low-end lawyer a credit card in those days. I'd asked our accounts department for more cash without success.

'Shanx Sahib said the client will be paying all bills,' the accountant explained. By the time the trip was over, City Law would have billed Telsta several thousand dollars for my services but I went there with an empty wallet.

I didn't render any service of course. I joined Adela for breakfast, which is the only time I saw her for the next three days. She asked me to get a good book and wait in the room while the partners held their commercial negotiations. I waited three days. It was the time before laptops became de rigueur. I saw a lot of Thai TV, consumed a lot of tom yum goong and kai satay with peanut sauce. I spent a lot of time warding off a procession of strange persons who knocked on the door and asked if I'd like a massage. Eventually, when they decided I was harmless, the ladies started to show up offering their own services. Some were really attractive but I was waiting to write a contract. I didn't blame them: anyone waiting without moving in a room for days on end is either hiding from something or waiting for something. At 8 p.m. on the third day, Adela called up to say the negotiations had failed. She said she was flying out in hours. She explained nothing. I started to think about my financial situation. Adela was truly taken aback. 'Telsta does not pay you?' What could I tell her? I started to choke. She got the point and, besides, it was not in her nature to be cruel. She told me she would settle the hotel bill and bid me goodbye.

I watched even more Muay Thai that night. Next morning, after a leisurely breakfast, I tried to call the airline for a revised booking. No such luck. My room telephone had been blocked. I called up reception. They said there was no credit card on record and demanded a cash deposit of 100 dollars. Hadn't Ms Adela Swensson paid last night? Yes, she had, but only up to last night. Today, I was on my own. With the airport taxi paid for and a breakfast bill to pay, I was probably down to 80 dollars already. I dressed hurriedly, packed my airbag, paid for my breakfast and walked out of the hotel. A public call office stood outside the hotel gate. I called up City Law. Our Supreme Court advocate-on-record Ashok Mathur answered the phone. His sister lived in Bangkok, not far from Lumpini Park. I was welcome to go to her.

Even though I was a complete stranger, Ashok's sister was most welcoming. I stayed with her for a bit and treated myself to the authentic 1990s-style Bangkok experience. Yes, I did Pat Pong and all that. Inspired by the cobra blood mixed with that nasty Thai whisky Lao Kao I saw selling in Lumpini Park, I went down to Soi Pradung Dao in Chinatown one hot humid dawn and had my own snake drained for my delicate consumption. I felt privileged. I had arrived, even though I was broke and hung in City Law by a slender thread.

The idyll ended when I returned to Delhi. Shanx disapproved of my pliant ways. 'This is completely contrary to my philosophy,' he thundered. 'You can't kill your client for billing. This is immoral. She is selling her employer down the river without reason.' I protested feebly: 'The client is not complaining.' 'Look, the client does not understand. If you understand, you are duty-bound to protest.' Battered repeatedly, I caved in. What should I be doing? Mathur wanted a comprehensive note written on the subject, so that he could discuss it with his superiors. I did a bit of plain speaking and faxed the damn note off to him.

Mathur couldn't find the note when he got to the office that day. He called me and I re-faxed it. Still no luck. I re-faxed to an alternative fax number we had in the office. He still didn't get it and called again. I wrote down an alternate fax number he gave me and re-faxed the confounded note. The peace lasted three hours, then Shanx was hooting down the phone. 'You've sent the damn fax to Telsta's legal department!' he laughed, 'every legal brain in Telsta is in a tailspin. Mathur is jubilant, Adela has gone incommunicado. At last, someone is worrying about this situation.' Through sheer default, I had become a master strategist!

Mathur called me not long after. He thanked me profusely for saving Telsta from this terrible situation. He said Telsta's CEO had already called him and set up a meeting to debate the issues. He then switched topics and asked me to join him in Kathmandu early the following month for a new deal they were doing there. 'It's a mobile network in Nepal,' he explained. 'Write me a standard draft joint-venture agreement so I know what to talk to the local partner about.' I was getting my reward for helping Mathur shaft Adela.

Björn Högström was on the phone the following week. Mathur had had a meeting with Telsta's top boss. He had reported that they had lost all decision-making control over their company, GMT, and had become hostages to their joint-venture partners. Adela had tried to defend the GMT situation but the CEO was not convinced. He had sought a specific legal opinion on a range of issues. Could I answer these questions please? Yes I would, and how! I wrote a strongly worded risk-assessment report, ran it by Shanx and sent it off to Högström. He called back to say I was fearmongering. Högström wanted us to meet him in London and finalize the note.

This must be one of those great fateful coincidences that usually happen only in Hindi movies because we met in the Grosvenor House Hotel in London which Subroto Roy purchased fifteen years later in 2010. As I sit here to write the first draft of this book, Subroto Roy is in jail while Sahara considers selling this property. When we met at the Grosvenor House Hotel, Högström tried to tone down the draft but we fought him tooth and nail over every word. Ultimately, he took what he could get and gave up the rest. He asked me to send the next version of the note under my signature and distanced himself from it. London was about as good a time as I'd ever had till then. I stayed back in City Law's rented apartment for a week, had Shanx feed me touristy meals in Veeraswami and Chelsea's Chutney Mary, drank myself under the table on Shanx's account on frozen margaritas in Leicester Square and went up and down Soho's mean streets. Getting the boss back in the loop was cool play.

It wasn't all fun and games though. The London office wasn't making any money. Shanx met his team there and was severely underwhelmed. He told them they were flapping about clueless, ending with a terrifying tantrum which shut down the office and ended a dream. It escaped me not that Deo and Neeru would soon be back in Delhi. What would happen to my new-found freedom then?

Back in India, we never heard another word about the GMT issue. I finally called up Högström. He said Adela had had her showdown with everyone else and won. She was allowed to make a new shareholders' agreement and she made sure City Law went out of the loop on GMT completely. Mathur was kicked out of GMT but they compensated him by giving him exclusive control over Nepal. In turn, Adela was kicked out of the P-Tech joint venture, which went to a new kid on the block named Karl Andress. Don't forget this name: he is next in my story because I had great times with him too.

What, you may ask, happened to Palanpuria? After all, they were one of the co-licensees in GMT. Nothing! Kathuria had predicted that the Department of Telecommunications would transfer the licence to his nominee Ray in a jiffy. They did. He took an equity position in Ray's company and Ray paid in the share of capital for both of them! I didn't get how Kathuria could have the licence transferred so easily. These licences weren't transferable. Years later, I met Suntel's finance guy on a flight and asked him. 'Kathuria was Sukh Ram's nominee, you dope,' he said. Sukh Ram was India's telecom minister at the time, who famously sold telecom tenders for cash and ultimately went to jail when they found Rs 3.6 crore in jute sacks in his official residence. Who knows what wheels turn within what wheels in incredible India! As it turned out, my tryst with devious deeds in high places had only just begun. Not long after, Mathur had me experience the same dubious deeds in a neighbouring country!

13

Kathmandu Knights

Mathur was as good as his word with the Nepal deal. Summer turned to monsoon as the time to go to Kathmandu came up. I had a shareholders' agreement to write, but I still hadn't actually laid eyes on one. Where was I going to get hold of a draft? I asked Pia, but she didn't have one. This I could believe because Deo had determinedly kept her on the litigation end of his law practice. That left Neeru, who had written shareholders' agreements her whole life. She gave me a look Queen Victoria would have approved of, and told me she didn't have one to show me. I knew when I was beaten. I went to see the remedy of last resort. Shanx said he didn't have one either, but he agreed to come by and help me write one! Reinventing the wheel was a City Law speciality. No, let me rephrase that: using square wheels was a City Law speciality!

As it turned out, this went well for me. Shanx spent the best part of a Saturday dictating the document while I hammered away at the keyboard. I have no idea why he did this, the most charitable explanation being that in the days before soft-copy databanks, he couldn't be bothered to get his secretary to wade through piles of dusty files to find a printed version I could use. What's more, he called up Mathur, extracted decisions on some harsh choices and then took the trouble of explaining why he was doing what he was doing. This proved invaluable. I made sure I let him know that he had enriched me immeasurably. I am glad I did because this is one of the last times anyone ever sat down and taught me anything. The learning curve in this profession is truly steep and it becomes harder when there is no one to hold the torch. If someone gives you a pearl of wisdom, be sure to prostrate yourself before him and kiss his twinkle toes. It's rare, and it's precious.

Kathmandu turned out to be a very lucrative and well-paid waste of time. The lousy flight connection to this ethno-chic mountain backwater ensured that we were there for a day before Mathur got in. Shanx began to succumb to all my vices, substituting beer for inflight lunch. The beer was hot and the can was greasy. Indian Airlines did not chill its beer. I asked for gin and tonic instead. The air hostess came back in five minutes: she had tonic but no gin. Shanx wanted to know if she had tea leaves but no hot water. Sometimes, he could be very cruel. I remember the flight mainly for the paradigm shift in the way he started to perceive my role in City Law.

He approached the topic in his usual heckling way. The Professor had turned down an appointment with an American lawyer who had flown in because it was Sunday. Shanx was incensed: 'He's not even a Christian!' he snapped in frustration. 'Mr Dubey, what is your strategy for City Law?' I told him I had a strategy for me, not the law firm. 'You know you are so self-absorbed, you don't see you cannot progress unless the firm gets its act together.' He wanted me to motivate all the other lawyers. Why would I want to do his job? 'I don't run motivation classes,

Shanx,' I said with my new-found self-confidence, 'management should mean perform or be fired. You don't believe in firing.' Shanx disagreed with that too. 'You are too bloody destructive. You don't value relationships and you will end any relationship any time, any day. This is not the way to do it. You must learn to persevere and work with people.' He was probably thinking of Dhoot, but that was about as insightful as anything he had ever generally said to me about my attitude at that point.

At the end of the day, in my scheme of things, his followers were not my baggage, they were his. The way I saw it, he could not stop my progress. Now he wanted me to do his job. In any case, the followers were lame-duck dogs-in-the-manger who resented any progress I made but were not willing to join me or run at my speed. From trying to suppress me and hold me down, Shanx was now asking me to pull everyone else up!

No placard awaited us at Tribhuvan International. We looked around for a cab, only to be attacked mercilessly by a pride of urchins who grabbed our suitcases and ran in different directions. Shanx fell on top of his briefcase like he had received a super-bowl-winning touchdown pass. I chased down my baggage, shaking collars while screaming hysterically. Finally, we escaped into the innards of a 1969 Datsun with interiors like Normandy after D-Day. 'Man, this is why Nepal is so religious,' said Shanx.

At the bar in the evening, I told Shanx he wanted me to train people with whom I had been fighting for the last three years and would probably have to again. He lamented my appetite for hostility: 'Have they invited every battle you have fought?' I said it was like Indian bureaucracy: to pull down an efficient officer who is better than you is a career compulsion.

'We didn't fight every fortified village in Bangladesh in 1971,' he reminded me. 'Leave the others where they are and progress.' Even he had written off the followers. That didn't help me. 'It's not possible for me to progress, Shanx. I can't work with these people and I can't manage all the business I have without them. Basically, they will not perform and they will not let me perform.' He saw the point. 'Okay, go get yourself some new junior lawyers. Make sure you get them in before Deo hits town next month. Let's make this lot irrelevant. Ranjeev, you and I can do it.' I am glad the alcoholic haze slowed me down. It was a while before I absorbed the enormity of the 'you and I'!

Mathur arrived a day after we did. He already had a local Nepali partner, a suave businessman called Duggal. Duggal laid out the red carpet. We had lunches and we had dinners and then we had some vague meetings in between. We ended up eating in a succession of speciality Newari restaurants where the exotica of choice was a local brew called *raksi*. Duggal displayed his panache and showmanship when he poured out the raksi in a three-inch-wide earthen bowl, whipped out a cigarette lighter and promptly set the brew on fire. He invited me to drink it while it was still burning, which I did without serious damage to myself: the trick was in blowing hard at it immediately before tipping the contents in! By then it had burnt so long the alcohol was all gone, leaving just water behind. I spent the rest of the evening drinking raksi by the bucket. By the end, I was bloated on both food and my ego, drunk on raksi and success. Not till much later did I learn that raksi was local lingo for *tharra*, the worst of the worst of country liquors, as likely to intoxicate you as to blind you if it's made from industrial alcohol. The risk haunts me still.

Duggal wanted a minority equity stake. He roped in the Army Pension Fund to hold another 20 per cent. 'To make things happen here,' he revealed, 'the king must participate.' We were facilitated by the army chief. He presented us with commemorative plates, he offered us cigarettes out of an inlaid silver box, and everyone made a speech. We had long confabulations over cocktails in the Soaltee, in the Annapurna, in the Yak and Yeti, but basically, at the end of the week, all we had was a vague discussion on shareholders' issues and an Expression of Interest letter from the Army Fund. Since the Army Fund was now in the frame, it was necessary for me to draft our agreements under local law. I asked for a copy of the Nepal Companies Act. I marvelled at its familiarity: had I been a Nepalese lawyer in a previous incarnation? Of course not! It was copied wholesale from the Indian Companies Act. But it was only half as long. Where were the rest of the provisions? 'They copied what they understood,' Duggal helpfully explained, 'and deleted the rest!' It's a nightmare writing agreements when half the law is missing. I found myself legislating for contracting parties, writing what appeared to be whole new chapters in Nepalese company law.

I made about a dozen visits to Kathmandu that year, but apart from capping Duggal's total equity obligation to Rs 6 crore, all I did was run about in Thamel, educating myself about the secrets of Kathmandu nights! Located west of Kathmandu palace, Thamel in the 1990s was a coming-of-age story in progress. In the flower-power era of hippies, free love, charas and Dev Anand's *Haré Rama Haré Krishna*, it had been the mecca of every backpacker. By the 1990s, it had downgraded into a cut-price shopping opportunity for budget tourists from small-town India looking for bargain garments and bhang-stuffed buffalo momos. I picked up bushels of sleeping bags, tents, downs, fleece jackets, gloves, and fur-lined trekking shoes on my successive visits, but even so there was still something bohemian about Thamel. I remember walking up to Rum Doodle on *Lonely Planet*'s recommendation to find a dead bar heavy with contrived 'atmosphere'. I was bored of the cardboard yeti feet autographed by celebrated Everest mountaineers and alarmed at the price of a third-rate Nepalese interpretation of Thai food. Quickly finishing my dinner, I slouched off in search of excitement to be drawn inexorably to the sound of wildly banging traditional instruments on the third floor of an anonymous building.

It was a hard-core Nepalese dance bar with a sort of low stage on one side, a dance floor, standard four-seater tables, and a lively clientele of sloshed locals. It was noisy and it was gay. A procession of artists enlivened the evening, singing folk songs while beautiful girls in ethnic drag danced! Weary men with regular day jobs and stress to relieve twirled and swayed on the dance floor in time with the professional dancers, making sure their hands brushed along their bosoms whenever the opportunity presented itself. The girls seemed to take it in good spirit, recoiling in mock horror while feigning embarrassment. I was captivated enough to keep going back for more every time I was in Kathmandu. No, no one solicited my custom and I didn't ask for or get offered any sex. More than a decade later, when I went through Tibet time after time in my off-roading phase in 2005–06, I went back to the same place and it was still the same good clean fun joint without sleaze or the veiled threat of looming violence.

Somewhere between these endlessly entertaining but fruitless Kathmandu visits, I acquired my first sustainable City Law junior: Sajan. He was decidedly from the tight-fisted end of 'English Medium' but he was ambitious and he was very intelligent. I had to tweak his attitude a bit—make him more service-oriented—but he was a quick learner. This took care of my trial-court practice, leaving me free to follow the fantasy I chose. When you look back at your life, you find little blessings that you never quite saw in the way you should have when they came along. Sajan was one of them. He worked hard and he kept an ear to the ground. Because of that I always knew what was going on in City Law. He was also good at riling people. My lack of talent in playing politics did not detain him at all. He understood what needed doing better than I did, and he did it mercilessly. In the space he helped create, I found the freedom to build a career, and I did. That is, till the potential-career-killer Deo returned from London, assuming like any self-respecting NRI that nothing had changed in India since he left.

Why did the London office die? Firms don't succeed because you open a shop and wait for customers. You have to go out and get customers. Every law firm rides on the back of a rainmaker. London didn't have one. Shanx didn't want to freeze his butt in an inhospitable land slogging to feed Deo and Neeru and, besides, what would become of his extensive Indian practice? Eventually, as the months went by and London continued to haemorrhage, Shanx had no choice but to pull the plug. Deo returned home, ready to dust his disused throne and park his sweet fanny on it.

But India had changed. Deo's leverage in the law firm had changed. His law practice had dwindled. I had changed. His main litigation lawyer was now a corporate commercial M&A lawyer. Everyone's attitude had changed too. Life went on after Deo left for London. Everyone concluded Deo didn't matter so much. Deo came down to earth with a rude thud, and he needed someone to blame. I was doing the work he and Neeru would have been doing if London had never happened. They got together to try and fix that. The months that followed were a procession of suspicious looks, unspoken curses and plaintive confabulations with Shanx.

Deo raised the inevitable 'partnership issue', which Shanx deflected because, at the end of the day, it was too late. Shanx shared some of this with me with as much dignity as he could muster. He wanted to promote me but he didn't want to disrespect his partner. He tried to balance the colliding agendas and the situation ended up projecting him as a waffler, unable to take a stand. I misread that situation as usual and became defiant! Again, it matters little. The learning if any is simply this: in life, you can never walk the middle of the road, Buddha be damned. You walk on this side, or that, because if you walk in the middle, you get hit by a speeding truck.

Thence started a weird struggle for controls of briefs. I only paid limited attention to this because the real game at its most entertaining best was unfolding in Chandigarh.

While meetings in Nepal dragged on, Karl took over the P-Tech joint venture. Karl could play the bureaucratic line like no one: you know, the one from *Yes Minister*, when, in answer to the question 'So what have you achieved?' the Cabinet Secretary draws himself to his full height and replies, 'Minister, in the civil services, we measure ourselves in activity, not results.' He wanted bi-monthly meetings in Chandigarh, and always on a Wednesday because he hated ruining his weekend. He would fly out on a Monday, have a pre-meeting with me in Delhi on Tuesday, and take the evening Shatabdi to Chandigarh, frequently with me in attendance. He held his meetings on Wednesday, travelled back with me on Thursday, then conducted a wrap-up meeting in Delhi before flying off the same evening (with two bottles of Old Monk XXX Rum which he loved) to be in his office, back home in Scandinavia, on Friday. It worked for both of us: I billed mega hours and Karl continued to demonstrate to Telsta how busy he was. In the bargain, he accumulated more frequent flyer miles than the world ever saw Bitcoins. Even more than Shanx, Karl helped protect me from Deo. With the kind of money I made for City Law, how could Deo argue about what kind of lawyer I ought to become?

Right off the bat, it was clear that Adela had not briefed Karl before he took over her duties. Like every straight-talking Viking before him, he took Harjeet and his fraudulent corporate gravitas at face value. Within weeks, Karl was checking out P-Tech's failed paging venture with another foreign company Aviran. As Harjeet told the story, Aviran had bid with P-Tech for paging licences across north India. That joint venture won nine circles across India, but Aviran refused to participate. Karl didn't stop to ask why. Harjeet offered Karl this equity and Telsta decided to look in. I was authorized to conduct a due diligence in tandem with Price Waterhouse. It was surreal. I had no idea what a due diligence was, let alone how to do it. Neeru wouldn't give me a checklist. I asked Shanx and he dismissed my query, saying we were to check if the company was following all laws. I sniffed around the office mainframe and found a standard-form early draft of a due diligence report City Law had done for another client. I arrived in Chandigarh with Sajan, clueless as a monkey in a Bar examination mechanically reading statutory records looking for default. We made synopses of board minutes and lists of share transfers, trying to mimic data we had spotted in the format we had picked out of City Law's mainframe. We behaved like low-end government inspectors on a forensic escapade and found nothing. In twenty-four hours, I was reduced to a feeble-minded geriatric while Sajan went about ingratiating himself with the PWC guys whispering, 'Kuch mila, kuch mila?' ('Found anything?')

The P-Tech due diligence was proof that you really can learn on the job. In the five days it took to do it, conversations with PWC showed us what was expected and—surprise, surprise—a perfectly respectable report came out the other end of the langur leap. I mean, it was a bit slow on cutting to the chase, but it got all the data down on paper with a fair summary of the unquantifiable legal risks. An equal amount of regret also came out of this due diligence because Telsta's technical due diligence team had several Nordic girls—two ash blondes to boot—who clearly were ready for the authentic oriental escapade and I failed to rise to the occasion. I accepted an invitation to join the girls at the bar after dinner and had them in splits with rough translations of raunchy Punjabi jokes. When late in the evening, the cute plump girl who simply loved the 'chicken la-bob-da' (which, as it turned out, was her rendition of 'murg lababdaar') drunkenly asked me to help her find her room, I took time out to visit the loo and skipped right out the back door. Should I bang a drum for marital fidelity, or lament a life less lived, or regret, inconsolably, a third-rate come-on that flattered only to deceive?

Whatever we or PWC did say, killed the deal. P-Tech didn't really have the manpower, expertise or money to create a paging footprint across the country. They gassed all the time but they were broke. Karl was credulous, but he was not stupid. When he killed the deal, he also killed his relationship with Harjeet. Harjeet had a typically emotional take on the whole deal: 'If I am not good enough to joint venture with in twelve states, I am not good enough to joint venture with in three states either.' He started to ill-treat Telsta in their existing company, and that in time led to the litigation I have described in *Winning Legal Wars*.

Subsequent events revealed that Harjeet's reaction could in part be explained by the enormous financial strain he was under. P-Tech was a sinking ship at the time, bloated with people who had purchased their jobs. It sold obsolete products manufactured to poor standards in a market that was rapidly evolving. P-Tech also invested heavily in paging technology, which globally was already giving way to mobile telephony. Harjeet dressed up his balance sheets to inflate whatever life P-Tech had left in it. When he could hold it together no longer, he skipped out of the country. Someone said he had been spotted in Boulder, Colorado, but who knows? We do know that some members of P-Tech's senior management were arrested for fraud and fought a long bitter battle to get bail. P-Tech ended up in the bottom drawer of the Official Liquidator.

Now, if you don't know how that works, think of a sci-fi worm from outer space that gets into your body and paralyses you immediately, then slowly—very slowly—starts to dissolve your innards and consume you from within till ultimately only the thinnest outer layer of your skin remains like a brittle shell. This carnivorous stripping is carried out under the genteel phrase: 'an orderly winding up of the affairs of the company'.

This is how the bankruptcy game is played. Unless he is completely daft or naive, the owner of any company knows long before it goes under that its days are numbered. Since he knows the business best, and has the early-mover advantage, he makes sure he strips his company as best he can. He sells off the choicest assets as scrap sales, writes down inventory claiming stuff as lost or untraceable, gives cash to his friends and round-trips it to himself claiming it as lost to a debtor, takes out cash as third-party payments when in fact the receipts are faked, and so forth. By the time the outsider stakeholders—shareholders and lenders—learn of the company's terminal ill health, the easy pickings are all gone. The promoter then throws up his hands and delivers a homily about limited liability companies.

At this point, outsiders get into the game. Some creditors think they can drag the promoter to court and give him a shake-down for cash. But it's often too late. The horse has bolted and the stable has none of the hay that got made when the sun was shining. Soon enough, the creditor learns that he is stuck in the orifice where the sun doesn't shine. At this point, the court has no choice but to deliver the company into the salivating hands of the official liquidator. This is not a smooth passage.

Between the time the court passes the order and the official liquidator finds his way to the company, the employees (who probably haven't received their salaries for several months) bring in the sledgehammers and take away anything they can salvage: stationery, office furniture, air-conditioners, ceiling fans, printers, computers. By the time the official liquidator finally gets his locks on the main gate, all he has left to receive is what is not easily carried away: heavy machinery, stocks of raw material and finished goods, market credits owed to the company and money lying in the banks.

The final kill now takes place. It's the official liquidator's job to liquidate and he does it with passion. If there is still cash in the bank, lucrative contracts are given to security companies to secure the premises. *Kabaria*s come to inspect scrap, riding in second-hand Mercedes purchased out of the profits of previous liquidation deals. Whatever remains is sold for as little as the official liquidator can possibly justify. Any cash he does make from these scrap sales is used as expenses to secure the rest of the assets. As the years tick by, the company doesn't appear to be liquidating very much but if you step inside, it dissolves slowly but determinedly. Eventually, when only the land and building remain, the final auction process kicks in. That's when the real-estate mafia shows up at the door, bidding in cartels, orchestrating everything. Any independent buyer trying to buy a distressed property from a bankrupt company outside the cartel either finds himself facing a death threat or pays for a factory he will never get possession of. Buying a distressed property outside of the mafia circle is the same as buying a lifetime of entertaining evenings with lawyers, billed by the hour. I will give you an example of this kind of hazard.

Years ago, a friend decided to buy a distressed property. The Finance Act of 1986 gave the government a pre-emptive right to purchase any property under income-tax law. This is how it worked. A seller signed an agreement with the buyer and then filed form 37 with the tax authorities asking that he be allowed to sell the property. If the property was underpriced, the appropriate authority pre-empted the sale and paid off the seller. The property was now put out to auction where, presumably, it would sell at a higher price and fetch a fat profit for the government. Since there often was a cash component to every property purchase in those days, selling property was really about having the means to manage the appropriate authority so they did not pre-empt the sale. Many sellers did not do enough management.

Buyers who did not have an ear to the ground thought there was an opportunity here. One of them was my friend Anand. He pitched for and won an auction for a prime property in Bengali Market. He deposited the earnest money at the auction venue. No sooner was he back home than the seller filed a case trumping up a bunch of specious arguments claiming that the auction process was fraudulent. The seller pleaded that he himself would pay more. He then kept the pot on the slow back burner for the next decade even as Anand kept burning up legal fees. The case was fought before a single judge of the High Court, then appealed to the double bench and ultimately reached the Supreme Court. It was then remanded back to the single bench of the High Court. Ten years was as long as Anand was prepared to wait for delivery. Fed up, he asked the seller for a settlement. The seller was more than reasonable, reasonable if you understand how the legal system works. He said he was willing to split the upside, calculated as current market price minus Anand's winning bid.

Anand was offended. For a guy who screwed the approval up royally while selling his property, fifty-fifty was an unfair offer. Anand decided to keep fighting. The case went through a second set of appeals. He won at every stage. When the Supreme Court threw out the seller's final appeal, he thought he now had the property. With the Supreme Court's order in hand, he approached the income-tax department. Did they honour the order and transfer the title deeds in his favour? You must be kidding. You are talking about the government here and they don't do Gandhigiri. The department now took the view that the property had become very valuable and couldn't possibly be sold for the price of the winning bid. In short, they decided not to give Anand what belonged to Anand, because the court did not deliver justice to Anand in a time frame that helped Anand. Inevitably, Anand started a new round of litigation against the income-tax department. He is now in his twentieth year of litigation over this rapidly deteriorating 200-square-yard bungalow in Bengali Market. Curiously, the court is not overcome with guilt, nor does it go out of its way to help the victim of law's delays. Anand's new case gets a lot of very long adjournments.

Let me get back to my story. Expanding corporate work and an endless travel schedule allowed me to reassess my trial-court practice. Most of it was SBI and not worth the candle. I petitioned the Dragons and asked to get rid of it. Deo had another tantrum. 'You *bhenchod* want to kill whatever *ikka dukka* trial practice we are able to muster up in City Law?' he spat disgustedly. I wasn't listening: it was just a formality with a very resentful man. Shanx was more nuanced. 'If you don't like the profile of your trial-court practice, why don't you network with SBI's head office and go up the value chain?' I had any number of good reasons. SBI's corporate-level work was handled out of Mumbai; Delhi would always be civil recoveries. The work was not taxing at any level: the main skill lay in getting the work. The rest of my practice was not lucrative enough to keep. I made up my arguments as I went along. I was not interested in litigation any longer. Litigation was inefficient and required me to sit around all day waiting for cases which would inevitably be adjourned. Shanx didn't fight too hard. I was on a roll and Shanx had little reason to argue with my revenue stream. I resigned from my SBI panel, called up my private clients and, in two weeks flat, wound up my old law practice. A sort of die had been cast.

Was it a good die to cast? I would like to think so. Giving up your existing practice is always risky in any law firm. Your leverage in the firm depends on the clients you 'control'. But I didn't give it up for nothing. I had developed an alternative revenue stream that was more valuable in this environment. City Law needed my new work more than it needed my tiny trial-court practice.

This doesn't mean that giving up litigation is a good idea in general. It probably was at the time and in the given circumstances. I had a proliferating M&A practice. It was not possible to meet that demand and still conduct trials in the subordinate courts. Besides, I was still getting to grips with M&A. I needed time to develop, and that was impossible if I was serving two mistresses. Litigation and dealmaking are very different businesses. Litigation requires you to split hairs and divide and subdivide points, looking for loopholes and failings. This is why litigation lawyers play zero-sum games, excel in laying minefields across the enemy's path and assume a do-or-die position. It's a kind of creative destruction. The job description makes litigation lawyers aggressive and hostile. Dealmaking on the other hand is a can-do and will-make-it-happen business. You try and iron over the wrinkles, find ways through the minefield, bring people together, talk 'we' rather than 'either-you-or-me'. You smooth ruffled feathers, soothe people with expressions of good faith and belief, address insecurities, and add two and two to make five. It's a kind of value creation. The job description makes dealmakers suave, smooth and non-invasive. You can be all of that, but you have to spend many years mastering each, before you can bring the three skills together in a single personality.

It took me four years to learn the basics of dealmaking. Once I got past the kindergarten, I came back to the beginning. In 1998, I resumed litigation work, but at a very different level. If you ask me to sum it up, you are not a lawyer till you understand litigation. Indeed, you cannot be a half-decent corporate lawyer till you go to a trial court and pay your dues and understand how exotic contractual clauses are viewed by judges on the ground. I demand that all the youngsters in my law firm go to court and get their ordeal by fire. I demand that they learn litigation before they learn corporate work. This is the only way airy-fairy Bulgari-spraying Arrow-adorned shaved-chest metrosexual yuppie lawyers are ever going to get into my office. Before sitting in posh Italian-marbled corporate law firms asking office butlers to bring their morning coffee, they have to first understand how the law is applied in the dark and dirty killing fields of Indian courts. If you don't have the balls for this, I tell them to become a law officer in a provincial PSU or something.

Of course, at the time, I was headed the other way. I had paid my dues in the court and I was on my way to learn deal-making. When my billing hit a crore of rupees in the financial year 1996, Shanx was forced to sit up and take notice. For a low-paid employee sitting in a garbage dump populated by chattering loonies with bad breath, I earned too much and controlled my clients too much to be ignored. Out of the blue, he came down one Saturday and asked me what I wanted! My response was pathetic. I pulled out a piece of paper, adding up my kitchen and utility bills + my car instalment + my fuel bill + incidentals + school fees, etc., added Rs 10,000 as savings and told him I needed to be paid Rs 1 lakh a month! 'Okay, done,' he said absently, a hint of an indulgent smile playing on his lips.

I hadn't said a word about being paid a percentage of what I earned or about the partnership deed he had signed with me and failed to honour. I may have fancied myself as a hotshot upcoming M&A lawyer, but I still didn't know a thing about making deals. He felt so comfortable with my naivety that he also immediately accepted my request to be moved back up to the spacious top floor in a room of my own.

Within a month, I was up in my old chamber opposite Deo's, complete with private bathroom (a lifestyle imperative I have retained ever since!). I had my own cupboard full of my own files of my own clients with my own private telephone line. At the same time, I also acquired my own laptop and another copper line with which I learnt the rudiments of dial-up internet service which VSNL had introduced six months ago in August 1995. I had completed four years in City Law, and while I would never become an effective equity partner, I was the second-highest individual billable head and finally being paid a decent wage. The worst was over. The future could only get better . . . and it did, and just how!

14

Greed Creed

Specialization is a double-edged sword. It may allow you to sell your own brand of high-priced super-expertise, but it also shuts the door to a lot of business opportunities. Obviously, if you only do one particular thing you are really great at, there's a bunch of other stuff you don't do, except badly. What happens when a client comes looking for skills in the areas you don't do? And so it was in City Law. I had set myself up as an M&A lawyer, but litigation kept coming back looking for me. I found I could take myself out of litigation but I could not take litigation out of me!

When Chris Cole showed up at our door one day and told me about his dispute with his Indian joint-venture partner, I did not hesitate a minute. Chris was general counsel to the American telecom equipment supplier Altel. Their history went back to the days when the Department of Telecommunication still dominated the sector in India. I could fill this book with hilarious stories of how appalling the telephone service was in those days. This started to change after Rajiv Gandhi appointed Sam Pitroda

194

as his technology adviser in 1984. Pitroda conceived a plan to increase India's tele-density through the indigenous development of manufacturing capacity. DoT started aggressively reshaping the technology drivers of India's telecom network in the late 1980s, and a whole bunch of private players set up manufacturing operations with DoT as the only customer. It was a hellish world of backroom deals, scandals and discontent, and the buzzword generally was 'foreign collaboration'.

An enterprising young Indian company, Bentel, mounted the collaboration bandwagon when it persuaded Altel to transfer its technology to manufacture a Subscriber Carrier System. Whoa, you say? Telephone conversations in those days were relayed by pairs of copper wire, one pair for each pair of talking heads. If you wanted the same pair of wires to carry more than one pair of voices, you would have to digitize them. The Subscriber Carrier System was the CDMA of its time. Altel had a system like that in its kitty and they licensed it to Bentel. Bentel set up a brand new plant in Alwar and Altel transferred the technology to Bentel, complete with kits and training. In due course, DoT floated a tender and asked for the supply of substantial quantities of Subscriber Carrier Systems. The blossoming love story had a twist: they wanted a 'Go to Snooze' feature. Altel's equipment did not have that feature.

Only one company in India had the feature! Not a word about this requirement was ever breathed by DoT to anyone till the tender actually came out. By then, it was too late for everyone to get it. Conspiracy theories sprang eternal. There were hints and allegations, whispers and mutterings, winks and nods. We do know that one particular company did extraordinarily well under telecom minister Sukh Ram, whom, as I have already mentioned, eventually got chucked into the slammer for storing bribes under his farmhouse bed. Bentel immediately demanded that Altel supply this feature. Altel didn't care about the operations in India because it was only trying to unload an obsolete technology on a third-rate company in a Third World country. Thus started a dispute, the essence of which was really this: did Altel sell an existing technology, or did it promise to support Bentel's telecom venture in India with whatever it needed?

Chris showed up at City Law's door because Bentel invoked arbitration demanding 5 million dollars in damages. He was shell-shocked. This was an itsy-bitsy technology transfer for some small-ticket licence fees. Where were these millions in liability coming from? We looked at the break-up. Bentel wanted Altel to pay for the land they had purchased in Alwar industrial area, the cost of the building, the cost of all the equipment in the building, all the profit they would have ever made if they had won every tender ever put out in India, plus a large sum of money for loss of reputation, mental anguish and post-traumatic stress disorder to boot. The claim made zilch sense to me. To win a tender, supply goods and make money, you need a factory. If you want me to compensate you for lost profits on possible deals, you need to pay for the factory yourself. But if you want me to pay for the factory, then transfer the damn factory to me and I will pay for it and the lost profit. Or sell the factory and if you make a loss, I will pay you that loss plus the lost profit. Bentel wanted to have its cake, eat it too, have Altel pay for it, and then compensate Bentel because Bentel got diabetes. It was absurd.

It was easy to see where Bentel was coming from. It was engaging in brinkmanship. All of us fear the entanglement of litigation. If someone tells you, 'I am going to sue you to death and then you will spend the next twenty years slogging through decades of long hot summers in Tees Hazari Courts,' you will probably try and settle the case. To top that, if he threatens all this, and adds, 'I will make you do all this, not in the convenient

confines of Delhi but in the local trial courts in Tripura next to
the Burmese border in territory controlled largely by Kalashnikov-
toting narco-terrorists,' you will succumb to this threat faster
than I can say Indian Penal Code. Now imagine if you are an
American. Where on earth is Alwar? Can you get an elephant taxi
there or do you have to ride on unsprung wooden bullock-carts
drawn by flatulent bullocks? Chris was very rattled and asked for
a compromise meeting. He wasn't going to meet in India either:
what if Bentel went to the police and had Chris arrested? We
converged on a swanky hotel with a name I can't remember off
Orchard Road in Singapore.

Please don't try and spot the hotel on Google Maps: it
probably doesn't exist any more, not the way I knew it. At the
time, it was the only major building on a flower-strewn tropical
paradise of a hillock about a kilometre from Robinson's in
Singapore's Centrepoint Mall on Orchard Street. Singapore
at the time was still an ongoing construction project. I stopped
there first in June 1987 on my way back from my honeymoon in
Hawaii, and it looked like Gurgaon does today. Many roads were
dug up, sparkling new glass towers in the commercial hubs were
divided by large empty plots full of litter, the malls were more
like Palika Bazaar and the traffic had a lot more variety: more
mopeds and rickety Matador-type vans. Most people travelled on
Haryana Roadways'-type buses and of course, Singapore's Mass
Rapid Transit hadn't opened yet, not till November of that year
anyway. Actually, that is the main reason I have always believed
passionately in the India story! By the mid-1990s, the project to
rebuild Singapore was well under way. Parts of Orchard Road
were still dug up but several of the newer buildings were up and
running. Smoking was banned in taxis, which smelt better, but
you could still buy knock-off branded clothes and pirated CDs in
some shops. It wasn't an expensive city either.

I had a dinner pre-meeting with Chris and we agreed that the only way to settle the issue was to debate the claim. We planned to cut the figures down to something realistic, based on potential liability under Indian law, and take the proposal back to the Altel board for final approval. It didn't work out that way. Bentel came to the meeting both bleeding-heart and hostile-aggressive. It tried to bury the absurdity of its position under a barrage of moral outrage. We tried to argue that in Indian law, the best Bentel could expect is that Altel put it back in the position it would have been if Altel had supplied 'Go to Snooze'. Just how many Carrier Subscriber Systems would DoT ever purchase and what was the profit on them? Bentel did not want to assess what it would have earned if it had won every tender DoT put out. We tried to stretch the logic this way and that, assume everything in Bentel's favour, but we just couldn't get past 250,000 dollars in total turnover. What profits would Bentel have made on this revenue? Would Bentel open its books in a limited way to demonstrate its profitability? Bentel wouldn't go there. It wanted to be paid for the factory it had set up, the foreign trips it had made, the people it had hired, the dinners it had consumed and the 100-dollar hookers it had humped in Dubai. In sum, it wanted to be paid for the factory and it wanted to keep the factory at the same time!

Chris admitted defeat in less than two hours, and then it was time to go out to lunch. Bentel's managing director was friendly, forthcoming and very optimistic over lunch. His confidence unnerved Chris, who then spent the rest of the day cross-examining me about my assessment of the potential liability. Exasperated at his continuing scepticism, I told him his potential liability was zero. I told him I would keep the case in court so long he would never pay anything but my fees. I told him to take the 5 million dollars, put it in a bank deposit on 1 per cent interest and give me the interest on the deposit to fight the case with. As it turned out, my legal fees never did exceed a tenth of that figure at the time, because frankly there was very little work to do.

Although I have discussed the strategic considerations in this case in *Winning Legal Wars*, a synopsis will reveal a great deal about how cases can be paralysed completely in Indian courts.

Back to India, I decided the best way to fight Bentel was to argue that we didn't have a dispute that could be settled in arbitration. The words 'Go to Snooze' or anything like it had never appeared in the Technology Transfer Agreement. What Altel had sold was what it had. Altel declined to appoint an arbitrator, forcing Bentel to go to court in Jaipur. In court, Altel argued that an arbitrator appointed under the Technology Transfer Agreement could not go beyond that Agreement in search of a larger legal obligation. For good measure, we also argued that the Jaipur court had no jurisdiction to decide anything since nothing had happened in Jaipur!

The thing with Indian courts is that you get to have lots of fun if you are a defendant. The guy filing the case has a heavy burden to prove stuff and courts are very reluctant to interfere. Culturally, Indians find it very easy to get an incurable case of analysis paralysis at the slightest provocation. Raise a jurisdictional issue and most courts will jam the brakes, mesmerized by this beautiful thing called jurisdiction. Worse, many courts can't seem to cut to the chase. If you want to be a good defence lawyer, practise the art of enmeshing courts in jurisdictional issue: it never fails.

I will spare you much of the gory story. After years of argument, the Jaipur court ultimately decided to appoint an arbitrator. Not that this changed anything. I filed an appeal and the whole Ferris wheel started up again. It was fun. The Oberoi Raj Nivas had just opened and they couldn't attract customers that far out of town. I made the best of the deal, driving down for a poolside conference before the hearing. After the hearing the following day, we did a wrap-up conference in the coffee shop. The local lawyers were happy to revel in the memory of such luxury and frequently forgot to send their bills. I had a blast working in such an opulent ambience and the client was happy to ward off a 5 million-dollar claim for another decade!

It wasn't over by any means. While the appeal was in its third year of paralysis, Altel further convoluted the legal confusion by asking a court in Alwar to independently determine if an arbitration clause existed at all under Section 33 of the old Indian arbitration law! I then became Neemrana's best customer, living out of the Kesroli Hill Fort up to ten times a year, for years on end. If the case got listed on a Friday, I made sure I addressed the high stress levels of the lawyer's life by lying prostrate all weekend on the beautiful lawns of Hotel Siriska Palace.

The years had not been particularly profitable for Bentel and it now found itself faced with a logistics nightmare, prosecuting cases in several jurisdictions which its enemy was happy to fund. Every small town in India has two lawyers who dominate, of whom one is the don and the other is the wannabe. You go to one or the other. If you know you are going to face a case in this or that small town, you make sure you anticipate events and hire the don first. Bentel couldn't find a lawyer who understood the issues, let alone fight this second case. In the face of this stonewalling, Bentel lost heart. The petitions slowly ground to a halt in both courts and, as they did, Altel also gradually demobilized. At the end of six years, both cases were dismissed for default because lawyers stopped appearing.

The Altel case was somewhat life-defining for me: life-defining because, for the first time, I started to feel on top of the strategic litigation game. I felt I could fight anyone, anywhere, anytime. Law practice had become more beautiful because now, by executing simple strategic steps, I had learnt to win.

As I look back on my career, the most fun I've ever had, and the most money I have ever made, has come from cases where Indian partners in cross-border deals have let their claims outstrip their business sense. Many Indian promoters still believe that they can extort money from foreigners through sheer intimidation. They try to block market access, instigate regulators to embark on investigations, get third parties to file false criminal cases, pay NGOs and RTI activists to go on fishing expeditions, and generally create a witch hunt at the other end of which they hope the foreigner will pay them to shut up. It doesn't work. It doesn't work because Indian promoters always want a lot more money than the foreigner can justify. If the foreigner can't earn back the money he pays the Indian promoter in the next few years in India, why would he pay the blackmailer off? The board would prefer to leave India than pay out the money and then find it can't earn it back.

That is one part of the story. The other part of the story is that it is harder now to prejudice anyone against foreigners. While our colonial masters bid us goodbye in 1947, the truth is that our hostility towards the foreigner continued well into the 1990s. Not any more. If Ratan Tata can buy a Jaguar and Lakshmi Mittal can conquer the whole steel industry, by what token are the Indian government or bureaucracy going to sustain their paranoid scaremongering? Besides, most of us would rather like to work for those sophisticated expats with their democratic, courteous ways and their long weekends when they don't hassle subordinates. Can't say that about our fellow countrymen, can we?

Finally, there is the legal end of the piece. Many of the draconian laws Indian companies could use to screw foreigners are gone, the Foreign Exchange Regulation Act being the worst of them. Increasingly, breaches of law which were crimes have become minor infractions carrying penalties while prison terms have become fines. It is true that the cops are still capable of giving those they don't like a very hard time but then, when they offer their services to the highest bidder, it's hard for an extortionist to stay in the pay-out race. In the upshot, when an Indian promoter exaggerates his claim and hits a foreigner with all he has, the foreigner finds a basis to create a generous budget with which he pays people like me serious money to jack the Indian promoter back.

~

I am not a Buddhist but that has never prevented me from being mesmerized by the yin-yang duality of life. While my career was zooming in City Law, my relationships with practically all my colleagues had reached a low point. The only exception were the younger people. Every junior, and his country cousin from Tanda Urmar, wanted to work in my chamber. On the other hand, everyone in middle management—the followers one and all— would have invested fifty-one Saturdays making offerings at the tantric-infested Bhairon Mandir behind Purana Qila, if they felt it would help squeeze me out. It all came to a head when Inland of India Pte Ltd wanted to form a joint venture with the Tatas to market steel in India.

The provocation was small but the event was symptomatic of everything that was wrong in my working relationships. Christopher Tucker representing Inland of India wanted his upcoming joint venture with Tata Steel written as a formal contract enforceable in India. Shanx made one last attempt to get me to work with Neeru. He had his agenda. I was getting all the work Neeru used to get before she went to London. He needed us to become a team. Given my tendency to handle independently any client he gave me, he also needed someone to keep tabs on what

I did with his new clients. I tried to play it fair, as I would define fair. I went to see her and found a sulking, resentful girl unwilling to engage constructively with me: 'You draft the documents and then I will see if I have anything to add.' I read that to mean 'it's your problem' though now when I think about it, she probably wanted to see my drafts, rip them apart and establish her authority over me. That would have been normal in any law firm. I went and short-circuited the destructive game by doing the documents and sending them off to the client. Tucker was a good lawyer. He papered over all my failings with his input. In three days flat, we had hammered together a great set of documents. In these three days, I had also been paid to be guided by a top-notch American lawyer on the finer points of contract-writing.

Neeru waited for a few days to hear from me, then went and complained to Shanx that I was sleeping on the job. This one truly blew up in my face, and from her viewpoint rightly so. I added fuel to the fire by protesting against the idea that I needed to have anything at all approved by Neeru. 'You want the job done and I have done it,' I let my new-found arrogance fly, 'don't ask me now to suck up to these people.' Shanx had to work hard to wrestle down his impatience. He said my whole philosophy was warped. City Law was a law firm. The main challenge was not doing the job: everyone did the job, one way or another. It is to carry people along. You have to work with them, make them agree. If someone is being very difficult, appoint him to the board of directors. If that is not enough, he said, make him the chairman of the board of directors. 'Everyone knows a chairman of the board has nowhere to go but down,' he explained, 'why don't you try kicking an inconvenient person upstairs till he is too far up to know what is really going on, and then do what you want?'

I didn't want to understand. I wanted to vent all my angst. 'At this rate, I will be carrying every chaprasi along.' He tried and then he tried some more. I behaved abominably. He said there was only so much of a debate with me he had patience for, but I should seriously consider my attitude. He said I had antagonized practically everyone. He said he spent a lot of energy defending me from Deo. Both Dutta and the Professor were barely on speaking terms with me. I had successfully upset everyone in his own team. 'Ranjeev, is it fair for you to expect that I will spend all my time protecting you from everyone else in this law firm?'

The truth is, I needed protecting from my own demons, but those very demons were taking me to places I would not have the courage to tread if I exorcised them from my soul. I breastfed on anger, and that was my strength.

Thirty-five years of law practice later, as I look back at my life, I see that everyone has a personal narrative on the events taking place in his life. We then interpret these incidents within the context of this narrative. As often as not, this narrative has only a passing resemblance to the truth—if there is such a thing as the truth. As I write this chapter, I find myself faced with a tactless, confrontational junior who simply will not take instructions. He argues about everything and work suffers. Most of the objections he raises are rubbish. I reason with him as best I can but, beyond a point, who has the patience? He has a different narrative. 'I thought this firm promoted independence of thinking,' he says accusingly, 'if you want me not to think, I will do that then.' So now this kid has added moral righteousness to obstinacy. This is typical. Clearly, you and I can only have a relationship if our two narratives about our relationship have a fair amount of common ground. If we can't agree, then, like the face-off between American imperialists and radical Islamists, all we can possibly have between us is bullets and blood.

~

As I wrote earlier, my father used to say that every man gets three opportunities in his life. The successful man is the one who grabs them. Getting into City Law was my first. Telsta was my second because, on the other side of it, I had a full-fledged independent corporate law practice. I was now ready for my third opportunity but I had no sense of when and how it would present itself. That still left open one key question. In any law firm, if you make a niche for yourself, do your own thing and leave others alone, will other people pay you back in kind and leave you in peace? I hoped that they would. As I was soon to learn, I was wrong. You may think you are leaving everyone alone. They probably find your neglect very threatening. Why doesn't he care, they ask themselves. What does he have going on that makes him so cocksure he doesn't need to engage with me? These questions festered like a sore through the corridors of City Law as I continued my relentless climb out of the dungeons and into the light. And while these questions festered, I found distraction in spending my time advising some really weird and wonderful characters. That included the nearest thing to a Dubai don that I've ever had the opportunity to run into.

15

Gangsters, Vultures and Angels

I love the way I am projecting myself as this uber-luxury champagne-breakfast corporate commercial lawyer with a lifestyle to kill for. I'm exaggerating and talking myself up. Not everything that came my way was quite that upmarket! That didn't make it less fascinating though. Early one morning on a particularly cruel April day, I was introduced to Sethi. I liked him instantly. He had the face of a bulldog, the backside of a water buffalo, and the self-confidence of Salman Khan taking off his shirt in a gay bar. He liked his food and drink, but his real weapon was his wit and his charm. He had been talked into buying a Bombay mini-steel mill positioned as a real-estate opportunity and now he was up to his neck in the sludge.

It had seemed a simple business proposition. The steel mill sat on a large plot of land in Navi Mumbai. The company was bankrupt and under the protection of the Board of Industrial and Financial Reconstruction, aka BIFR. All the buyers had to do was make deals with all the creditors, negotiate a discount on the debts and pay everyone off, taking the company out of BIFR supervision. They could then get official approval to convert the land to residential use, allowing them to build swanky high-rise homes for the rich. All their funding calculations were based on the floor area ratio they could get, and it seemed like millions in the bank. Of course it wasn't as simple as that, it never is.

The problem was pretty much what every vulture fund experiences in India. The bankrupt company owed money to everyone: employees, suppliers, contractors and customers. It hadn't paid municipal taxes, sales tax, excise duty, income tax and whatever other tax it is conceivable to pay in India. It hadn't paid wages to its workmen for years, deposited the legally mandatory provident fund or contributed to workers' insurance. It hadn't paid for the electricity it had used and had huge loans to repay to bankers. This was hardly unusual. Every bankruptcy in the world is at one level the same. The difference was that half the creditors had all kinds of crazy draconian powers of pre-emption, seizure, auction, sale and every other scary financially ruining disaster you could think of. Everyone wanted their money back before everyone else and while they did little in practice to get it, every conversation with them ended with hysterical threats of dire consequences. Vijay Mallya would know. This reality stood quite opposed to the one found in mature economies with advanced bankruptcy laws where a regulator supervises the revival of a sick company, hammering home a Rehabilitation Plan across all creditors, and then ensuring the turnaround.

Ironically, Sethi wanted to pay back the creditors but found he couldn't. It wasn't a matter of discounting a debt. The creditors wouldn't accept a part payment in 'full and final settlement' till you bribed their officers to make the deal. The cultural consistency in bribe-taking was alarming. You would expect bank managers, provident-fund inspectors and electricity departments to be on the take; they have for decades. Here, even the union boss wanted to be paid cash to accept part payment of outstanding wages in full and final settlement of all claims. It was a nightmare. How was Sethi to settle with all these bloodthirsty creditors?

Actually, his problem ran deeper than that. The deal had been put together by a street-smart man-about-town called Khorana, who hadn't the money to buy the sick company. Sethi and his friend Chadda formed a consortium and funded Khorana on good faith. Once Khorana received most of the funding, he began exhibiting the usual symptoms of advanced avarice. He backtracked on key elements of the deal between them, and he withheld information of the company's affairs on the ground. Sethi wanted to understand better what he had gotten into and he needed legal help to navigate through it. We offered to put down the total deal in binding contracts between Khorana, Chadda and Sethi.

I am a great believer in management by tantrums. If you are a latently violent, unpredictable bastard who doesn't bleed for other people's feelings, you can be a very good manager of the mild and the meek. People who dislike unpleasantness would rather do what you want, when you want, how you want, than face the ruckus you would create. When the same technique is brought to bear on legal negotiations, the results can be scary. The negotiations between these three were admirable exhibitions of competitive tantrum-throwing. There was no talk, only shouting. There was no debate about risk distribution, only hysterical protests of hurt feelings. There was no attempt to be reasonable and fair to all, only the exhausting spectacle of a mixed-martial-arts-type full-contact contest where he who continued to scream long after everyone else had won the point. They call it 'Superior Cardio' in mixed martial arts. I learnt then that law practice is about working across cultural boundaries. The three protagonists were talking in hundreds of crores. They were all wealthy men with kids studying abroad and wives serially shopping at Harrods. At least two were urbane and educated. It wasn't that they didn't know better. Their behaviour was culturally contextualized negotiation. How would anyone take you seriously if you did not throw a tantrum?

There were days we made little progress, on others we ran for cover. Khorana was obstructive and Chadda became increasingly exasperated with Khorana's petulance. Sethi unsuccessfully tried to keep the peace. It kept going downhill. Eventually, one afternoon, as the pitch of the conversation became steadily more shrill, Chadda vented his annoyance at Khorana's refusal to yield on a perfectly fair point with a resounding slap. Khorana's head snapped back and a nasty weal appeared instantly on his cheek. Khorana started to cry, shaking with shock. Chadda exploded even more, picking up one of Sethi's faux Ming vases to smash down on Khorana's head. Sethi rushed up and caught Chadda from behind, pinning his arms. Khorana screamed that he wouldn't take a beating. Chadda screamed he would beat him till he received a refund. Khorana said he didn't have money to give him. Chadda said he had a gun to show Khorana. Sethi pleaded with both for calm and the brotherhood of man. I sat through this entire drama as still as a cattle thief astride a horse with a rope around his neck, minutes from being lynched under the old oak tree. Not a lot came out of that. Khorana conceded the point and the merry tantrums started again on the next point. As the Turk famously said to Michael Corleone, it wasn't personal.

Sethi later said that Chadda hadn't been kidding about the gun. Chadda had once been the close associate of a Dubai-based Mumbai don, or some such. After that day, I made sure my bills were delivered to Sethi alone. At least Sethi's primary negotiation tool was audio!

Hundreds of billable hours later, we got the documentation done but the business restructuring didn't work out too well. Most of the creditors were paid, but several others filed actions in court and progress got bogged down. It's the old land-acquisition problem: the last one-acre plot is always the hardest, and most expensive to buy. Outstanding creditors could approach one of a half-dozen forums to stall all progress till they were paid, and they made sure they did. Indian courts and tribunals did what Indian courts and tribunals do: order long adjournments and progress very slowly, if at all. I have long believed that analysis paralysis is a central feature of the Indian mindset, exactly like Arjuna poised on the field of battle asking himself if he should be killing his cousins. This question reared its head bang in the middle of a stand-off between two great armies ready to spill blood. Some timing, eh? If you are trying to get something done, pre-emptive action is about the only viable strategy. If you let the courts in on the conflict, you lock the time clock down so that it barely moves.

The last time I asked Sethi about this venture, he said they still hadn't unlocked the value in the real estate.

As City Law hummed along nicely, my journey through the legal labyrinth plunged me relentlessly towards the nadir of cynicism. Sometimes the jolts could be really rude: arbitration was one such. Most of us corporate lawyers writing high-value contracts had long been arbitration fans. It was supposed to bypass the procedural complexity of civil courts, access the best legal minds as arbitrators (even if they had been retired), and offer quick solutions to commercial disputes. I saw all these objectives achieved when a client, Pure Helium, sued ONGC sometime in 1994 asking to be paid more for gas supplied to Bombay High under a global tender because the rupee had devalued against the dollar. It came down to an interpretation of the terms of the tender and there were no witnesses to be examined. We appointed Dinesh Kothari, a Middle-East-trained financial wizard, as our arbitrator, thinking that experience of cross-border contracting and foreign-exchange risk management across geographies would push arbitrators to a more commercially pragmatic decision. ONGC in turn appointed retired Supreme Court Justice V.D. Tulzapurkar. The arbitration tribunal asked parties to complete pleadings in six weeks and, when the paperwork was done, invited us to argue our case at noon in Mumbai on a sprightly January Monday morning.

That day is etched in my mind. I woke up at 4 a.m., rang for a taxi at 5.30 a.m. and made it from Vasant Kunj to the check-in counter of Palam airport at 5.55 a.m., one hour before the flight. Try doing that today! Everyone smoked in business class those days and if you survived the heavy nicotine environment, there were always the heavily aromatic toilets to deliver the fatal blow. The client was there to pick us up at 9.15 a.m. but the journey from the airport to the arbitration venue in the Fort took longer than the one from Delhi to Bombay by plane. What a dump, I thought, little knowing that Delhi would be worse twenty years later.

Justice Tulzapurkar was a kindly soul, soft-spoken and warm. His age had done nothing to dull his mind and he conducted the arbitration with a calm sense of gentle purpose. Kothari was a thoughtful measured man, very picky about the words he used, very concise about the thoughts he expressed. I ran through the pleadings and documents in half an hour and the law in about the same. ONGC's arguments lasted no longer. The arbitrators asked short pithy questions. Two hours later, we were on our way to Khyber restaurant in Kala Ghoda. We drove off at 4 p.m., hit the airport at 6 p.m., reached Delhi by 9 p.m. and received the award by post two weeks later. The entire process from invocation of arbitration to award had taken five months and a single hearing.

But arbitration was not always as seamless. I once had the good fortune to represent the construction contractor of a power plant in Haryana before a recently retired High Court judge. My client wished to be paid for work the owner had asked him to do outside the contract: the owner claimed it was included in the contract price. The contract was not more complex than ONGC's arbitration and this dispute too could be resolved without witnesses. I naturally assumed that this interpretation of contract case would be over in a year. I was wrong. I should have smelt it as soon as we met for a preliminary hearing. There was way too much hail-fellow-well-met bonhomie between the arbitrator and the owner's representatives. The judge was way too ingratiating. Tall, thin and squirrelly in his demeanour, he made Cassius look like a novice in the lean and hungry department. He ordered the parties to pay him 'per sitting'.

This was new to me since most arbitrators charged by the hearing. As it turned out, a sitting lasted two hours all-inclusive, and a good part of that was spent burrowing into piles of biscuits, sandwiches and samosas washed down with oversweet HMT (half-milk tea). To be fair, the judge always held hearings in his own home and his wife always laid a generous table. That said, if you are being paid Rs 50,000 per hour to supply snacks and beverages worth a few hundred rupees, how gutted would you be? We trudged to his home for hearing after hearing, only weeks apart, never to be there longer than two hours and never taking less than forty-five minutes to drink the brew and talk trash about politics. It had the client tearing at his blackheads every time.

Through all these hearings, there was little for the defence lawyer to do but interject some wholly irrelevant rustic homily from time to time to keep his end up. Clearly, he hadn't read his case and didn't need to, since the judge thoroughly indulged his time-wasting irrelevancies. He was a friendly if rather gross character from Chandigarh, and his main brief appeared to be to buy time by filing applications for adjournments. The judge didn't mind at all, as long as it was understood that he charged for a hearing whether or not the parties wanted to be heard. Many an afternoon have I spent enjoying samosas at a scuttled hearing because the lawyer was unavoidably detained in Chandigarh at the last minute.

Three years and perhaps sixty hearings into the arbitration, I was able to conclude my arguments. At this point, the judge applauded my efforts and suggested that I should briefly go over the matter again, just to be sure he had understood it well. Flummoxed but pliable, I prepared my summary and returned for one final hearing, only to find the judge asking crudely tangential questions as if he had comprehended nothing at all. He almost said as much with a cunning glint in his eye, leaving no doubt in my mind of his intentions. As shameless sods go, he was in a class by himself, and I knew I was roundly beaten. To add misery to defeat, I knew that the law would do nothing about it. So off I went to the client and told them that they needed a senior counsel to manage the judge.

The client wasn't delighted with the suggestion. He didn't like to 'change horses mid-race', but I did my share of insisting. We ended up with the truest gentleman the Calcutta Bar may well have ever known: Jayant Mitra. Regrettably, all it achieved was a shift of responsibility. The judge continued to play the dud. He made Jayant-da repeat all of my arguments, and then made him repeat himself. Another year into the arbitration, I told the client that my presence served no purpose and went off in search of greener pastures. I bumped into Jayant-da many years later on one of those Kingfisher flights where they served lobster tails for lunch in business class. He was still chipping away at the case, still uncertain if it would ever be finalized.

Here is the deal with arbitration. What happens to your arbitration depends almost entirely on the arbitrator. Because we want the courts to keep out of the arbitrator's hair, we have together set up a system by which it is practically impossible to have any recourse against a rogue arbitrator; and there are more than a few rogues out there. If you pick a good guy, you will get a great result. I have had great arbitrations before honest, upright, God-fearing judges. I can't say that about a great many others I have done. With each passing year, I see a steady deterioration in the quality of arbitrations we are experiencing. Some are absolute nightmares, enough for me to put my mouth where my client's money has already gone.

I recall City Law doing a 300-crore-rupees arbitration, between a telecom PSU and a service provider, before a retired Supreme Court judge who was the sole arbitrator. Each party spent about 30 lakh in fees over sixty sittings in six years, and then the arbitrator died. It took all of fifteen years to see the end of this one, in which time I went from being the 'basta vakil' to the managing partner of a law firm! I am managing several arbitrations right now that have lasted longer than seven years. Tell me about the seven-year itch!

Unless you intend to shaft your partner and rip him off even as you sign the contract, you would do well not to sign arbitration agreements. Arbitrations as often as not best serve the purpose of those who don't want justice to be done.

Because of the scary mismatch between City Law's public profile and its actual domain expertise, it remained a brilliant hunting ground for anyone who was prepared to bust a gut and address the skill deficit. I spent vast amounts of time rushing into meetings rendering service in areas I didn't understand at all. On top of that, I frequently found myself dealing with people who truly were good at what they were doing. Inevitably, I got derided, mauled and slaughtered. My counterparts went away laughing but I picked up valuable knowledge every time I stumbled and fell in the open sewer of my ignorance. And as I stumbled from one area of practice to another, never quite knowing my butt from my elbow, I paid for my legal education in humiliation, but I learnt a great deal.

Fairly early on, I had the privilege to learn about the world of private equity financing. The idea is exactly what it calls itself: a bunch of private investors buying into the equity of a growing company. It's a simple model. A financial institution, a bank, a cash-rich company or a very rich investor sponsors the creation of an independent trust fund and appoints a fund manager. The fund manager raises capital from other companies, banks, financial institutions, HNIs, pension funds, and so forth till it has a fat corpus of, let's say, Rs 1500 crore. The fund manager tells the contributors that the fund will use this money to buy shares valued at, say, 100–200 crore in ten to fifteen companies, and then use its expertise and business network to help these companies grow. The basic aim of this exercise is to partner with the owners of the businesses to grow the businesses, and with it, the value of the fund's stake in the businesses. At some point, when these cheaply purchased shares become really valuable, the fund sells its stake and exits the company, making a tidy profit. By way of example, take the PE player ChrysCapital. It invested Rs 300 crore to pick up around 11.2 per cent stake in the pharmaceutical company Intas Pharma. In 2014, ChrysCapital sold 10.16 per cent stake in Intas to another PE player, Temasek, for Rs 880 crore, tripling its money.

It's a simple profitable business, you would say—except that it's only intermittently profitable and never simple. As I was to learn through bitter experience, the PE business suffers from a severe case of the Abhimanyu syndrome! Getting into the *chakravyuh* of investing in companies is a whole lot easier than getting out profitably. The inefficiency of the justice machine is one major reason why. In those good old days, PE funds wrote in all sorts of creative 'Put Option clauses' into their contract. Put option clauses are a weird animal. If I invest in your company, a put option clause will say that no matter what the price of the shares in 2025 AD, I will be entitled to 'put' the shares to you at Rs 10,000 per share or whatever and you will have to buy these shares from me at that price, even if the shares were completely worthless at that point. The Securities Contract law in India did not allow this kind of contract to be made. This led to endless acrimony.

If you had asked me for a legal opinion at the time, I would not have advised you to sign these types of clauses because Put Options were then not legal in India. Still, when NIF, a Japanese-bank-sponsored PE fund, wanted to sue a web-based share trading platform to enforce its Put Option, NIF hired me and I rode in on my white steed Gangnam-style and to my own surprise, forced a settlement. It's about the only time I successfully fought a full-blown litigation for a PE fund and found it possible to do my job without having the client run about like a headless chicken. Why would that be, you may ask. My answer at the time would have been that the 'structure' of these funds discouraged them from ever going to court. A bunch of investors put money into the fund. They understood that the fund manager would make some risky investments; in this game you will win some and lose some. If the fund lost, they expected the fund manager to cut losses and move on. What they most definitely didn't expect is that they throw good money after bad. Even if a lawyer ever managed to talk a PE fund into going to court, especially if the fund is a minority shareholder, he would have to carry the case even as the client had severe self-doubt as to its wisdom.

Promoters of companies which took in PE money were very quick to sense how weak the funds were, for they often purchased a small percentage of the company's shares and they never had management control. Some of their procedure and reporting orientation also left the promoters with the impression that fund managers were sarkari babus. The fund needed to engage with the people who had put money into the fund; they did this by regularly sending detailed reports of what they were doing to their investors. Pestering company officials seeking more and more information quickly led promoters to think that this was more or less all the fund managers ever did. With this rising contempt came an urge to behave dishonestly. Between the irritation and the vulnerability, PE funds become a natural source for rip-off schemes. It helped that they were very reluctant to litigate.

Then how come the Japanese fund successfully enforced its Put? I don't know. Maybe it's a Japanese samurai thing! More likely, the sponsoring bank had a lot of its own money in the fund, so they were thinking like bankers, not like a fund managing other people's money. In another case I did, where a London-based bank had merely sponsored the fund, the results were very different when it came to a dogfight with a plastic packaging company from Gujarat. I knew this investment well because I had written the document, managed the due diligence and negotiated the legal stuff. I liked the promoters: they were old-school and seemed very honourable. Some years later, it became obvious that they were anything but. They siphoned money out of the company by over-invoicing imports, moved the dollar-denominated kickbacks to

Mauritius and round-tripped the money back as FDI. There was a lot of that going on then, as there is a lot of that going on now.

In fact, many lawyers would argue that most of the FDI one sees is Indian money. If, indeed, everybody and his pet poodle has a Swiss bank account, as AAP would have you believe, why would they leave the money idle? Presumably, if you are smart enough to make that kind of money, you are smart enough to get it to work for you while you lounge about scratching your crown jewels. If you want your money to work for you, how many markets offer you higher potential returns than India? And in how many markets would you have the same comfort level that you do in India?

Anyway, when we found out about this, I asked Shanx to accept a nomination to their board of directors. Shanx was superb at orchestrating screaming solos in board meetings and a lot of people used his services when they wanted to unleash a wave of intimidation as part of their corporate strategy. He was as good as his reputation, though the promoters thwarted him somewhat by smiling through it, allowing him to exhaust himself and disregarding whatever he said. Meanwhile, I used the evidence we had of misappropriation of money, and the board proceedings, to make a case I could take to the Company Law Board. This is where my litigation self-belief took a beating.

We filed a case with solid documentary evidence showing that the promoter had misappropriated money. We built up a good legal basis for why the company should be managed differently. We had the case argued by an eminent senior lawyer, and the Company Law Board was pretty sympathetic too. Despite all this, in the background, the fund experienced severe existential angst. You can't fight a case if a client is flogging himself with a whip fashioned from his own anticipatory defeat. We wouldn't get clear instructions, any creative idea we had would be drowned in a rash of objections, and no one quite knew what the deliverables for the litigation were. The whole thing fell apart very quickly.

This is when I truly came to understand that most people who go to court have little comprehension of either this tool or the use to which it can conceivably be put. Unto this topic, I now turn.

16

The Naked Truth about the Law

Most people are incredibly ignorant about what lawyers really do for a living. They think we are here to help our clients get justice. This is rubbish. What we really do is help our clients to get the courts to apply the law, or violate it or circumvent it. At any rate, what lawyers don't do is worry about justice or try to deliver it. Not every layman understands that law and justice are two very different things. Let me explain.

Consider a typical bungalow at the edge of (let's say) Delhi. Once upon a time, a long time ago, the land on which this bungalow stands was beautiful forest. Then along came a primitive tribesman and decided he wanted to live here. So he burnt down all the trees and built a nice spacious hut. In this way, the land that 'belonged' to no one was now his to the exclusion of everyone else. That is tribal law for you: you take what you like and it's yours. At any rate, it's yours till someone stronger comes along and boots you out.

And boot our tribesman out, no doubt, someone did. Now, as time passed and ancient Delhi became more politically organized, tribes appointed chiefs who then acquired a lot of authority over the members of the tribe. In time, the biggest bully amongst these chiefs crowned himself a feudal lord and started to, yes, lord it over everyone else. In time, this lord announced that he was the true owner of all the land and everyone who occupied it to grow crops on it must pay him. If someone did that on the streets of Chandni Chowk today, we would say he was running a protection racket. At the time, the lord called it taxes! When the peasants resisted, he used his sword and his nasty violent sidekicks to intimidate the peasants into agreeing that they were only tenants. In one sense, nothing really changed. The feudal lord may have changed the ownership of the land but the guy cultivating the land was the same sorry peasant, still sweating away on the land and still getting exploited by everyone. This is how the world was, for as long as anyone remembers. There were no courts to go to except the court of the feudal lord, and he wasn't waiting with bated breath for someone to walk in his castle door and accuse him so he could condemn himself to his own dungeon. Where was the justice in any of this? That is feudal law for you: if you are the top bully and you say you want something, then that is the law.

Not that this lasted too long either. It was very temporary. In time, feudal lords got together in larger political combines so they could go and gobble up other people's land too. The strongest of them became the king and he had the last word on who would own which piece of land. The land was snatched from feudal lords he did not like and given over to those he favoured. The dispensation lasted as long as the king lived. Every time the ruling dynasty changed, the new king kicked out one feudal lord and gave the land to another feudal lord whom he liked more. In turn,

the favoured feudal lord gave money, soldiers and horses to the
king. Where was the justice in any of this? This is law for you in
monarchies: arbitrary rules created by kings to confer favours on
nobles who supported them in war and in peace.

Eventually, the local kings were replaced by foreign rulers.
When the East India Company became the new king on the block
in India, it took the land from the nawabs, rajas and *badshah*s
and gave it to a new class of princes who it called zamindars. No
doubt, the sons of the same tenants continued to till the land. The
new king expected the zamindars to extract every bit of juice from
the rural fruit and, sure enough, the zamindars did it with gusto,
using local thugs to intimidate the peasants. Everything you ever
saw in a 1960s Hindi movie about life in the rural hinterland is
exactly how it was. The only change was one oppressor replaced
another. If there was a law court to go to, the court would have said
that the king had the sovereign power to take the land and give it
to another and there was nothing to be done about it. Where was
the justice in any of this? Law is nothing but muscle-flexing kings
and company bahadurs doing what they wanted simply because
they could.

Then at last, India achieved independence and the tenants got
a vote. These new kings did not need the support of princes or their
soldiers, but they did need votes, which the peasants had. It made
sense for democratic governments to curry favour with tenants
and abandon the owners. New laws were now created, placing a
low ceiling on land holding and redistributing the 'surplus' land
to landless peasants. The zamindars mustered courage to go to
court but were lectured about the dawn of a new India. Where
was the justice for the zamindars in any of this? Law was nothing
but old wine in new bottles: arbitrary rules created to curry favour
with the new majority supporters of the new rulers under a new
political order.

As time went by, cities started to grow and soon edged up to villages. Villagers had by now figured that elected rulers were not going to do anything for them or their country. They figured political promises were made to be broken. The peasants decided that if the politicians wanted something, they would have to buy it for cash. Where were the new rulers to get the cash to fund their elections? Besides, the peasants were also selling their land to city dwellers. The new settlers had the votes too. It all came together beautifully. Upwardly mobile owners of new houses in new colonies provided the votes and colonizers and builders provided the cash. One day, the local government of one town issued a notice acquiring a whole village for a song and sent in the police to take possession of it. Taking possession of course means kicking everyone out of their homes. When the peasants went to court, the court told them that 'due process' had been followed and that the land was required for the 'public purpose' of generating housing. So the new rich urbanites got their bungalows in south Delhi, the politician got paid off, and the peasant ended up in a slum. Where was the justice in this? This was just a gang of wealthy people, their political frontmen and profiteering builders snatching assets from small landowners because they could.

Meanwhile, the world changed again. The bungalows were few and the demand was great. The owners split the bungalows and started renting out flats. The rulers realized that there were more tenants with votes than landlords. The political classes now ditched their landowner sponsors and promulgated rent-control laws. Suddenly, owners of flats couldn't chuck out the tenants and the tenants could pay the same rents for the next thirty years. The landlords who went to court and challenged the law were read a lecture about social engineering and protection of the weak. Where was the justice in this? This was just a bunch of cunning politicians expanding their appeal to the majority electorate at the cost of their former sponsors.

It's still not over, because the fat lady hasn't sung yet. In the mid-1980s, the tide once again started to turn. The pace of construction had slowed considerably. Builders didn't have too many bungalows to build. People who bought new houses wouldn't let tenants live in them. Actually a lot of these house-owners lived as tenants in other people's houses while keeping their own houses vacant! Landlords were screaming blue murder and builders wanted the real-estate sector to pick up its pace. Beginning 1988 or thereabouts, the politicians started amending rent-control laws. They killed these laws using two strategies. First they decided that tenants who paid rent above a certain amount could be chucked out. Second, they allowed rents to rise slowly so that eventually everyone was out of the rent-control net. What did this mean? Richer landlords who had bigger properties and collected higher rents could chuck out their tenants quicker than poorer landlords who had rented out small properties with smaller rents. Tenants who went to court to challenge these amendments were delivered a lecture about coveting the property of another and the changing needs of society. Where was the justice in this? It was just a bunch of rich owners and richer builders who banded together and screwed the tenants right back.

～

Let us ask ourselves what is really happening here. In this dynamic world of ever-changing laws that rob one person and reward another, only one thing is certain: in every case, a powerful group of people get together and make laws to get what they want and bulldoze over the rights of everyone else. We call these dominant guys the political elite. We need to recognize that man is ultimately a political animal, and in the use of the expression 'political', we speak of the acquisition, control and exercise of power over our fellow men. Societies are structured around those who exercise the most power. How is this power exercised? This power is exercised by creating new laws and then using these laws to screw other people. Thus, judicial systems set up by societies are intended primarily to serve the paramount interest of those who dominate those societies. It's possible that some sections of this elite may have more than a streak of do-good humanism in them. When this happens, they support all sorts of initiatives to work towards a better society. When the elite does not have more than a streak of do-good humanism in them, everyone else is profoundly pulverized to powder.

In any democratic society, the powerless basically have two choices: take to the streets in protest or go to a court for help. If they protest on the street, they face a lathi charge, an arrest, a jail term and, perhaps, even bullets. Shorn of the sugar-coated oratory, these protests are received with violence which encourages them to give up and go home. If they go to court, they are told 'the law' is against them. A judge may see the injustice, but he would hardly ever be able to help the fall guy. What can a judge do? He can hold that the law is illegal, but he can only do that if there is another 'higher' law in favour of these underdogs. Frequently, this higher law is the Constitution of India. If that is not an option, then it's curtains for the powerless. This is the harsh reality that every court faces, whatever its personal feelings on any subject.

That is not how the reality is projected though. Going back to our example of the bungalow in Delhi, during these sixty years since Independence, in almost every judgment on land ceiling, land acquisition, rent control or abolition of rent control, the overwhelming tone is righteous and rhetorical. Everyone knew that at each step, the lawmakers were following their self-interest.

Yet no court ever said, 'Look, this law may be a crime against one section of humanity and we understand why the politicians are playing the voting numbers game, but we must enforce it because that is what courts are here to mainly do.' In every case, lofty language and elevated moral posturing informed the court's decision. This is denial wrapped in moral oratory.

However, neither moral posturing nor moral outrage at moral posturing leaves us any wiser. It's the bottom line we have to recognize, so let us summarize it one more time. Almost every law favours one person and penalizes another. How we define justice depends on whose trumpet we blow. The courts enforce unjust laws all the time. Even if we forget about who is favoured by what law and get back to the basics, we still have to admit that courts have been established to enforce the law that has been enacted. So you can get a judge to deliver a legally correct decision but, unless the law is just, you can't get him to deliver a just decision. The judge runs a court of law; he doesn't preside over a court of justice.

It's important to understand this. The courts have been created to enforce the law. Laws flow from agendas of dominant groups of people: society's elite groups. These elite groups create laws in their own self-interest. Such laws cannot be fair to everyone, nor are they intended to be. If you are a judge, you work for an institution. You may not agree with the laws that the court is expected to enforce, but you can either do what the institution is set up to do or you can walk away. Either way, you cannot subvert that institution and do whatever you like. It does not matter if what you do is just or not. If what you do is not legal, you cannot do it. When the law is unjust, and many laws are, where is the question of anyone going to court to get justice?

～

Unfortunately, people who end up in a court case don't always understand this. Given the hard work it takes to go there, you wouldn't dream of going to court unless you had a huge perception of wrong, injury and injustice. If you are fighting a court case, the whole environment is clouded with a sense of outrage and moral righteousness. You would never admit you just may be wrong. Worse, you probably think that courts are here to right every wrong. Not just that, you probably think you are a better judge of what is right and wrong than the court is. You would be upset if the court did not totally agree with you. In fact, everyone in court on both sides of every case thinks exactly like you would. The result is a very confusing mix of angry clients, bewildered witnesses, cynical lawyers and exasperated judges. Justice is not what always gets done at the end of the day.

Now I am not suggesting that justice never gets done. I am definitely not suggesting that judges and lawyers are not trying to provide justice. Sometimes they succeed and this is good. But just as often, they can't succeed. I am not saying they don't or don't want to. I am saying they can't. There are many reasons why they can't. First, they can't because all laws are not just, as I earlier mentioned. Second, legal procedures are also never just. It all goes on endlessly. In our attempt to be fair, we are so fair to the person who is wrong that the person who is right gets his butt wiped with sandpaper. The procedure makes sure that everyone—and his favourite pet monkey—gets to say whatever rubbish he wants for as long as he wants till he runs out of things to say. So much is said that by the time it is all said, no one knows what anyone started out to say. And many of those who did the saying, listening or suffering are long dead or senile. It's ridiculous.

That said, it doesn't matter if it's ridiculous. If you go to court thinking that this is where you are going to get justice, you had just better accept that this is your tool of choice and you are going to have to live with the limitations of that tool. You can't buy a bike and then worry about rain all the time. A hammer doesn't run your arithmetical calculations for you; a computer does not fix a nail into a wall for you. The court is what it is; you have to deal with what is on your plate. Once I understood this, I started to get seriously good at running legal cases. The results came almost immediately, of which the proof was to follow within months.

Part III:
Rocking Steady

17

War Games in the Himalayas

As I said, having developed the correct 'mental attitude' to work, I suddenly found that I was able to deliver results to my clients effortlessly, without breaking a sweat. By the time my next life-changing client showed up at my door, I was itching to prove to myself how good I really was. That client was Weizmann, and its appearance resulted in two main consequences—it tested all my litigation skills and helped me make pots of money for the Dragons.

Weizmann found itself in trouble almost immediately after coming to India because it tried to compensate for earlier sins. It took too long to decide to come to India, and when it did, it wanted to do everything very quickly. Weizmann was at the time an engineering multinational with ventures in forty countries but it waffled about entering India till everyone else had already set up shop here. This was weird because it was a top global player in the auto-component manufacturing business. The market wanted Weizmann. By the time Weizmann figured out what it wanted, the big boys of the Indian car industry were all hitched up with their foreign bedfellows. Weizmann could either partner with a pipsqueak or 'learn' the local market the hard way on a greenfield project. Weizmann decided to go slumming instead.

In time, it acquired a publicly listed sick company near Chandigarh in Himachal Pradesh. This company was protected by the Board of Industrial and Financial Reconstruction (BIFR). Let's try and understand BIFR a little better. Traditionally, India did not have a bankruptcy protection law. In 1985, our parliament passed the Sick Industrial Companies (Special Provisions) Act. It was supposed to do what its name suggests: give legal protection to bankrupt companies till they can restructure and nurse themselves back to good financial health. What the law actually achieved in practice is another can of worms. As far as Weizmann was concerned, Gupta, the promoter of this sick company, was a flamboyant maverick who charmed everyone except the man-eating leopards he was authorized to shoot on government request from time to time. The first time I met him, he gifted me a photograph of himself with a look of sneering triumph holding up the head of what he called the 'Man-eating Leopard of Kyunkleshwar' sprawled across the bonnet of his green Maruti Gypsy, its face frozen in the agony of its death throes. I was revolted, but then, I was a new convert to the conservation movement and could not be philosophical about the inevitable extinction of these magnificent beasts in the wild. The fact though was that Gupta was a man of personal courage. Man-eaters usually have to be followed through thick underbrush on foot before being shot. Gupta had big balls.

Weizmann didn't buy Gupta's company for his balls: it bought the company because he had driven it into the ground and they thought it was cheap. They also bought it because it owned a state-of-the-art production line which Weizmann wanted. Basically, Weizmann didn't want to twiddle its thumbs for a year awaiting delivery of a new production line while it started a greenfield project. The Buddha says men in a hurry always take longer! Weizmann made the deal, picked up the majority of the equity and appointed the majority of directors on the board. They then got BIFR to rubber-stamp the rehabilitation scheme.

The honeymoon lasted a month. Before Weizmann's professional management had time to settle into their new jobs, Gupta went wink-wink nudge-nudge and told them about his magnificent financial jugglery, which had allowed him to reduce his disclosed losses to a quarter of the real figure. He thought he had done pretty well to keep the company from liquidation, but Weizmann was appalled. They authorized a forensic audit. What came out of the woodwork is exactly what tens of thousands of companies were doing in India and still continue to do. At the top of the list of rogue tricks was an accounting tactic called 'Non-reconciliation of Debtor Accounts'. The company produced rubbish for ten years which it could not sell. When this rubbish came back unsold from dealers, Gupta showed it in his books as still lying with dealers awaiting customers, not as rejected goods. He justified it by saying that a sick company under rehabilitation was too busy to reconcile its accounts. As far as Weizmann was concerned, Gupta had misled them by claiming that a lot of money was owed to the company by the market when the goods were already back with him. Even when Gupta did admit that he had his goods in his own factory, he showed it as stock-in-trade, not junk. He explained it away by calling it 'Non-reconciliation of Inventory'. Either way, Weizmann was confronted with the reality that Gupta had sold them an overvalued company, claiming to own more stock and be entitled to receive more money from the market than it did.

To top these two accounting frauds, Gupta also showed fictitious production and sales. To this category of accounting fraud, he gave the name 'Pre-booking of Sales'. How did he do this? He showed next year's production as booked for sale this year! He didn't think this was strange: after all the orders had been verbally received in this year and only dispatched next year! Weizmann could not digest this contrived rubbish about non-existent sales in a non-existent market to non-existent customers. To these major items, you could add the usual smaller scams that promoters of sick companies run, and he had three significant ones.

First, Gupta and his dodgy directors drew modest salaries but claimed large cash expenses on the company account. The accounting department was awash with fake vouchers without supporting documents towards travel, miscellaneous expenses, foreign trips, foreign exchange withdrawals, entertainment and so on. Next, he re-routed creditor payments to his personal accounts. He had a large number of unpaid creditors on the street. Gupta paid them by bearer cheque and pocketed the money himself. Finally, Gupta advanced loans to lowly employees and diverted the money to himself. Gupta said BIFR was forcing him to do all this. He said that he needed to round-trip the money back to the company to sustain the endless 'promoter quota' equity injections BIFR thrust on him. Weizmann could conclude that they had a devious and unscrupulous partner.

The real problem wasn't that Weizmann suddenly found itself in bed with a scoundrel; it was that it now had unlawful carnal knowledge of dirty deeds in the dark recesses of a basement it had purchased. This was a listed company. Weizmann was sitting on a time bomb, and they had a reputation to protect. To be silent was to become party to the fraud and join Gupta in perpetrating it upon the lenders, BIFR and public shareholders.

That apart, if Weizmann did not speak up, Gupta would soon be in a position to blackmail Weizmann. They could not clean out the toxic accounts without perpetrating another cluster of frauds. What was Weizmann to do?

In these sorts of matters, there is never a choice. What would you do if you found a skeleton in the house you just bought? Would you inform the cops, or just rebury the corpse? Weizmann bled out its heart to C.S. Mathur, one of Delhi's most respected Chartered Accountants, and he decided they needed a law firm. City Law walked into it wondering if Weizmann had the stomach for the inevitable war to come. Weizmann said they did. Since Weizmann already owned 65 per cent of the company, the fight would really happen at board meetings. Weizmann appointed chartered accountants and lawyers as alternate directors to the board and told their own directors to stay out of India for the moment. Effectively, Weizmann's gladiators occupied board seats, ready for full-contact warfare.

Effective control of a board does not mean effective control of a company. CEOs of companies have many powers that the board has given them. You can take the powers back but then who is to run the company? Weizmann had to terminate Gupta's services as CEO and they had to install one of their own men. Frankly, in a perfect world, it would be great to kick Gupta off the board of directors, but in the practical scheme of things, this was a problem because the law wouldn't allow it without a shareholders' meeting. A shareholders' meeting in a publicly listed sick industrial company is always an unpredictable animal. Those shareholders had invested in a good company and now it's sick: they have frustrations to vent and Weizmann didn't fancy being a target of that kind of emotional *atyachaar*. Not being able to remove Gupta did not mean that Weizmann couldn't 'strip him of his powers' for his misdemeanours if it could. To make it foolproof, they needed him to admit in writing that he had done these things. How were they going to achieve that? If Gupta found out that Weizmann had it in for him, he would go scurrying to court faster than you could say *'Draupadi ka cheer haran'*. Moreover, BIFR was the bigger 'unknown unknown' here. The company was still under BIFR protection: change the board status and you could end up with a bunch of bureaucrats conducting cavity searches with a magnifying glass. Weizmann needed to disrobe Gupta ritually, for a reason everyone could see. A confession would do very nicely.

Weizmann actually got the guy to confess. It was the Satyam story long before there was Satyam. Weizmann told Gupta they wanted to hold a board meeting to decide how to handle his financial disclosures. They asked him to prepare his own 'explanation' for submission to the board. Weizmann didn't care how hard Gupta justified his actions as long as he admitted he had done it. Once the cat was out, it would chew Gupta's frisky bushy tail for lunch. Gupta was bewildered: what was the point of an explanation? Everyone knew how these things worked! Every Indian company has the same dressed-up accounts! What are you trying to achieve? Weizmann played possum. This is not an Indian-owned company any more, Mr Gupta, they explained, and so we do it our way. Gupta threw up his hands in exasperation. Everyone knows these foreigners are crazy. In two days, Gupta and his finance director had signed and delivered their own company exit plan!

It was now time for Weizmann to ritually wash its hands in public and crucify Gupta. Weizmann could not circulate an agenda with an item on throwing out Gupta and his finance director! Subversion was necessary. We prepared a resolution on 'consideration of accounts' and added Gupta's explanation in the Notes as the lethal injection. The die was cast. The board met in one of the conference halls of Delhi's Hyatt Regency. Gupta came in whistling flamboyantly like Dev Anand in a 1960s romantic comedy, not a care in the world. It was a full house with eleven directors, six of them Weizmann nominees. The orchestration was perfect. Weizmann directors tore into Gupta's Explanatory Note like they were hyenas feeding on a fresh kill. Independent directors appointed by lending banks abstained from uttering a word. Like a good whipping boy, the BIFR director wanted the board to decide nothing, referring every issue before it for decision to the bureaucrats at BIFR. Gupta was largely shell-shocked, dumbfounded by what he must have seen as a betrayal.

To cut a long story short, the board booted him, and his finance director, out of their executive positions, leaving them naked and powerless. Weizmann was now in complete management control. The memory that remains though is of Gupta bravely standing there consuming his post-meeting lunch, only speaking to those who approached him. He was seething with rage. I should have been sad at our duplicity, but I was as jubilant as is possible for any truly amoral professional singing for his supper. Somehow, the post lunch tiramisu tasted just that much sweeter. It's best for us lawyers always to remember that butchery is our business.

The days after this Hyatt Hotel Haldighati *yudh* were awfully quiet. Gupta filed a complaint before BIFR but his confession letter shut them down pretty quickly. In private, BIFR stated that it was here to rehabilitate the company, not settle shareholders' disputes. In a country where the judiciary doesn't function very efficiently in settling commercial disputes, what do you expect a bunch of bureaucrats to achieve when the going gets rough and contentious? Weizmann progressively sank its teeth deeper into the innards of the factory, as its newly appointed German-speaking NRI CEO Kaustav Sarkar strutted about like a boot-camp sergeant—a latter-day Asrani in *Sholay*—throwing his weight around, making an ass of himself. Everyone hated the man. He was hostile, antsy and paranoid. For the second in command, he hired his wife's brother! Yes, the guy behaved like an Indian politician.

As for us, we practised our sarcasm on him. Since his lawyers were his directors on the board to which he reported, he had no one to complain to. For sure he did dumb things, but Shanx really treated him like garbage. Two months into his appointment, we were all in Timber Trail Resort in Parwanoo munching on his newly unveiled business plan for the company. The directors were not amused: he had forgotten to budget any money for marketing or sales. How did he expect to sell in the market if he had no marketing budget? The directors rejected his plan, and sent him back to rewrite one, as if he was Johnny Misdemeanour caught speaking to Tom in the class when the teacher was explaining something. It was pathetic.

In truth, he did try and get back at us. He tried to participate in lawyers' meetings, but found himself without the database to carry on the conversation intelligently. If you don't know enough of the law, no matter what else you know or how smart you are, you are going to look like a dunce. He asked dumb questions, then argued with the answers, then got trashed for his comments. Eventually, Weizmann told him to concentrate on business and let us manage the litigation. His last gift to us was to recommend that we use his landlord's son as our lawyer in Chandigarh. I felt bad for what we lawyers did to him, so I agreed, but it was a blunder. In fairness, it was a very lucrative blunder but I got whipped for it and rightly so too. You don't hire a fancy law firm; throw megabucks at it only to then eat a stay order.

The bullfrog snot hit the fan because the company lost its auditor. If you helped Gupta make his sagging accounts look like Shah Rukh's six-pack abs, you would be sacked too! We needed shareholders' approval to appoint another. Then there were new additional directors to confirm to the board. Weizmann convened a shareholders' meeting, and we all trooped down to Mount View Hotel in our best suits to mingle with public shareholders and 'gauge the mood'. It was not to be. Twenty minutes before the meeting, Gupta came in, a court process server in tow, flashing a 'stay order': the Shimla High Court had prohibited the company from taking orders from its own shareholders! Given all that the Supreme Court had been saying about 'shareholder sovereignty' over the years, this was of another order of unreality. I didn't pause to take in the stick that would inevitably come my way for not anticipating this. I jumped into the nearest cab with my youngsters in attendance and hightailed it to Shimla.

It wasn't that hot a case. I must have read it five times over. Gupta repeated 'joint-venture agreement' (and his role in it) on every second page, repeating it like a Sanskrit mantra he didn't understand. Basically, he was saying that he had a role in the company etched in stone, which no one could change no matter what. It was our job to explain to the judge that what he had done was enough to send him to the dungeons. The problem was we had to do it in a court located in a holiday resort. Shimla High Court in those days was a fun place. Judges lived a stress-free life and worked in a brand-new building sitting on what used to be a grassy knoll not far from the Oberoi Clarkes Hotel right by the Ridge market. They lived the Brown Sahib's life in spacious Raj-era bungalows and walked to work when the mood took them. When they were not listening to long-suffering businessmen complaining about the arbitrary ways of state-level bureaucrats, they were listening to lamenting bureaucrats asking for more privileges and equal treatment under this or that service rule. It was tender matters and service matters all the way, and Gupta's company matter stuck out like a sore thumb. The court's rustiness with this branch of law showed too. Mostly, it showed that since Gupta had his stay order, he wanted to hang on to it for dear life. He dragged his feet, and we suffered adjournment after adjournment, while happily tucking into the pepper pork chops at the Clarkes day after day.

Of course, we shouted ourselves hoarse every time we suffered an adjournment. The joint-venture agreement was a private agreement between two shareholders but this was a publicly listed company with many shareholders: why had the rights of these public shareholders been suspended? Why was the court stopping shareholders' meetings of a public company at all? How could a court force a company to use the services of any servant (read Gupta as managing director), let alone one who confesses to doctoring accounts? The court could compensate Gupta by giving him his salary for the remaining period of service, but how could it grant a stay order? Gupta's lawyers used all the diversionary tactics in their arsenal to avoid a hearing. Why not let BIFR decide this question? Why not let an arbitrator decide it in arbitration? The judge understood what Gupta was doing. 'I am prepared to suffer the labour pains of hearing you both,' the judge quipped, 'but let it be understood, at the end I have to deliver something!' The entire court was in splits of laughter. Eventually, the court's patience gave out. It decided that the partners were free to go to arbitration and fight their supremacy battles but the shareholders' meeting of a public company could not be delayed any longer.

Given the enormity of the problems every court has to deal with, humour in court is as therapeutic for judges as it is for lawyers. Sometimes, it can be at the expense of lawyers. One of my favourite Tees Hazari judges who made it up to the High Court was this sardonic Sikh with a peculiar talent for plain speaking. Let's call him Justice Singh. The story goes that his marital life fell apart because shortly after he brought his bride home, his father-in-law sent a favour-seeker to him with a chit instructing him to help the guy. Justice Singh was nothing if he was not principled. He declined to interfere, which put two immoveable sardarjis on a collision course. His father-in-law gave him a choice: help the man or lose the wife. Justice Singh preferred to abide by his principles, living the rest of his life by himself. He served long as a district judge and was one man who took a dim view of the role of families in breaking up marriages. I loved him because he was very kind to youngsters like me but I loved him all the more because he would cut through to the chase like no one. For example, when it came to granting adjournments.

Lawyers ask for adjournments all the time. The system doesn't exist to render quick justice: it exists to serve the purposes of the service providers—judges, court clerks, lawyers, etc. So if getting the case heard on a particular date of hearing doesn't work for us, we'll find a way to take a 'date', and no, the irony of 'dating' a judge is not lost on me! Now, you can't just walk up to a judge and tell him you don't want to work. He will decline right away and push you around. It's a game so old we've all forgotten why we play it, especially since we all know that perhaps one hearing in four is ever likely to be effective. Still, to get a 'date', you have to spin a yarn.

I recall sitting in his court one day as Justice Singh presided on the civic side of the High Court. A young woman lawyer stood up to speak as her case was called. 'Lordships, I am for the plaintiff and

I had filed an application seeking documents from the defendant.'
Justice Singh looked bored. 'What documents do you want?'
The lady now launched out. 'Me luds, to explain the situation,
I had filed a suit where I had prayed for temporary injunction
and damages in July of so-and-so year. Thereafter, lordships, the
defendant appeared in May of that year. Thereafter, lordships,
he filed his written statement (of defence) in September of that
year. Now, in para XYZ of this written statement, he has relied on
certain documents which I do not have a copy of. So, lordships, I
had filed an application in October of so-and-so year. Now to that,
my lords, in paragraph xx of his reply, he has said that he does not
have the document. Now, my lord, without the document I can't
argue my case so . . . May it please your lordships, I may be granted
these documents . . .' she slowly trailed off. There was utter silence
in court. What was the point of this long explanation?

Defence attorney Mr Luthra, a true gentleman who had taught
me Hindu law back in law school, slowly got to his feet and offered
his thoughts in impeccable English. 'My lords, I have stated that
I do not have these documents. There is nothing more for me to
add.' The lady was dissatisfied. 'But, lordships, I cannot argue
this case unless I have read those documents.' There was another
silence. Mr Luthra cleared his throat. 'My lords, if it is my learned
friend's grievance that I am deliberately not supplying documents,
the court will make me suffer the consequences of failing to do
so.' The lady was still dissatisfied. 'But, lordships, I cannot argue
this case without these documents!' Now everyone was confused.
'Lordships, I truly don't understand what my learned friend wants
when I don't have the documents,' Mr Luthra offered. Another
silence followed. Justice Singh scratched his cheek, a mischievous
smile playing behind his fuzzy beard.

'You know, Counsel,' he offered in his Punjabi-accented
English, 'George Bernard Shaw said at the end of his life that he

had studied women for sixty-five years.' We all waited for more. 'And he said, still, after all these years, I do not know what a woman wants.' Mr Luthra stood very still. 'Do you expect,' the judge continued, 'to have better luck than an intellectual as great as Shaw?' Mr Luthra was not one to disrespect a colleague. He stood silent. In the absence of a retort, Justice Singh concluded, 'She wants a date!'

Of course he was right and because she had been so ingenious in positioning her request, she got what she wanted. I do urge you to make allowance for the tenor of the times. None of us were gender-paranoid in those days in the way we are now and I wouldn't want you to think poorly of Justice Singh.

Courts could be entertaining in all sorts of ways. About the most fun we had in the Delhi High Court was in the court of Justice Narang, perhaps the most data-dense judge it has ever been my privilege to experience. He was a storehouse of knowledge, down to every possible intricate detail. You couldn't get half a fact past him; he would seize the opportunity and expand on what you were saying. If you were wrong on a bit of it, he would fill in the blanks, and then some more. Many eminent counsels have squirmed as he has cut them to size, nuancing what they were saying with masses of facts. Others have had to suffer long scenic drives around the shores of this ocean of knowledge with no particular destination in mind. Counsels in his court were judged by their ability to get him back on track in a finite timeline. Sometimes, they ended up with mud on their faces.

Like the time he heard an application under IPR law trying to stop counterfeiters from using the name 'Kama Sutra' on women's wear. A company called J.K. Ansell launched Kamasutra condoms in 1991, accompanied by a very visually explicit advertising campaign featuring Pooja Bedi and Marc Robinson, selling sensuality and pleasure rather than the birth-control measure it actually was. How could the already over-populated sexually hyperactive, largely repressed society of the time not be obsessed by the steamy scenes and provocative imagery? It took the market by storm and sales of the brand zoomed to the top in months. Duplicators were on to it in no time, trying to sell Kama Sutra kachhas and Kama Sutra kurtas by the bushel. J.K. didn't like that, so to the Delhi High Court they went.

Delhi High Court has long been and still remains the best place to get legal relief in IPR infringement cases. Not this time. Justice Narang was unmoved. 'It is one of the greatest treatises about love ever written in the world,' he thundered. 'I am not going to give you exclusive rights over a 2000-year-old work of classical literature.' The lawyer begged and pleaded. 'Lordships, my client has spent this many million on the campaign and has placed advertisements in so many magazines and so many newspapers,' etc. etc. Justice Narang only sneered. 'Young man,' he said, 'for 2000 years, millions of couples have experienced the epitome of sexual love as a result of Vatsyayana's great book. This book is a central part of our culture, a vital part of our collective knowledge, an inalienable part of our identity as Indians. Today you say that you are superseding the collective historical experience of generations of people with your advertising budget?' With that, he launched into a half-hour scenic detour of what the Kama Sutra says and what it means. Now let me admit that I tried to read the damn book. It is unreadable. It doesn't even titillate. It's eighteen positions of this and seventeen positions of that and how to flutter your eyelashes in between. It's tedious, but to hear Justice Narang describe it was as enriching as any lecture I have ever heard on classical literature. Truly, if you want to experience intellectual giants, this is the profession to pursue.

To return to my leopard-shooting adversary, Gupta's day was lost in the Shimla High Court but his spirit was not broken. He now started the guerrilla tactics type of war, where he aimed to harass and harm, but with no real expectation of winning a major battle. I learnt then that even if you are down and more or less close to out, it profits you never to quit, never say die. If your enemy will not pay you because your enemy cannot function without your cooperation, he will pay you to go away because dealing with the allegations you fling around becomes unbearable after a while. Gupta made sure Weizmann was enmeshed in litigation after litigation. Since he could not stop the upcoming shareholders' meeting, he financed a small public shareholder to try his luck. This guy filed a stay order in a nondescript court in Solan. Unless you drank a lot of beer or rum, you are unlikely to have heard of Solan. It's next to Barog, the highest point on the Kalka-Shimla road and home to a beautifully situated hilltop hotel called Barog Heights. They aren't kidding about the 'heights'. I would know because I have spent more time eating greasy chicken masala there than most people have had hot dinners.

How did I find out that a case had been filed in Solan? I had wised up after I was hit with the first stay order. I had a lawyer appointed to check the court's filing in every district court in southern Himachal Pradesh, plus Chandigarh and Delhi! The case was filed at 2 p.m., the local lawyer called me at 4 p.m., I took the Himalayan Queen from Old Delhi Station at 10.30 p.m., I reached Kalka at 5.45 a.m., I picked up a leisurely breakfast at Timber Trail in Parwanoo at 7 a.m. and changed into my black coat and bands. At 9 a.m., I was cooling my heels in Hotel Himani at the gate of Solan District Court waiting for someone to come and unlock the doors! The case was a walkover. I told the local lawyer I wanted time to argue the matter. He shrugged. No problem. The local lawyer didn't wait for the case to be called: he simply walked up to the judge the moment the judge sat down to start court proceedings and asked for a week. The judge nodded. That was it. By the time the week was up, I had filed 200 pages of pleadings and another 400 pages of documents in support. Any judge deciding that case would have to deal with 600 pages, a truly scary prospect. Plus he would have to deal with a *bara vakil* from Delhi who probably spoke some Latin gibberish and confused everyone with convoluted English-*vinglish*. Crudely put, I buried the case under the record.

~

Gupta wasn't done yet and, with each day, my respect for his spirit grew. He instigated marginal employees to start an agitation. He financed litigation by third parties with a grouse against the company. He made a third attempt to get another stay order, which I again picked up in time and stalled the action. I spent the next year scurrying up and down the hills. If Indian Railways had launched a Frequent Shatabdi Rider Programme, I would have earned a lifetime supply of tickets. I spent thirty days in Oberoi Cecil in one year. When I booked for the tenth time that year for a hearing two days before Christmas, they called me up and encouraged me to bring my family at no extra cost. I did. I frolicked about the pool with the kids as the judge posted the case to the next day, then spent the evenings listening to *Coco Jambo*–type pop-for-duds music in the lobby lounge. The hotel gifted me a set of pictures and a bottle of champagne, which I shamelessly exchanged for an Islay malt. The clouds gathered low and heavy, and we all prayed for a white Christmas. It was not to be and when I left on 26 December, Citibank declined to honour my credit card! How's that for a KLPD?

It wasn't Citibank's fault. I had exceeded my credit limit and, City Law's dysfunctional accounts department being what it was, there was no easy fix ready. The hotel was graceful to a fault. They said I could send them a cheque later, but the whole experience so humiliated me that I never stayed in the Cecil again, preferring to hide my shame in Clarkes! There was no way to hide the legal costs though, and Weizmann was really hassled with Gupta's proliferating attacks. How can any director go on and on suing his own company, even instigating others to do so? They thundered that they wanted Gupta chucked out of the board. It wasn't possible. You couldn't remove a director without getting shareholders' consent. This would give Gupta a chance to defend himself before those same shareholders. Remember, these were public shareholders. It would be like letting the bulls run through Chandni Chowk in time for the evening prayers on a Friday. Besides, if you were a parochial type, thoughts of a latter-day rapacious British East India Company would be in your mind, wouldn't they?

At the end of the day, a settlement had to be made. We resisted. The battle had been won. They were making crocodile bites out of mosquito bites. Every business has its share of irritants. Even if your partner isn't a leopard-shooting hotshot, there will always be some other masked joker playing Phantom in a purple suit with laughable black undies on top: why let it get you down? No can do, said the client. They had had enough. Just as their impatience got them into trouble in the first place, their lack of patience sent them suing for peace. Not that Gupta hadn't earned it. He had made enough of a nuisance of himself to deserve a generous settlement. I wasn't there when they went to talk to him. I am sure he was more surprised than most: I mean he hadn't been THAT much trouble. But there was learning in that too. You never know how much trouble you are to the other side because you aren't keeping the appointment the other side is. If making trouble is your strategy, you just have to keep making it dispassionately. If your name is Gupta, it will pay off sooner rather than later. This is how it ended, with Gupta bringing an end to one of the most exciting periods of my life in City Law.

Of course, every ending is only a new beginning. In the years since this case, I have asked myself what really happened to me here. I can think of several answers. The first great lesson I learnt was of the supremacy of logistics. Litigation is mainly about getting the organization right. In the years since, I have dealt with no end of multi-jurisdiction, multi-court, multi-action, multi-party complex litigation. When push comes to shove, it's always the same thing: you have to manage a lot of lawyers in a lot of cities, and, as often as not, that is the management of a lot of very fragile, very oversized, very sensitive egos. You also have to be able to work with a disparate variety of thought leaders steeped in their regional cultural prejudices. You have to be willing to hear trash about what works and what does not. You have to be ready and willing to put up with half-assed legal knowledge in the name of experience. You have to humour the humourless. Then, when everyone has exhausted themselves, you still have to be able to dispassionately get down to it and digest the masses of facts emerging from a dozen courts and the point and counterpoint in each of them. You also have to then be able to put them all together and write the pleadings and the notes on argument in each of them yourself. That's the only real secret of successful complex litigation.

Beyond the management of such cases, the Weizmann case became for me the ultimate song of hope for the weak and the powerless. In Gupta's actions, I learnt that it is entirely possible for one poorly financed man to fight an entire corporation, if he picks his battles well, and knows how to manage his costs. I learnt that the bigger the enemy, the bigger his cost in managing any battle. If you are a little guy, you decide what you do, whereas with him, a general meeting of lawyers, management, accountants and compliance officials was required to get anything done. Chances are pretty good you will lose whatever you do, but your giant of an enemy will bleed money and, ultimately, if you keep fighting well and losing well, he will wilt. It has not been my good fortune to fight for too many small guys, but when I do, it's always fun to roger royalty royally. When it comes to fighting the government of India, you pretty much use the same tactics you would if you were fighting a way more powerful enemy. That is what I did next.

18

Korea Rope Tricks

You generally notice radical paradigm shifts well after they have occurred. This is why many flourishing businesses suddenly find they've gone out of fashion long before they've noticed how the wind is blowing. Ask Blackberry and Nokia. It's happened to many of my clients too. As a lawyer I have had a ringside view of the legal fallout of these shifts. Clients who were flush with cash—who paid me generously to do legal workshops for their key employees—suddenly found themselves awash in litigation, unable even to pay my bills! More likely than not, they kept using my services while delaying payment till they had run up quite a debt. At this point, they generally told me that my services were deficient and then sacked me, replacing me with a nondescript small-timer from nowhere who claimed to offer the same service for a quarter of the cost. Two years later, when he couldn't deliver on the service, he was sacked in turn, but by this time both the unpaid bills and the quality of service I'd provided had long been forgotten.

I am not alone in absorbing bad debt, but not every lawyer takes it lying down. I once helped Pearl Tours and Travels run a deal with the defunct airline Canada 3000. When Canada 3000 went down within days of the World Trade Centre twin towers, their lawyer hit the High Court with a petition attaching all the airline's office furniture in payment of his legal fees. The Hindi metaphor 'grabbing the underwear of an escaping thief' came to mind! On my part, I have never sued a client for failing to pay my fees, nor have I ever withheld original papers that the client has placed in my custody. There is no special reason for this. Lee Falk told us that Phantom is rough with ruffians, and I guess I should be too. Somehow, I just don't want that life. When you are dealing with people on whom fate does not smile, you can either walk away from the bad karma or join fate in screwing them. I don't like to screw the terminally screwed. The downside is that I have tens of crores of bad debts in my books. I keep telling myself that I have consigned a hundred dodgy clients to hell for ripping me off! I actually believe that you always pay the price for the things you do, one way or another. That still leaves you free to laugh at the fate of a lawyer who is unable to collect crores in debt his own clients owe him. Bang a drum for the efficiency of the Indian legal system, and the faith of its key service providers!

But I digress: we were talking about paradigm shifts. If you are suitably menopausal—meaning about fifty years old—you will recall Akai's entry into India circa 1994. Colour TVs and music systems were high-priced lifestyle luxuries at the time, selling for multiples of tens of thousands of rupees. Akai dramatically dropped the price of consumer electronics in 1994 to a third of their ruling prices, selling colour TVs for less than Rs 10,000, and hi-fi 1500-watt 3-in-1s for Rs 15,000. From a turnover of 2500 TVs in 1995, they went on to sell 450,000 sets in 1998. It took us Indians some time to figure out that this had little to do with the

Japanese company: a Mumbai entrepreneur named Mulchandani had licensed the brand and was selling us junk. By 2000, most of us had trashed our Akai TV sets and 'stereo systems' in disgust. No matter that Akai went bust in India, Mulchandani's tactics made high-end electronics accessible to the middle class for the first time. Never again could an Indian company diddle us by selling junk products at premium prices.

Akai wasn't alone in setting India's consumer electronics sector on fire. In September 2005, LG announced that it would blow Rs 9 billion in capital expansion in India in the next three years. In December the same year, Samsung entered India with another big bang. With little cash to spend while I was still employed by City Law, I paid not the slightest attention to them, till some years later our client Spark Electricals started delaying payment of our bills. Now that was a sign I could read like a frisky mouse in a blouse! Inquiries revealed that the Korean companies were screwing Spark on prices. Spark, which was set up in India in 1991, was a global leading manufacturer of white goods. They had a manufacturing facility in Haryana and sold state-of-the-art products. What was going on?

As I dug deeper, I learnt that Spark's competitors were selling goods 10–12 per cent cheaper. Since everyone was sourcing parts from the same or similar vendors, how could others sell the same goods at a cheaper price? To answer this question, you have to understand how India's sales tax regime was structured at the time. Under our Constitution, the central government and each state government is entitled to collect sales tax. State governments collect tax on sales occurring within their borders while the central government collects tax on 'interstate sales'. The state governments are, of course, notoriously bad at managing their finances. They compensate by charging higher and higher sales tax. By way of contrast, the central government keeps its tax rates nice and low.

Naturally, everyone loves an interstate sale a whole heap more: thinking local and buying global so to speak!

It didn't end there. From time to time, both the Union of India and the states tried to promote industry in 'backward areas' by offering sales tax holidays. Daman and Silvassa were two very good examples at the time. If you set up a manufacturing facility in a tax haven, you paid no sales tax on both local sales and interstate sales. But setting up new factories in tax havens costs a lot of money. Besides, the tax holidays only last a few years and it is not financially viable to spend a lot of money setting up new factories so that you may earn marginally more for a few years. The only real solution then is to keep your existing factories going but to send almost-ready goods to these tax-haven factories to screw in the last few assemblies of your product, whatever it is.

Naturally, in a competitive sector like white goods, every manufacturer rushed to set up 'screwdriver' facilities in these desi tax havens. These were bare-bones sheds built on a wafer-thin budget. They kept their very expensive main factories entirely intact. They partly assembled the machines, shipped the sub-assemblies to their screwdriver factories and finished the job in the tax haven. They then offered direct sales from these tax havens to the customers' homes, taking advantage of the tax-free holiday in these havens. That's where the problem came in.

Of course, not everyone had a friendly neighbourhood tax haven to gain competitive advantage from. As the joys of these tax havens became more widely known, people figured they could run a similar scheme from the many union territories that dot India. Central sales tax is always lower than local state sales tax. If you were a Chennai-based dealer selling white goods, you could sell your stuff 10 per cent cheaper by shipping it from, say, Pondicherry, a union territory, than you could by making a local sale. In time, this tax artistry became the default transaction format for goods being sold in price-sensitive markets, like those of consumer durables.

If you lived in Chennai and wanted a washing machine, you had two choices. You could either drive down to Pondicherry and buy the machine, ferrying it back yourself, or you could place an order with the Pondicherry dealer and he would make a smooth interstate sale to you. That was the theory. In practice, no one went down to Pondi to buy a washing machine because no one wanted to ruin the rear suspension of their sexy new white Maruti 800 by loading a fifty-kilogram machine into it, or worse, the old Lambretta (the type Subroto Roy loves to display) which did transportation duties for the family before the Maruti 800 came along. If a manufacturer wanted to make a sale, he had to offer his customers a cross-border courier, who collected the money from the customer's home, zipped across to Pondicherry, bought a washing machine with a local bill and then delivered it the next day to the customer in Chennai. How much imagination does it take for us to realize that in practice, people were paying the Chennai dealer and he was delivering the washing machine with a Pondicherry bill the next day? In fact, was the machine ever in Pondicherry or had the bill book been moved to Chennai? Of such stuff are tax frauds constructed!

Okay, forget about the local Pondicherry sale, because by law, the dealer could just as easily make a cross-border sale. The problem is he now has to manage his inventory in both Pondicherry and Chennai. That's only possible if he can predict the proportion of people who will be happy to pay Tamil Nadu tax and those who prefer to pay the lower central sales tax in Pondicherry. In practice, the dealer would get it wrong several times a month. What happened then?

Check out the scenario. A customer wants a washing machine as of yesterday but he isn't going to pay Tamil Nadu tax. 'No

problem, *saar*, we will deliver from Pondi in twenty-four hours!'
The customer smiles and exits, dissolving in a cloud of high
humidity and coconut oil. The dealer then calls Pondi. 'Sorry saar,
ille machine in *stockaye.*' Now what? The customer isn't going to
wait for the next regular stock transfer of a hundred machines to
Pondi in the ordinary course of business. No problem, man, send
four machines now to Pondi in a small tempo and bring one back
tomorrow! I'm not joking: everyone was doing it. If the diesel
cost of a round trip was lower than the difference between local
and interstate sales tax, the customer would lap it up gleefully.
You know this is true: we Indians are stingy in a very mindless
way. How long would it take for the dealer to figure that he could
leave the washing machine in Chennai and save on the diesel?
All he had to do was create a 'movement document', something
to show that a tempo had moved from the state and another
had moved back the next day. How do you think the sales tax
department inspectors on border check-posts build those lovely
chocolate-cake Madrasi Baroque houses in the Tamil Nadu
countryside?

As the years went by, exactly like the signature nightgown of
a high-end designer label, this simple tax dodge acquired all sorts
of beautiful frills. To cut delivery times, if the Chennai dealer had
ten washing machines to deliver, he placed an order of twenty
in Pondicherry, ten of them disclosing fictitious customers on
fabricated addresses. As and when a customer dropped by for a
washing machine, he switched names in his sales records and sold
a machine meant for Zeiglveit B Schtoonk to . . . well, Zambar
Bhootalingam Subramanium. Eventually, it all came down to
Invoice Musical Chairs. All the machines were locally supplied.
If you purchased one, you got your machine immediately and
an invoice two weeks later because the dealer needed to create a
paper and 'machine movement' trail before he could give you the

invoice. Most customers were paying cash, aka tax-free money, so who cared anyway?

This is how the index of Gross National Happiness is increased, and Spark in its ignorance rewarded its employees for its sparkling sales performance. Spark was sitting on a time bomb. Eventually, the tax sleuths would blow the scam wide open and then there would be billions to pay in taxes. The curtain went up on this impending disaster when in a random survey of one of Spark's outlets, local tax authorities found a little black book which revealed which machine ordered by which fictitious customer and on what date was delivered to which other customer and against which order. They grabbed the book. Three days later, they raided every Spark dealer and every company property and the scam had split wide open.

~

For a start, Spark's regional legal executive wanted to know what was going on. I used to do a lot of forensic stuff in those days, so I set off with my youngsters and off we went sniffing up every Spark alleyway. I'm not kidding about the forensic stuff. I sat under a tree filling papers while my enthusiastic youngsters stripped down to their boxer shorts and climbed up stacks of cartons fifteen feet high to read serial numbers of machines in the loathsome leather-dye-stained lanes of Tangra in Kolkata. I sat in an airless room on the outskirts of Pondicherry and spent days poring over the incoming and outgoing registers of the company. I went to Daman and had Spark deliver its entire production record to my room in a beachside hotel. I then spent most of the night poring over the fine print while outside my door, a gang of delectable Gujaratis danced away the night, doing their bootleg garba to Hindi pop hits played ear-splittingly loud. Too late did I realize that beachside hotels in Daman are addas for thirsty youngsters from neighbouring booze-free Gujarat who came by the busload at weekends and partied till the wee hours. To our credit, in a month, we had cracked the whole damn scheme down to its knucklebones.

Shanx wasn't amused: he served on the board and could be sued for any tax dodges the company was running. He decided to go over the heads of the local management directly to the head office in Singapore. We arrived in Singapore within a week of asking for our appointment, laden with papers. The regional compliance guy wasn't going to take it on his head: he kicked the matter upstairs to the regional finance head. The regional finance head wasn't going to take it on his head either: he kicked it up to the Asia-Pacific CEO. This procedure took several weeks and two more trips to Singapore complete with platefuls of chili crab at Clarke Quay. By the time someone ready to deal with the situation looked at the problem, the potential liability was probably another million.

Eventually, on our fourth trip to Singapore in as many weeks, we had a grand Star Chamber impeachment ceremony. The Asia-Pacific head sat at the head of the table, affecting the stern stare of a provincial school principal. He was a mousy man, formerly of finance, much taken in by the new corporate fad of being thin. He tucked his mouth under the conference table from time to time till it reached his knees munching on a cereal bar, trying to kill his hunger pangs. All the other Asia-Pacific supervisors maintained a fraudulent air of moral outrage, dishing out ethical homilies, knowing full well their salaries came from the profits the salesmen had generated. The Indian CEO sat slumped in his seat, a little bewildered. Clearly, everyone had followed his orders to increase sales without telling him how they were going to do it. I found myself playing Rajat Sharma in *Aap Ki Adalat* without the sarcastic barbs. I reeled out the facts, addressing each regional head in turn, laid out the liability created, and pointed out the obvious illegalities they had committed. The regional heads denied nothing, trying to brazen it out. Do you want sales or don't you? Give us cheaper machines to sell, or let us do what the Koreans do!

It was never going to work. Credible deniability lies at the heart of the compliance regimen of every company. Once the cat is out of the bag, you have to fill body bags. Spark lost three of its four regional sales heads in an hour. The only one who survived managed the East—he didn't have sales enough to fake anything—and his incompetence became his greatest asset! One year later, the Koreans ate up much of Spark's market share, exactly like they do those small slithering live octopi back home in Seoul. Spark's sales were reduced to half the previous year's numbers.

Declining sales came with expanding legal costs. Time only worsened the legal outlook. Our interviews with Spark's Pondicherry sales manager revealed that he had received some sort of invitation from the local sales tax office to which he had gleefully responded without telling his bosses. It seems he had gone there seven or eight times, making sure he signed their register every time. He claimed they asked him inane questions over tea and biscuits. It soon became clear that, unknown to this somewhat naive employee, all his visits to the sales tax officer were being showed as formal legal hearings. I wasn't surprised. If you handle cases with the government long enough, you come to realize that it will cheat, lie and defraud its citizens without a second thought. In the upshot, we went careering into the office of the Pondicherry sales tax department only to be told that they had reopened all of Spark's sales tax demands seven months back and were going to raise new demands. They were as good as their word. One week later came the news that they had disallowed all interstate sales for the current assessment.

It was by no means the worst of it. The next meeting with the local sales tax officer delivered another bitter blow: he flashed a draft unsigned order which he said covered all the reopened assessment. He had made up his mind, he said, but wanted to make sure that procedures were followed 'so that justice is seen to be done'. Just to make sure we believe completely every depiction we see of corrupt bureaucrats in Hindi movies, he added for good measure that he would be delighted to meet any Spark official at home in a personal capacity over a cup of tea so that he could demonstrate his goodwill to the company. Spark didn't need a second invite. A mid-level Spark official was knocking at his residence the same evening, to be told that they should prepare to receive a demand of Rs 40 crore. The way sales tax laws are structured, your accuser is your judge. You can take it that if you get a notice, you are going to get a demand. To appeal that demand, you generally have to deposit 25 per cent of the demand. Everyone knew this. Since the pre-deposit to have a 40-crore-rupee order heard in appeal was Rs 10 crore, the sales tax officer added that perhaps it was a good idea to consider how much they would be willing to spend to avoid all this trouble. He concluded by delivering a well-aimed homily: he was always ready and willing to help everyone, and litigation was not a solution!

While these shenanigans played out down south, we continued our fortnightly round trips to Singapore, reporting on developments and the state of our investigations. We were still poring over the records across the country and had, by now, established that Spark's sales were generally what they claimed to be. Where they did not match, there were few if any documents on record to show whether they were interstate or local sales in the customer's town. About 20 per cent of the unknown customers had not collected their machines personally. They had sent their representatives with unusual names like Babu Lal and Ram Kumar to collect their purchases. Each of these Babu Lals and Ram Kumars collected an awful lot of machines. Curiously, all the Babu Lals and Ram Kumars within the state of Tamil Nadu owned, between them, only about three ballpoint pens. And all these authority letters seemed to have been written using the same two or three pens. There was no way I was going to produce these records before any court.

When you don't know how to defend a legal case, the best thing you can do is seize the initiative and go all aggressive on technical rules and regulations. It doesn't have to be airtight. If it has good 'dressage'—meaning it looks good till you take the clothes off—it's good enough to file successive appeals all the way to the Supreme Court. That kind of process takes ten years to run and in the meantime you could witness the dawn of the Age of Aquarius! We filed reams and reams of papers demanding that the department disclose how it had reopened assessments without a 'reason to believe' that tax had been evaded. We complained about 'violation of rules of natural justice', i.e. no one had asked us if they could reopen the assessment. We complained about the 'assumptions and presumptions' the department had made without any evidence to support them. We argued that the standard of evidence to reassess a tax return went beyond establishing dodgy downstream transactions: as a manufacturer, our responsibility ended when we handed our machines over to dealers. It was all very sublime stuff—hoopla wrapped up in a brilliantly woven fabric of such great beauty so that you could never tell where the aesthetics ended and the crass business of clothing an ugly sagging body began! But then, what is advocacy if it is not that?

When we got to the hearing, we faithfully reproduced the strategy smart lawyers use when dealing with an ill-trained dishonest halfwit bureaucrat. We carried in cartons upon cartons of 'machine movement' papers, guaranteed to keep the guy engaged for a very long time. We produced long briefs of arguments and longer lists of case laws. We pitched the case up to its most elevated jurisprudential level. Once we had him thoroughly confused with the law, we then said we wished to support our arguments with facts. We proceeded to open cartons and cartons of files, referring to this, then that. The glassy hazy look was by now deeply set in his eyes: the man had faded out. He eventually roused himself and said we could show these papers to his subordinates another day. Perfect!

Round two was a repeat of the first. The subordinates were disinterested in reading the papers, and weren't going to do so unless someone bribed them. Here's the deal with petty bureaucrats. Many have purchased their jobs. This is no joke. Former Haryana Chief Minister Om Prakash Chautala is in jail serving time for selling jobs. The Vyapam scam is another incarnation of the same universal reality. People who purchase their jobs come to the office to collect a salary; how else would they recoup the money they've paid out to get the job! If you want them to work, they need to be paid in cash on top. There was no one to pay these tax sleuths. We didn't want them to read the cartons of papers we'd brought, so there was a lot of tea-drinking and debate about Anna, Amma and Karunanidhi. This went on for several hearings. By the time the case went back to the main sales tax official, the debate had been whittled down to centre on Spark's ability to prove delivery of machines to actual customers. This Spark gracefully accepted, and then took time to compile the proof. A day later, we asked the department to let us have copies of all Spark papers which showed that there was any irregularity at all in delivery of machines. We said that we wanted to make sure we missed nothing: that we explained every document where the government thought we were wrong.

The tax official didn't like that. He said as much. His order recorded that Spark was asking for copies of all documents so that they could 'tailor-make a defence' and 'explain away' their evasion. In conclusion, he asked us to file our delivery documents before he would show us anything. Yes! Yes! Yes! We now had what we needed to start the appealing circus, and by god, we were up and running. In less than a week, we were before the High Court arguing a writ demanding documents. We got our stay. All we had to do now was sit on it, which in India is of course a no-brainer.

When the case did finally get heard, the sales tax department dumbed it down, which is always a good idea when you are in court. We Indians are an emotional people, and we don't need to think too hard about what appeals to our sensibilities. All we need is to go and see a Bollywood film. As a lawyer, all I need to do is project an oversimplified emotionally appealing bipolar vista of my case versus the one projected by the enemy. At the end of the day, I need to be the hero, not the villain. Indians rarely sympathize with the bad guys. The department did a good job of demonizing Spark. Spark had evaded taxes. It could not prove delivery of machines. It needed to manufacture evidence. It didn't want to be caught in a contradiction. It wanted to see everything the department had so that it could manufacture a story consistent with the department's records. The department should not be forced to disgorge its documents before Spark has disclosed its complete defence.

Spark took the opposite tack. This was an astonishing situation. This was not a game about a winner or loser. The issue is a little more complex—which is, did I pay my taxes or not?

I believe I did. I filed my sales tax returns and you closed your assessment. Now, years later, you have reopened your assessment. You say I evaded taxes. You are not telling me why you think so. You are not showing me anything that indicates such a thing. You now want me to defend myself without telling me exactly what I am accused of. Show me what you have and I will prove my innocence in relation to that very thing. That is not all. A reopened assessment is a quasi-criminal proceeding. I don't have to prove anything. You have to prove I evaded payment of sales tax. If you don't prove it, there is nothing for me to prove. If you don't show any document, your case will fail anyway. I can't prove my innocence. No one can prove a negative. So what on earth are you talking about?

In the end, it all came down to the principles of natural justice. No man can be expected to defend a charge against him when he has not been told what it is. Everyone is innocent till proven guilty. The matter was heard over many hearings, bit by bit, the way it often goes in the High Courts. Ultimately, the High Court took the view that the department couldn't run a 'barter trade' in documents, nor could it behave like a naughty kid in a school bathroom saying, 'You show me yours and I will show you mine'! In conclusion, it ordered that Spark be given all documents in a month.

The department took several months to find the documents. We reviewed them. Many of them were internal records of various shopkeepers. They showed that shopkeepers had been diverting machines. I didn't care a fig because it wasn't Spark's job to police the shopkeepers: the department was welcome to sue them. In the back of my mind, I had a better defence. Sales tax rates are determined by the nature of the transaction: not on the mindless doodling of a bored shopkeeper trying to entertain himself by writing fanciful fiction in his little black book! Try proving that what the shopkeeper had written had actually happened.

Some of the documents were a little more damning. They consisted of third and fourth 'carbon copies' of Spark's shipping documents: lorry receipts, invoice copies, customer order copies, receipts of machines delivered, stuff like that. Once again, there were some really busy Babu Lals and Ram Kumars. Again, I didn't really care beyond a point. My shipping documents instructed the transporter to deliver the machine only to the invoice address. If the truckers were diverting machines in collusion with shopkeepers, what could I do? All I needed to prove was that I had asked the transporters to do the right thing. If the department wanted to hang me, they had to prove that this was untrue. For good measure, we made sure we put it on record in our arguments that the department had the power to call for the transporter's records. If they had not done so, they must have had very good reasons.

As the case meandered through the prescribed procedure, a journey I did my best to complicate and prolong, it all came down to who carried the burden of proof. Did I have to prove that the machines had been delivered to the invoice address? And if they were not, was I guilty only because I had failed to ensure that they were delivered there and nowhere else? In short, did I have a legal obligation to police transporters so that they did exactly what they were asked to do? Did I pay sales tax on the transaction structure I accepted, or did I pay it on what happened to the machines after they left my factory or shop? Eventually, we ended up before the High Court again on these questions.

Now, you and I know that Spark's sales guys were up to some monkey games because that is what I told you. If I hadn't told you that, you could have read the case papers with the arguments on both sides and never known. When High Court judges don't know what to do, they 'admit' the case for regular hearing. When a case is admitted to regular hearing, it comes up when its turn comes up. That can take a very long time. In 2013, Prime Minister Dr Manmohan Singh fairly disclosed that India had 30 million cases which at the current rate of disposal would take 466 years to decide. To put it very bluntly, the case got buried. I checked with the company several years after the admission order and no one expected the case to be heard any time soon.

There are, I guess, several morals to this story. I am often asked if I have ever willingly defended the guilty. It's a naive question because everybody has the right to a fair hearing in court, and that is not possible unless he has a lawyer to represent him. I know that many lawyers refused to defend the guilty in the Nirbhaya rape case, and who can blame them for refusing to defend the indefensible? That said, in the school where I studied, I was taught that no one was guilty till it was established by due process of law, and till that day I was duty-bound to defend everyone.

Then there is the question of knowledge. I knew what had happened in the Spark sales tax better than the sales tax department did. If I went by my knowledge, the case was indefensible. But I could never be certain how much the department knew. I had to test that knowledge and, if they did not know enough, they could not hold Spark guilty. This is often the case. I may not believe in the case I am fighting, but if I believe that the enemy may not know enough to prove its case, I will happily fight it. I therefore never accept a case based on my knowledge of it. Maybe I do accept cases based on my knowledge of the other party's knowledge of it!

So isn't it true that lawyers will willingly prove lies? How many leering Punjabi uncles asked me what I do, and then triumphantly declared, 'So you are a liar?' It's so epistemologically mindless I don't deign to react to it with courtesy any longer. It is not my job to ensure that the truth will be established or that justice will be done. If anything, it is my job to use the law, and its procedure, to make sure that the 'truth' that gets established is the one that works for my client. At its root, for us lawyers, there is no truth: there are only plots and stories. It is my job as a lawyer to bring out the evidence I have and project it the best I can so that the story that I want to establish becomes the 'truth'. That is the true soul of the ethical void.

Perhaps now, it is possible for us to sympathize with Bill Clinton. He is a trained lawyer, and reacted like one when he said, 'I did not have sex with that woman.' Thanks to that subtle distinction, we can all enjoy a very long semantic debate about what constitutes 'sex with a woman'. For the same reason, I don't think it's a great idea for lawyers to be running a country. With our utter amorality, we can argue anything with utter conviction, and irresistible persuasion, even if it runs India into the ground: it's great television, but it's not in itself great nation-building.

Spark's story didn't end there. Two years after the case broke, they the client started to bang their heads against the walls of their moral prison, suffering with remorse! I was told to recommend a procedure by which we could pay the evaded taxes. I have dealt with Europeans and American extensively since 1992, but my hair still stands on end when I see moral righteousness start to eat its own tail. For a people who firebombed their fellow men to smithereens for five long years in Europe and Vietnam, not eighty years ago, culminating in the annihilation of entire cities in a mushroom cloud of destruction, this kind of simplification still leaves me cold. What is charming in a Graham Greene novel is disastrous in real life. In India, you don't get a medal for admitting you are wrong: you get hanged, or at the very least shaken down.

Have you ever seen anyone admitting after even a minor car crash that he was wrong? You can't. If you do, the cops will make your life so miserable you'll wish you had lied instead. So you shout and you scream and you pretend outrage, knowing fully you blew it royally.

The client wouldn't understand this. I told them it wouldn't be just sales tax any more: it was going to be penalties too! So what? It was still the right thing to do. I said it isn't just penalties: it's also the implications on old assessments of other taxes. That didn't cut any ice either. Beside myself with frustration, I then wrote a longish note telling them that we could not voluntarily pay back taxes because we did not know how much to pay. To establish that figure, I would have to look at every document of every transaction, literally from the cradle to the grave. I asked for six months to do this and set out a budget of several crore. Voila! That killed that story off pretty quickly. They were happy to pay off any taxes they should have paid but didn't, but that didn't mean they were going to spend some serious money finding out how much they should have paid but didn't. What started as ethical compulsion, ended up at Kafka's door!

Spark wasn't the only one who ended up at Kafka's door. My career at City Law reached there too. Even as I continued to make money hand over fist for the Dragons, I wore out my welcome. Much quicker than I had anticipated, the tide turned against me and moves were made to cut me down to size—or squeeze me out of City Law.

19

Law-Firm Politics

Most lawyers working for law firms face the Seven-Year Existential Itch, one way or another. It had been seven years since I joined City Law. While I didn't feel the itch to move, the Dragons started to get antsy. The problem is universal. Like every other business out there, law firms have to select a business model and there are three very different trajectories to choose from. This choice is critical because it then determines how lawyers conduct themselves within the law firm, and in the market. This is how it goes.

A lot of small law firms want to remain small and cohesive. These may consist of people whose dreams—and perhaps skills— are finite. They have achieved what they want and have now reached equilibrium. Perhaps some of their partners want better work–life balance. They increase their volume of work, if at all, at a certain limited rate. They work super-hard to keep their partner-level relationships stable. They work even harder to protect and promote the good health of their staff. They know that their security depends on the stability and reliability of the platform. If this is what City Law wanted to be, the partners would have created a small cohesive team of like-minded individuals and nurtured the team till the end of time. They didn't.

This small-law-firm model has its critics. Many people argue that businesses never stay static: they either grow or contract. This is Bill Gates's 'only the paranoid survive' type of argument. It's possible to argue against this view. Can we view law firms as we would technology firms? A great many small law firms in the big cities today are very stable and very profitable. The partners of these small law firms may never own a bungalow on Pali Hill, but they have a 'normal' life, and most of them definitely do not bust a gut working eighteen-hour days till they fall down dead on the street with the resounding finality of a premature obituary in the papers the next day.

At the other end of the spectrum are large law firms that are doing everything Bill Gates would approve of. They establish a fair-sized pool of equity-sharing partners who drive business development. They also supervise large sweatshops delivering work to clients and potential partners to existing partners. They induct new partners from time to time and they just keep growing. They are the magic circle of the legal world, much admired, much envied. Their lawyers lead a glamorous globe-trotting lifestyle. They stay at the best hotels, eat the finest lobsters, own the best cars, screw the best-looking bodies, vacation when they can at Davos, and work on briefs that get reported in the pink papers. When they finally retire, if they are not already dead, they do it in golf-course luxury properties in the best neighbourhoods. If you want to be this kind of person, you would be a fool not to join a very large law firm and slash and stab your way up to the top.

This model too has its critics. Lawyers from these law firms are very sharp and very perceptive and—very unidimensional.

Conversational life on Saturday evening—that is, if they have such a thing as a Saturday evening off—dies when the topic moves beyond politics and the price of real estate. There isn't more to life than what you own and what you can buy. If this is what City Law partners wanted, they would have become extremely transactional in the way they conducted their relationships. They would have promoted excellence, cauterized the unskilled, hired more skills at prices marked to market, and generally worked to create a very professional service-oriented entity. In such an entity, there would have been no space for this ragtag bunch of misguided misfits and mischief-makers to run amok, destroying value that others were creating.

Between these two extremes are many mid-tier law firms that try to be a happy synthesis of the best features of both the boutique and the magic-circle law firms. They try to have the lifestyle of the small law firm, the wealth of a large law firm, the family time of the small law firm, the client list of the large law firm, etc. This business model too has its critics, who argue that they want it all, and just like Freddy Mercury in the video, they run the very real risk of ending up like cross-dressing the transgendered with black moustaches in pink frocks. There's a lot of them though. These days, we have a new rising class of professionals who advise these mid-tier law firms on how to grow. They help them improve their websites and business development handouts, target their marketing efforts, make pitches, acquire partners and generally engage in a kind of mergers-and-acquisition-driven expansion with other law firms that, more often than not, does not succeed.

It's possible to see why: many mid-tier law firms have insufficient comprehension of the price that is to be paid to become this, or that, kind of law firm. Ultimately, it isn't about what you do to the law firm; it is about what *you* must first become to be able to run a law firm like that. The law firm doesn't run the manager; it's the other way round. In the meantime, what you get are law firms in a continuous state of merging and demerging. They are not really doing it out of any hard-nosed business calculation. It's a game of pretend. They merge to get a chance to poach each other's clients. They then spend all their time protecting their client list from their new-found partners. When a few months pass and fundamentally nothing changes, they split up and go their own way. Delhi is littered with the empty carcasses of law firms that got thrown together for a bit, but then went up in smoke and great balls of acrimonious fire, leaving shattered dreams and broken promises.

City Law didn't seem to know what it wanted to be. Its partners didn't seem to have agreed on what they were going to do with the law firm. Deo was temperamentally a small-law-firm man, Shanx was temperamentally a magic-circle, mega-law-firm man, and, between the two of them, their mutual contradictions found voice in a deafening crescendo of cognitive dissonance. In the vortex of this dissonance, I tried to build my little kingdom. It was possible, but it was exceedingly unpleasant.

Many a time, the people involved in medium and large law firms are really a bunch of competitors trying to murder each other while presenting a picture to the outside world of a cohesive band of brothers pulling together as a team. It is as vicious on the inside as it is easy amicability on the outside. Everyone wears a tie or an evening gown, pretending to be urbane and sophisticated, and talks amicably about the state of the economy while plotting and planning each other's destruction. They are pretending to have a pleasant evening on the town, and are dressed for it, but what they are actually doing is sizing up their next kill. The question that confronts every youngster is this: if you are fighting everyone around you in your law firm, how do you get ahead? Since Indians are basically an intelligent people, you don't get too far only because you sound smart or went to the right school or whatever. You need a force multiplier and that comes in two avatars: what you are or what you can do. How you conduct yourself in a law firm basically depends on which force multiplier you think you can bring to the table.

Start with what you are. Your force multiplier could be your father who is a judge and great for your firm's profile. You will be amazed how many youngsters in large firms survive mainly because their dad is backing them, one way or another. A second force multiplier could be that your father is a customer of the law firm. Pound for pound, if you are directly or indirectly bringing more business to a law firm than they are paying you, you are a cash-positive asset who won't be dispensed with whether you deliver any work or not! Sadly, if 'who you are' is not equal to a force multiplier, you had better start to do stuff to have a future in a law firm. What's that?

Naturally, at its most basic, you have to have the skill to get the job done. No law firm has use for a person who knows nothing. Every youngster tries first and foremost to acquire marketable skills. Anyone who loses focus on that basically loses. Spending several years loitering about the corridors of a law firm is of no use. I get the odd youngster who comes into my room and wants to be paid what his contemporary on the other desk is being paid because they are equally 'senior'. He thinks seniority matters. I tell him seniority is not intrinsically more marketable in a law firm than it is in a whorehouse. Indeed, quite the contrary! I don't care about his ego. I care about what skills he possesses and whether I can sell these skills to my clients and make some money. But that is also not enough. There is a lot of skilled labour going around.

India has no use for a 130mm Bofors howitzer unless we can drag it to the border and shoot it at someone. Reliable delivery of skill is a force multiplier, mere skill is not. Are you the guy someone can call at 10 p.m. on Saturday night and ask to deliver a complex job first thing Monday morning? Are you the guy ready, willing and able to cancel that long-planned summer vacation with your parents, wife and children to Europe because a client finally looks like it is getting funding for its new dream project?

Anyone wanting to get ahead in a law firm has to see the legal world exactly as the managing partner sees it. For the managing partner of a law firm, it's all about keeping the client, and that is about delivering the service. In today's world, it's not enough even if the client is a buddy: you still have to deliver the job to whatever unreal expectation the buddy has, or the buddy is your buddy no more. It's a dog-eat-dog world out there and since the partner's main job is to get business, not just deliver labour, he only cares about people who either help him bring the business or deliver the labour anytime, anywhere. So when you start out in a law firm, unless you have the ability to attract clients, you have to become an indispensable labourer who will dance naked in a top hat if the partner asks. Just hope the watchers are not gay, that's all.

Unfortunately, this formula is only good till you are three years in the profession. By then, you really should be capable of managing other younger lawyers. If you don't have the skill to do this, you will remain a primary labourer and your progress in the law firm will grind to a screeching halt. At this point, younger people will start pushing you from below and, if you don't spruce up your act, they will push you over.

Even if you do lead, you come up against some fundamental contradictions. You lead, yes, but those you lead are getting smarter all the time, pushing you more. There is a point beyond which getting better and better at your work brings diminishing returns. There is such a thing as being good enough. Now what? At this point, your youngsters can do most of the work you do, and they cost the firm a whole heap less. Being good at delivering the work or managing the youngsters is now not enough. You have to start developing business. If you don't develop new clients, you have no USP in the law firm any more. Delhi's basements are full of almost-good-enough lawyers who once worked for major law firms and know the job well, but really didn't become full-equity-owning partners because their marketing skills were modest. These are also the guys who have converted corporate commercial advisory work into the cut-price operation that it has become, but that is another story.

Absurdly, evolving into a marketing man brings on even more all-round insecurities for everyone. If you can bring five new clients to the law firm, you are also fundamentally charismatic enough to take away five clients from your law firm and create your own. Existing partners are always apprehensive of a competent lawyer with six or seven years of experience in managing a team and delivering work and developing clients too. They have to offer him partnership or push him out. The key driver of this decision is the relationships you have developed with the existing partners. If they like you, they will call you into the inner room. Most smart youngsters make partner in seven to ten years of law practice and, if they do not, one way or another, they move on.

The firm's existing partners do have a third choice, but they have to implement that early if they are to have any chance of making it work at all. That choice is to undermine this upcoming star so that while he may have some loyal youngsters working for him and a few clients who back him up, he is never quite able to stabilize his law practice enough to become a real threat to anyone. That is exactly the situation I found myself in at that point.

Here's the deal. As the Mahabharata so eloquently demonstrates to us, most people are driven by their psychological compulsions, not any rational evaluation of the choices that confront them. What happened to me was unexceptional. My partners loved the money I made, but hated the fact that I might wake up one day and want to keep that money. They needed me to deliver the work, but they were afraid that I would walk away one day, taking my skill with me. To keep me from developing too much self-confidence, they kept me in a permanent state of instability. When they had access to my clients, they also made sure that they let the client know that I had severe limitations. They let me carry on my new-found law practice as best I could, but they made sure that logistic hurdles kept me enmeshed in the day-to-day stuff, unable to think strategically or long-term. They let me have my young assistants, but they made sure they never paid them enough. Indeed, they made sure they let them know that if they wanted sensible wages, they would have to work for me but report my activities to them. At the same time, they could not keep themselves from introducing me to new clients. After all, who would do the work? So we had a law firm that seemed to promote me publicly, undermine me privately, and agonize over what to do with me when the sun went down and the demons came out in the dark. That was a lot of balls to keep up in the air indefinitely.

I found it frustrating and pointless. We could not expand the law firm if we spent time stabbing each other in the back. We could not focus on our work if we bogged each other down with trivial politics. I must have spent a couple of hours every week protecting my youngsters from some devious mind-game unleashed to undermine them at the behest of a mischievous partner. Perhaps the partners didn't need to ask anyone to do this. Perhaps like King Henry II, they only had to look at Thomas

Becket and say, 'Who will rid me of this man!' and sure enough, some professional mischief-maker would get busy trying to score brownie points with the bosses by rogering my juniors.

At the time, I had built a simple narrative to this logjam. The problem wasn't me; it was the partners' insecurity. They had signed a partnership deed with me but failed to honour it. By doing this, they put themselves in the position of being petrified of a payback from me in the next seven years for their treachery. Having signed a partnership deed and gotten nothing out of it, I wasn't going to ask them to sign another. Basically, their sins were coming back to haunt them. To fix the problem, it was not me they had to address; it was their insecurity and their perfidy. All they had to do was treat me like a full equity partner, declare a profit and pay me, and then there would be no conceivable reason to leave. But such is the frailty of men that they can never see that they are the architects of their own misery.

∼

If I had known then all that I know now, I would not have been at all surprised that the Dragons had the knives out for me. Since my law practice was running a decade behind my peers, this didn't happen to me when I was six years in the profession: it happened when I was sixteen years into it. I was an older man and the Dragons were even older men. Beyond a point, I found it tiresome to have to deal with the Dragons who continued to undermine me, spitting into the plate out of which they were eating. At the time, I couldn't see that their response was rational according to their narrative. The followers added to my anger-management debacle. Being good groupies, most took their cue from the Dragons. Thus, I continued to take artillery fire from everyone while putting money into their pockets. It couldn't last.

In professional life, you are only as good as your alliances. When you get past the embellishments, we humans are only apes with enhanced cognitive capabilities. We are no different from chimpanzees running in small hierarchical bands, rarely more than fifty in number, leadership determined not by brute physical strength, but by alliances. Naturalists will tell you that it's not always the strongest ape that gets to lead the band: it's the ape which makes the maximum number of social friendships and convinces these friends to follow him. Call it coalition-building. There is no evidence to suggest it's different for people. Indeed, that is exactly what politics is today in India. It's the same for lawyers too. If you are an easy person to dislike, you are unlikely to become managing partner of a magic-circle law firm even if you are the greatest lawyer on earth. If I wanted to progress in City Law, or outside it, I needed my own band of loyal followers. I decided to cement my relationship with my merry band, and then confront the Dragons' angst about my future in City Law.

In sum, to respond to the upcoming challenge, I took two steps. First, I created a work group loyal to me, and second, I insulated my work from everyone else, as far as I could. It was a very small group, where only two people really mattered. The mercurial half of this yin-yang team was Sajan, who had progressed hugely as a professional since I first took him on. Short, dark and verging on the plump side, he traced his roots to Hathras in Uttar Pradesh, with sensibilities that came straight out of the small-town alleys of the state. He could be amazingly crude, but he could also display a fine sense of what the British used to call 'native intelligence'. He had strong legal instincts and incredible energy, so getting him to go out and rock the world was easy meat. Handling his temper, his impatience and his abrasive tongue took some patience though. He was also very good at engaging with City Law's underbelly, keeping me posted at all times of the teapot rebellions in the gutters. His energy and his hostile aggression propelled him to becoming my litigation point man, with great success.

Rajesh was his counterpoint. Barrel-chested, heavy-jawed, deliberate, Rajesh was a natural-born chess player. He could always see three moves ahead and he was very mature in how he conducted his relationships. He had incredible self-control and a fine understanding of human nature. When he joined, he had been slothful and frequently uncommunicative, but as the years went by, he began to mature into a well-grounded professional. His chief failing was his resistance to conflict, and he was deeply risk-averse, but this worked for me because he got along with everyone, and, sooner or later, everyone who couldn't get through to me communicated through him. Even Deo loved him. With his superior education and better command of English, he naturally gravitated to the corporate side of my law practice.

I have always believed that the basis of all relationships is trust, more than common interests. People driven by common compulsion will cooperate, but as their compulsions change their relationships transform. I needed stability, so I invested in developing an emotional bond with my juniors, seeking a paradigm in which lawyers do not normally operate. The three of us moved around as one. We went out of town a lot, hanging out together from morning tea till we hit the sack! We swam in the same pool at the same time, explored the same restaurants in the same towns, and unhesitatingly shared all business data of any relevance to our mutual destiny. This enabled me to chase whatever was the flavour of the month for me in legal work, while they kept everything else stable. As much as it is possible for people of three different backgrounds and of wildly varying ages to be, we became very close, and it worked like magic, setting the stage for what was to come.

As I entered into a critical, decisive phase of my future at City Law, I felt strong because of the stable team of supporting lawyers I had put in place. I believed that I was ready to take on whatever the Dragons chucked at me. At the same time, since I continued to respect the Dragons for their great intelligence, if not their ethical values, I half believed they would start to play fair with me. They knew I had a profitable client list. They knew I knew the job. They knew I was a great billable head. They knew I had developed a national network of contacts. Why on earth would they not play fair?

It was not to be.

20

The Lingering Kiss Goodbye

There is no such thing as reality. The world is nothing but clusters of narratives at loggerheads with each other. I have spent a few hundred pages in this book telling you I was underleveraged, overworked, underpaid, over-profitable and, at all times, undermined by those who spent the money I earned. The Dragons may easily have had an entirely different narrative. If you asked Shanx, he could say I was who I had become only because of what he had made me. He could say that he encouraged me as best he could despite my severe professional limitations and his partnership compulsions. He could say my ambitions way exceeded my skills. He could say I would be nothing without the head start he gave me. He could say I was the proof that anybody can be turned into a productive lawyer, given the right support.

In saying all this, Shanx would be speaking the truth. This is how alternate narratives are built, and they are all equally credible.

On balance though, Shanx's narrative may as well be another half-truth. He protected me because he needed me to do some of the work that came his way. He encouraged me because he could see the upside. By any objective standard, as I battled my incompetence, my woeful lack of skill, the predatory environment in which I operated, I battled nothing harder than a bunch of perverse colleagues who did more to undermine me than to improve their own performance. He helped me, because to get what he wanted from me, he needed to help me. The tragedy of City Law was that everyone thoughtlessly acted out their compulsions, with no reflection on what it was that they really needed to do if they wanted the law firm to go somewhere.

Remarkably, the end didn't come because I received the same salary for five straight years; it came because I couldn't get decent salaries for my team. I brought up the topic more than once. Deo reacted by projecting himself as a modern-day Pontius Pilate ritually washing his official hands of my juniors. Shanx in turn insinuated that it was hard enough for him to combat Deo's snivelling and bitching about me, let alone give my juniors more money. I told Shanx more than once that my team should be paid out of my revenues. Shanx couldn't do that because Deo never earned anything at all and he needed my revenues to pay the rest of the law firm, and Deo himself too. He moaned about Deo being City Law's biggest 'loss plan', arguing that to pay my team of lawyers, he would have to pay all the lawyers, most of whom were dysfunctional. He couldn't promote meritocracy because to do that, he would have to demote Deo too, and Deo was the first among the equals in this animal farm.

Looking back, the whole crapshoot was a carefully constructed hall of smoke and mirrors designed to keep me locked into my position. The two were probably sitting together slapping their thighs and laughing about screwing me over. Deo had an evocative expression for it: '*Sheeshe pe utaar do*'. It suggested a guy with a bottle up his arse who can neither sit comfortably on it nor stand up. At the time, I lacked the gumption to call their bluff. My head swirled in a chop suey of gratitude, insecurity, dependence, despondence and resentment. I just couldn't cut through the crap, nor clearly see how adroitly Shanx was manipulating everyone to his personal advantage.

It took me years to figure out the racket: Shanx had three main sources of income. He served on the boards of several listed and private companies. He did not do this out of the goodness of his heart. He charged substantial director's fees. He kept these fees to himself. He also generated a lot of work of the type law firms do. He contributed this work to City Law and let City Law keep this part of the revenue. Finally, he also generated a lot of 'assignment-based' work. This is work he did on a 'success fee' basis. If he helped you buy a company, he would quote you a success fee (let's say 1 per cent of the total price at which you purchased the company). In this fee, he included the legal work as well. This meant that very often, when he quoted for an assignment, he included work that City Law would have otherwise done for legal fees. In effect, money that would have gone to the firm went to him because of the way he quoted his fee. As the years went by, this put pressure on City Law's finances even as Shanx's own income increased all the time. To hammer the final nail in City Law's finances, he did his best to convert every one-off legal job which came along into a success-based assignment. If it worked out, he kept that too. Basically, he was ripping off his own law firm.

As a result, he actively contributed to the declining revenue of the law firm as the years went by. Deo couldn't complain, because Shanx was the king of rainmakers. Deo understood this as clearly as he understood that with me positioned where I was, he skated on very thin political ice. Shanx told Deo the best he could expect was for him to contribute some clientele to City Law. It was for Deo to figure out how to garner the revenue and spend it wisely.

Since most of it came from me, Deo could give it to my juniors, or he could keep it for himself! Ultimately, Deo's ability to secure his revenue stream depended on making me indefinitely sit on a bottle.

For a guy who was really fed up, insecure, neurotic and emotional, I eventually saw the whole picture with remarkable clarity. Talking to Deo made zero sense: his good health depended on nothing changing. That wasn't true of Shanx. He could keep most of his income only as long as I continued to contribute enough money for Deo to cover the law firm's costs. If I threatened exit, Shanx would have to finance Deo. Perhaps understanding this scenario would help Shanx rethink his priorities. I decided on one last conversation with Shanx before I pitched for make or break.

My 'ultimatum by way of consideration' came when we were all in Singapore that November. I had done two days of meetings, after which my wife had joined me for our customary twice-a-year gastronomic debauchery weekend. I called Shanx up and he was happy to see me in the evening. We met in a bistro on Orchard Street. I brought up the burning issue. I told him he needed to think about my future. I told him I had committed eight years to him and it was for him to see how my loyalty was to be rewarded. I said I had created the team and all we had to now do was keep it stable. I was the picture of humility. I grovelled. I begged. I pleaded. I pumped his ego. On his part, he appeared very majestic in his reticence. He gave me the space and the silence to run my script. He nodded periodically and tut-tutted sympathetically. His eyes were soft and indulgent. My wife sat motionless through all this. I hoped he got one hell of an ego kick out of it, especially with another woman sitting there while her husband kissed his ass. I thought I got through to him. He said he would think about a way out. We parted with a warm handshake. It was not to be.

As the weeks went by, nothing changed. Another 31 March came around. My team received salary raises of a few thousand rupees each. As for me, no one asked, no one gave! The youngsters complained bitterly. In desperation, I went to see Shanx again. The conversation was short. He affected his stern I-am-not-negotiating tone and body language. He said the finances of the firm were what they were and he didn't have the budget. Clearly, my ass-kissing had not penetrated to places it was meant to go to—it had only made me look more vulnerable, weaker. His lecture became steadily more patronizing. He proceeded to evolve the topic from an exposition of the firm's finances to a critique of my flawed character. He told me if the youngsters wouldn't work for me at the salary they could afford, I should get rid of them and start working with the followers instead. He said the problem wasn't the salary, it was my attitude. Basically, he slammed the door shut on me.

Retribution now followed rejection. Bottle-seating strategies intensified. Files of clients I didn't completely control disappeared. My clients started calling up. One or another member of the firm had been in touch with them through a common source. Was all well between me and the firm's partners? Meanwhile, one of Shanx's flunkies went to work on Sajan, harder than ever before. He was actively told to start working directly with Shanx if he wanted a proper raise. Sajan held off, fearing he was being used, but became sufficiently unstable to keep all options open. Meanwhile, Goofy, an independent lawyer who worked closely with City Law, touched base with Rajesh and floated the idea that he was looking for more help. He let fly that my days were numbered and he would be better off thinking of the future. Would Rajesh be interested? Rajesh stalled, waiting for developments. Clearly the word was out that I was the Peking duck for the honey roast that night.

It didn't work of course. Indians are great strategy guys, but hate implementation. Catch the yapping mouths on any morning walk and each one of those jokers will hold forth eloquently on what is wrong with the country, let alone the colony. But ask any one of them to take on garden supervision duties and your morning walk will be very lonely very quickly. No matter how little I did, I was still an important asset for City Law. Unless they could find someone to do what I did, neither my law practice nor my team could be touched. Goofy didn't want to be me and Deo didn't have the discipline. Getting a guy from the outside would cost more than I did. City Law's venerable Dragons floundered about trying to figure out a way of holding me down on the bottle. It would have been funny, if I wasn't the fall guy. Tulsi Das tells us that a kind of madness grips those on the path of self-destruction, or so Ravan's brother Vibhishan said. The Dragons didn't see that they were plotting against themselves.

∼

At this poignant moment in City Law's history, I had my epiphany in Singapore. If this was a movie, I would add the score from George Lucas's *Star Wars* to emphasize the importance of it. I remember this whole period of my life very well. I had spent a longish spell in Stockholm about that time. After I finished my work there, I spent the weekend with a cousin who was posted as the Indian ambassador. I did the touristy thing around the countryside with my bhabhi dutifully reading out long tracts from her tourist guidebook as we were driven across the frozen countryside in a car as long as a yacht. It was very cold and I felt the world had turned very surreal. Soon after I came back,

I drove to Rajasthan to manage a trial court matter which was threatening to fall apart. I then had four days in Delhi before I jetted back to Canada for a week to identify some documents and get an affidavit for a petition I was filing before the Company Law Board. I spent one of those nights shivering on the sidewalk in my pyjamas on a cold February night because a carelessly thrown cigarette somewhere in the hotel had set off a fire alarm at 3 a.m. I was already too zoned out to understand that you do not run out into the street in your pyjamas in sub-zero temperatures in Canada in winter, fire or no fire.

On my return, I rushed to Bangalore to firefight a works contract claim. Within days of returning to Delhi, I was called for a two-hour meeting in London. I took the overnight flight, landing in Heathrow at 4 a.m. Since central-London hotels don't, in practice, give you a room before 3 p.m., I spent several hours sitting in the lobby. Unknown to me, as I did so, the mango pickle I was carrying for an NRI niece spilt on to my starched white shirt. When I noticed it an hour before the meeting, I ran about in a frenzy trying to buy a shirt. After the meeting, I met my niece for a pub meal, delivered what remained of the achaar and then took a flight back the same day. By then, the adrenalin had pushed my metabolism into some sort of infrared zone.

I had exactly two nights in Delhi, on the other side of which I took a flight to Bombay, rented a car and suffered a six-hour bone-rattling ride north to Silvassa, capital of Dadra and Nagar Haveli.

The acrimonious meetings there did nothing to soothe my nerves. I had a sleepless night, then another meeting the next day, followed by the ride back over the same potholed road. I checked into the Leela near Mumbai airport that night, tried to get a few hours of sleep, failed, spent an hour walking in a garden which by then looked like a night scene in the movie *Avatar*, dragged

myself out of the hotel at midnight and took the 2 a.m. flight
to Singapore. Some ten hours later, I was in another day-long
meeting. By the time I hit the sack that night, I was really primed
for my epiphany.

Something woke me up about 4 a.m. At least that is what my
watch said. My throat was dry. I looked for a drink of water. The
bottle was empty. I looked out of the window. It was dull and
humid: the vapour hanging heavy around the lamp posts in some
sort of concrete jungle. Where was this? Where was I? In rising
panic, I grabbed the room keys and went down to the lobby in my
boxer shorts, looking for water. There was no one there. I stepped
out of the hotel. I still didn't know where I was. I walked up the
street and there, in the distance, I saw it: 'Robinson'. I was in
Singapore! I sat down on the sidewalk, shaking with relief. I must
have sat there a long time. A very thin glow appeared at the edge
of the horizon. I dragged myself back to the hotel lobby and then
it was obvious. The pretty young things were behind the desk,
smiling hazily at me, wondering if this dishevelled desi had had
quite as raunchy a wild night as it appeared.

This moment of complete disorientation set the stage for
a reassessment of my choices. If I kept going the way I was, I
would lose my mind. Why was I doing this, and for whom? What
eternal reward awaited me for wasting what remained of my life
in this limbo? How did it profit me to delay taking a decision?
Why did I think that I could talk to people who didn't want to
understand? How can you talk to people whose self-interest lies in
not understanding? When people are blinded by arrogance, what
did I expect to make them see? What compulsion was driving me
to this wanton self-destruction? By the time I left Singapore, I
wasn't debating exit any more: I was thinking exit procedure.

I have always been a fan of Sergio Leone and really love *The
Good, the Bad and the Ugly*. If you want to shoot, shoot, don't

talk! So I went to meet the youngsters in my work group. I told them I was going to leave: did they want to come along? I left them with no illusions about where they were going, nor did I lie to them. I had Rs 6 lakh in the bank, a three-bedroom flat in Vasant Kunj, and nothing else. We could all survive three months on that kind of money. I hoped to move my client list with me, but it was going to be chancy. The youngsters didn't take long to ponder. For them it came down to a simple fact: they did not *trust* the Dragons. They shrugged unconcerned. Where was the choice?

~

There is an inexorable logic to exit procedures in any law firm. You have to be completely blind not to see it. First you cut off communication with your peers, so they don't know what appointments you are keeping. Then you cut off traffic between your work and your peers, so your clients lose touch with the rest of the firm. Finally, you stop billing through the law firm, accumulating the numbers so that you can cash out and bankroll yourself after you've quit. It is a testament to the quality of management at City Law that the Dragons remained blissfully unaware of what I was doing. No one noticed and no one brought up the behavioural change. I used the time to increase contact with my client base, dropping broad hints that entrepreneurial ambitions were beginning to overwhelm my senses as though of hemlock I had drunk. My clients laughed good-naturedly about the inevitability of it all, promising support and whatever else.

In three months, City Law's cash flows started to go down the toilet. Why were the coffers empty? Ah, Dubey is sulking, is he? Let's encourage him a little. One morning, a billing clerk showed up at the door. He looked very sheepish. He'd probably been dressed down for not doing his job. I would have fallen about laughing, banging my fists on the floor if my future wasn't so uncertain. For years, my legal team converted its hours into invoices and submitted them to Accounts as fully finished bills: all Accounts did was print them out on letterheads and mail them. For years, I had cried myself hoarse complaining about Accounts being completely dysfunctional. In all these years, no one had ever walked through my door offering to help me send bills to my clients. What was the clerk to do but squirm at the door and look like he had swallowed the hind glands of a skunk?

I contrived to be livid.

'In five years, you have never come into my room asking for work; why are you suddenly so desperate to earn your salary?'

'Sir, I was told you had bills to prepare.'

'Who told you I had bills to prepare?'

'Sir, Deo Sir said you had bills to prepare.'

'Deo said that, did he? Don't ever come to my room uninvited. When I have a statement of billable hours for you, I will call you. If someone else is calling you, you make sure you get his hours, not mine.'

The clerk visibly crumpled. My naked attack on Deo's billing was an affront. Disregard had turned to ridicule. It had come to a head. It wasn't twenty-four hours before I had my reaction. On 7 August 1999, Shanx stormed into my room, slamming the door. He did not sit down. His eyes were on fire. He was shaking with rage. He didn't say very much. 'Ranjeev, I don't want to discuss anything. All I am telling you is that you'd better stay within your limits.' He spun on his heels and he was gone.

I sat slumped in my chair for some time. Somewhere in the deep recesses of my mind, even as I plotted my exit, something inside me had hoped that somehow it would still work out. Shanx's whirlwind visit cauterized that hope . . . terminally. It was over, right now. It took me twenty-four hours to exit. I loaded half of my clients' files into my car that evening. The next day, a Sunday, I went back to the office, loaded the other half, and I was gone. My parting thought as I left City Law for the last time was an emotional purgation. I had done everything in my power to stay, but after eight years of slogging, this dream had ended. The conclusion was inescapable; you cannot live your life by your rules in a world someone else has created. I would now make my own world, run by my own rules, centred on the idea of a law firm the way I think it should be run.

In the years since, I have tried to be as good as my word.

Epilogue

Some things are universal about migrations. For a start, you don't migrate till you've done a lot of rejecting. Migration is not a choice: it is the logical consequence of doors that have shut. My real migration only began after Shanx shut City Law's door on me. I still ask myself whether I would have stayed if he had kept the door open just a little bit. Here's the other thing about migration. Just because every door has shut and you have packed your bags does not mean that you really know where you are going. Migration is an act of desperation, not vision. Those who claim otherwise are only using hindsight to validate the risk they took leaping into the unknown. All I knew when I exited City Law was that whatever I did, it would not be as painful as what I had left behind. So I decided to do what I had recently learnt—run my own law firm.

For an international law firm, it was rather a deceptive start. We had a havan (a Hindu religious ceremony) in the spare bedroom of my Vasant Kunj flat and christened our new law firm Vista Legal. It wasn't the most creative name I've ever thought up but, frankly, the whole idea that clients get legal service from brands rather than competent professionals struck me as ludicrous at the time. What's in a name? I could have called myself 'The Fall Guy Formerly Known as The Pseudo Partner of City Law' and would it have mattered? Cheesy and unimaginative as it was, at least it was no worse than the half-Sanskritized claptrap that law firms call themselves these days, that is when they are not engaging in lunacy in Latin, or evoking the wisdom of Babylon and Israel. We opened bank accounts and printed stationery. My future had arrived!

That is not to say that I had any illusions about the future. The years of stress had taken their toll on me. I was perpetually on the edge of a nervous breakdown. I had little self-belief and a very great deal of hostile aggression. Any shrink would have diagnosed me as clinically depressed. Nevertheless, since I now had a law firm of my own, I had to stop raging at the Dragons and begin thinking about the future. I started to think about stabilizing Vista Legal. It was true that we had a client list, but clients, unlike diamonds, aren't forever. Like lactating cows, they yield milk for a period of time and then dry up. Marketing a law firm is the same as animal husbandry: you artificially inseminate and then, after a while, the milk flows! In a dairy farm, insemination is a continuous process. To inseminate, you need a lot of equipment and technology. In terms of a law firm, that meant a swanky office in a smart central location and a lot of cash to finance marketing. I didn't have either. Hell, I didn't even have a sperm bank! If I didn't figure out what to do pretty soon, I wasn't going to attract any international business. If anything, my work would steadily become domestic, I would come under price pressure and, before I knew it, I would get consigned to a basement in South Delhi.

What about joining another law firm?

I didn't know too many other law firms. At the time, there weren't that many worth joining. Those that I did know I did not like. But there was one lawyer of whom I was a big fan.

Pound for pound, he packed the most charisma I have ever seen in a compact body. I remember once spending a couple of hours with his charming and very pretty wife in a homoeopathic clinic waiting for the doctor to see us and she regaled me with stories of how her parents went into catatonic shock when she'd said she wanted to marry him. 'Think about it,' she said. 'He didn't look like anything! But, you know,' she added thoughtfully, 'my husband has this magnetic, irresistible quality!' Even though she was an interested party, her judgement was spot on. So I went to see him.

He was very forthcoming. Perhaps he sensed my neurosis. He tried to soothe me. He talked about his vast expansion plans. He talked about the structure he dreamt of creating, the departments and the pyramid of skills. I listened to him mesmerized, exactly as I had listened to Shanx over the years. Then I told myself I had heard it all before. Somewhere in all this, he asked me what business I was bringing. Here comes his evaluation of how much money he can make out of my clients by hiring me, I thought to myself. I said I couldn't say, but I would like him to think about what I was worth without the business. He said he would discuss it with his guys. We had several exchanges after that. I could see I had failed to impress him. Several thoughtless things I said didn't amuse his guys at all. I had the distinct sense that he engaged with me only because in his wisdom, he knew that no one my age leaves a law firm without taking a few clients. In the end, when I failed to flash my client list at him, he politely ran me out of his office.

I am deeply indebted to this gentleman because he inadvertently helped me to make a radical shift in perspective. For too long, I had viewed the whole City Law Dragons-and-me monkey circus as a personality-driven game of thrones. At last I realized that no one wanted me for my legal skills or, at any rate, such skills as they could believe I had. It didn't matter where I went searching for a job. I would be evaluated only for the business I brought. My client list could buy me a position in a new law firm, but I would have that position only for as long as I could retain control over my clients. I had just finished fending off attacks on my client list by the Dragons: why did I think any law firm I went to wouldn't do the same thing? Even if they didn't, given the client churn, if I could not bring in new business, I would be sacked as soon as my existing clients left. If I did have the ability to bring in business on a continuous basis, why would I give that business to another law firm? It just made more sense to run my own. The trick was not to question the decision to run my own law firm: it was to focus on finding business.

It took a while for the Dragons to figure they had a problem on their hands. Shanx was travelling and Deo was disconnected from my work. He noted our team's absence and thought nothing of it, assuming that we were out of town on a job. When Shanx came back, they went into my office and found bare cupboards. They didn't call me; they rang up my team and asked them in for a meeting. The message was clear: Ranjeev is gone but it isn't a great loss. They said business would go on and the team would be taken care of. No doubt, some nasty things were said too. The boys never told me. They just said they heard out the Dragons and ultimately said they didn't want to go back to City Law. With the resounding finality of that refusal, they shut their own door on City Law. In doing so, they opened my door!

It took a while for the consequences to appear on my horizon. Two weeks to the day after I left City Law, I had my call from Shanx. I had expected a call, but I hadn't developed a plan for it.

Shanx sounded very relaxed, very confident. 'Time for a meeting, don't you think?' he said nonchalantly, as if nothing of any great consequence had occurred. I agreed, and we decided to meet in the Meridian once again, where it had all begun. History may not repeat itself, but historic conditions surely did.

Of the many wonderful things I can say about Shanx, I can certainly say that he never lost his poise, no matter how much pressure he was under. He also had the startling ability to press the right buttons of the person he was dealing with to get what he wanted. His tack with me was supremely emotional. 'What went wrong between us, Ranjeev?' he opened very softly, 'we had a long-term plan and then somewhere, we both lost focus.' 'I never lost focus, Shanx,' I shot back. 'You just don't value those who serve you.' 'You don't *serve* me, Ranjeev,' he purred, 'in fact I was telling my wife about this and she asked me why you would leave. Aren't you guys *friends*?' I found myself having to explain my conduct, when it wasn't my conduct that had triggered the exit. When finally I ran out of things to say, he said he was not going to deny anything I said, simply because he must respect my feelings even if he could contest my interpretation of the facts. He said we had to be practical and we had to look to the future.

I guess I was ready to listen to him. 'You have seen the corporate world, Ranjeev,' he said. 'You know the future is consolidation, not fragmentation. How can you be better off on your own, rather than using the force multiplier of all of us working together?' 'We aren't working together', I protested, 'I worked for you and you didn't want to recognize its value.' He didn't want to go there. 'Let me put it this way: what can we do now so that we can have the same success together?' I continued to look sceptical. 'If the money had not been a problem,' he asked me gently, 'do we have a problem we can't fix?' He was right of course, but at the time, I didn't see the simplicity of it all. I focused instead on my trunkful of resentments. I said I did not agree with the way he ran the law firm. I didn't agree with Deo's parochial perspectives. I didn't agree with the people he chose to surround himself with. I went on a bit. He nodded, repeating every time that the problem could be fixed. I didn't like the way City Law functioned? Okay, so run your own law firm. You don't like Deo's parochialism? Set up your own office. You don't like my colleagues? So go recruit your own. He was compelling, irresistible. All my grave objections dissolved into trivialities. Ultimately, I had no answer to his offer: if you don't like City Law, start your own City Law! All he wanted in return was a share of the new law firm. That left open the question of where this office would be. He said it couldn't be in Delhi because we already had a City Law there. I could pick NOIDA or Gurgaon.

I am a small-town boy. I don't like apartments. I feel bungalows are a more graceful way to live. I had spent all my adult life thus far in apartments. I had long nurtured a desire to live in Gurgaon. I had travelled the world and I understood that the suburbanization of Delhi was inevitable. I had also shouted from the rooftops since the early 1990s that Delhi would inevitably become an inner-city slum by 2020, the same way Chandni Chowk had. People jeered at my beliefs: many still do.

With Shanx offering a real chance to move to the suburbs, my resolve to do my own thing began to falter. From a client perspective too, that made perfect sense. Shanx had valuable clients in Gurgaon. He had neither the time nor the legal skill-sets to service them. He didn't understand indirect taxes or industrial laws and he didn't want to waste time on micro-managing litigation or regular corporate commercial advice. If I opened an office there, a lot of money could be made. I said I did not have the money to start an office. He said he would fund it. He said I could be an equal partner. He was offering that I run my own law firm, built with his money, servicing his clients.

All he wanted in return was a share of the profit. What could be more reasonable?

Still, I felt nervous and out of control. I kept obliquely voicing apprehensions about him keeping his word. He dismissed that out of hand. 'I accept that mistakes have been made. We could have done this differently but I want you to understand this once and for all, Ranjeev,' he said with rare candour, 'at the end of the day, it was always only about the money. You know I like you. It was never personal.' I found myself speechless, unable to figure out exactly where he had positioned this new scam he was unleashing on me. He thought I had absorbed enough for one day. 'Anyway, I don't want to rush you or push you,' he said. 'You need to find your comfort zone. Think about what I am saying. Meanwhile, I think Deo wants to spend some time with you. He will call you and you two can get together.'

I didn't come out of that meeting pumping my fists in jubilation. The offer didn't validate me. I had extracted myself out of an eight-year-long vortex of emotional instability only to find that it was pulling me back in. Yes, there was opportunity here, but I was wiser for my previous experience. I told myself I would never find peace unless I pursued the simplicity of an autonomous life. There would be less money, but the tiny kingdom would be my own. Not everyone plays tennis to become the Williams sisters. The experience of playing the game can bring as much joy as the success you get in winning it. The experience of being king is the same, no matter how small the kingdom. There will always be a bigger fish. Why exchange that to resume a dance with the wolves?

~

Deo didn't take too long to get in touch. He sounded exactly the way he had when I asked for his help at the Vasant Kunj D4 paan shop eight years ago. He was soft, warm, humane and conciliatory. He wanted to see me and he wanted us to make a new beginning. I invited him for a drink. I was so relieved I whipped out the best Islay malt I had. We did some serious drinking. We talked about the firm. He accused me of nothing, said nothing to demean me and put his heart on the line for me. We laughed about some work we had done together. I sort of apologized for some of the things I had said and done. He waved them away. 'These comedies are situational, Ranjeev,' he said, 'you can't affix the personality on the basis of the event.' We both turned maudlin as the evening progressed. Eventually, he got to the point.

Deo repeated several times that he had always tried to be fair to those he walked with. He said whatever his sins were, a lack of compassion was never one of them. He was all heart, and many of his friends would agree. 'However harshly you may judge me,' he said, 'I did nothing that my position did not require me to do.' I let that one ride. Self-righteousness is a common Indian disease, I told myself. The majority of us have it. He said he had tried to be a good partner to Shanx. The two were very different people but he was the one who worked hard to cross the gulf and get to the other side. When it came down to hammer time, he said, he always did what Shanx wanted, because that is what partnership is about. This too was doubtlessly true. His compulsions were obvious to everyone. If your meal ticket depends on a moody rainmaker, you take a lot of attitude from the rainmaker. Basically, he was saying I had demonized the wrong guy. I started to see him from a whole new perspective.

As I look back on that poignant evening, I recall most his piercing gaze and wavering voice choked with emotion as he said, 'In life, there are many moments when we become *nadaan* [naive] for no reason we can explain, Ranjeev: when judgement fails us,' he paused. 'But this I will say to you with great *tajurba* [experience]: you must never underestimate the overwhelming power of the instinct for self-preservation.'

Deo melted me in a way Shanx could not have done. Shanx made a business case. I distrusted Shanx at that point, so I wrapped his business case in suspicion and cooked it in cynicism. Deo came across as a man coming to terms with a new reality, rather than driving it. I began to see the human side of the dilemmas he endured. A sub-stream of defeat underlay his story. At worst, he had thoughtlessly acted out his compulsions but in doing so, was he any worse than the rest of us?

Not that Deo's redemption changed very much for me. I had been on the receiving end of a scam for eight long years. These guys had sold me a chocolate-brownie fairy-tale story in the past and locked me into a meat grinder: I wasn't going to buy another bullshit dream only so I could discover that they had in their closet another far more sophisticated meat-grinder. Still, the fact remained that the Dragons were ready to fund my office, put clients on the table and share profits with me. They were ready to play fair and be equal and the opportunity was there for the taking. Was this the third of the three opportunities that my father had talked about? I knew my youngsters would be apprehensive, but they trusted me: they did not need to trust the Dragons or be victims of their devious games. There was a Faustian deal to be made with the devil. What was there not to like about this deal?

I stood frozen, unable to move, confronting what was doubtless a life-defining moment.